Mastering Splunk

Optimize your machine-generated data effectively by developing advanced analytics with Splunk

James Miller

BIRMINGHAM - MUMBAI

Mastering Splunk

First published: December 2014

Production reference: 1121214

Published by Packt Publishing Ltd.
Livery Place
35 Livery Street
Birmingham B3 2PB, UK.

ISBN 978-1-78217-383-0

www.packtpub.com

Credits

Author
James Miller

Reviewers
Christopher Brito
Dr. Benoit Hudzia

Commissioning Editor
Akram Hussain

Acquisition Editor
Meeta Rajani

Content Development Editor
Akashdeep Kundu

Technical Editors
Taabish Khan
Mrunmayee Patil

Copy Editors
Relin Hedly
Dipti Kapadia

Project Coordinator
Kartik Vedam

Proofreaders
Simran Bhogal
Maria Gould
Ameesha Green

Indexer
Mariammal Chettiyar

Graphics
Disha Haria

Production Coordinator
Arvindkumar Gupta

Cover Work
Arvindkumar Gupta

About the Author

James Miller is an IBM certified and accomplished senior project leader, application/system architect, developer, and integrator with over 35 years of extensive applications and system design and development experience. He has held various positions such as National FPM Practice Leader, Microsoft Certified Solutions Expert, technical leader, technical instructor, and best practice evangelist. His experience includes working on business intelligence, predictive analytics, web architecture and design, business process analysis, GUI design and testing, data and database modeling and systems analysis, and the design and development of client-based, server-based, web-based and mainframe-based applications, systems, and models.

His responsibilities included all the aspects of solution design and development, including business process analysis and re-engineering, requirement documentation, estimation and project planning/management, architectural evaluation and optimization, test preparation, and management of resources. His other work experience includes the development of ETL infrastructures, such as data transfer automation between mainframe systems (DB2, Lawson, Great Plains, and more) and the client/server or between SQL servers and web-based applications. It also includes the integration of enterprise applications and data sources.

In addition, James has acted as Internet Applications Development Manager, responsible for the design, development, QA, and delivery of multiple websites, including online trading applications, warehouse process control and scheduling systems, and administrative and control applications. He was also responsible for the design, development, and administration of a web-based financial reporting system for a $450 million organization, reporting directly to the CFO and his executive team.

In various other leadership roles, such as project and team leader, lead developer, and applications development director, James has managed and directed multiple resources, using a variety of technologies and platforms.

He has authored the book *IBM Cognos TM1 Developer's Certification Guide*, *Packt Publishing*, and a number of whitepapers on best practices, such as *Establishing a Center of Excellence*. Also, he continues to post blogs on a number of relevant topics based on personal experiences and industry best practices.

He currently holds the following technical certifications:

- IBM Certified Developer – Cognos TM1 (perfect score – 100 percent in exam)
- IBM Certified Business Analyst – Cognos TM1
- IBM Cognos TM1 Master 385 Certification (perfect score – 100 percent in exam)
- IBM Certified Advanced Solution Expert – Cognos TM1
- IBM Certified TM1 Administrator (perfect score – 100 percent in exam)

He has technical expertise in IBM Cognos BI and TM1, SPSS, Splunk, dynaSight/arcplan, ASP, DHTML, XML, IIS, MS Visual Basic and VBA, Visual Studio, Perl, WebSuite, MS SQL Server, Oracle, Sybase SQL Server, miscellaneous OLAP tools, and more.

I would like to thank my wife and soul mate, Nanette L. Miller, who has given me her everything always.

About the Reviewers

Christopher Brito lives and works in Philadelphia, PA, where he designs and develops systems that manipulate and display operational data in real time. He got started with Splunk in 2009 and is the author and maintainer of splunk-client, the most popular Splunk search API client for Ruby.

Dr. Benoit Hudzia is a cloud/system architect working on designing the next-generation cloud technology as well as running the Irish operations for Stratoscale.

Previously, he worked as a senior researcher and architect for SAP on the HANA Enterprise Cloud.

He has authored more than 20 academic publications and is also the holder of numerous patents in the domains of virtualization, OS, cloud, distributed system, and more. His code and ideas are included in various SAP commercial solutions as well as open source solutions, such as QEMU / KVM hypervisor, Linux kernel, OpenStack, and more.

His research currently focuses on bringing together the flexibility of virtualization, cloud, and high-performance computing (also called the Lego cloud). This framework aims at providing memory, I/O, and the CPU resource disaggregation of physical servers, while enabling dynamic management and aggregation capabilities to native Linux applications as well as Linux / KVM VMs using commodity hardware.

www.PacktPub.com

Support files, eBooks, discount offers, and more

For support files and downloads related to your book, please visit www.PacktPub.com.

Did you know that Packt offers eBook versions of every book published, with PDF and ePub files available? You can upgrade to the eBook version at www.PacktPub.com and as a print book customer, you are entitled to a discount on the eBook copy. Get in touch with us at service@packtpub.com for more details.

At www.PacktPub.com, you can also read a collection of free technical articles, sign up for a range of free newsletters and receive exclusive discounts and offers on Packt books and eBooks.

https://www.packtpub.com/books/subscription/packtlib

Do you need instant solutions to your IT questions? PacktLib is Packt's online digital book library. Here, you can search, access, and read Packt's entire library of books.

Why subscribe?

- Fully searchable across every book published by Packt
- Copy and paste, print, and bookmark content
- On demand and accessible via a web browser

Free access for Packt account holders

If you have an account with Packt at www.PacktPub.com, you can use this to access PacktLib today and view 9 entirely free books. Simply use your login credentials for immediate access.

Instant updates on new Packt books

Get notified! Find out when new books are published by following @PacktEnterprise on Twitter or the *Packt Enterprise* Facebook page.

Table of Contents

Preface

This book is designed to go beyond the introductory topics of Splunk, introducing more advanced concepts (with examples) from an enterprise architectural perspective. This book is practical yet introduces a thought leadership mindset, which all Splunk masters should possess.

This book walks you through all of the critical features of Splunk and makes it easy to help you understand the syntax and working examples for each feature. It also introduces key concepts for approaching Splunk's knowledge development from an enterprise perspective.

What this book covers

Chapter 1, The Application of Splunk, provides an explanation of what Splunk is all about and how it can fit into an organization's architectural roadmap. The evolution aspect is also discussed along with what might be considered standard or typical use cases for this technology. Finally, some more out-of-the-box uses for Splunk are given.

Chapter 2, Advanced Searching, demonstrates advanced searching topics and techniques, providing meaningful examples as we go along. It focuses on searching operators, command formats and tags, subsearching, searching with parameters, efficient searching with macros, and search results.

Chapter 3, Mastering Tables, Charts, and Fields, provides in-depth methods to leverage Splunk tables, charts, and fields. It also provides working examples.

Chapter 4, Lookups, covers Splunk lookups and workflows and discusses more on the value and designing aspect of lookups, including file and script lookups.

Chapter 5, Progressive Dashboards, explains the default Splunk dashboard and then expands into the advanced features offered by Splunk for making business-effective dashboards.

Chapter 6, Indexes and Indexing, defines the idea of indexing, explaining its functioning and its importance and goes through the basic to advanced concepts of indexing step by step.

Chapter 7, Evolving Your Apps, discusses advanced topics of Splunk applications and add-ons, such as navigation, searching, and sharing. Sources to find additional application examples are also provided.

Chapter 8, Monitoring and Alerting, explains monitoring as well as the alerting capabilities of the Splunk technology and compares Splunk with other monitoring tools.

Chapter 9, Transactional Splunk, defines and describes Splunk transactions from an enterprise perspective. This chapter covers transactions and transaction types, advanced use of transactions, configuration of types of transactions, grouping events, concurrent events in Splunk, what to avoid during transactions, and so on.

Chapter 10, Splunk – Meet the Enterprise, introduces the idea of Splunk from an enterprise perspective. Best practices on important developments, such as naming, testing, documentation, and developing a vision are covered in detail.

Appendix, Quick Start, gives examples of the many resources one can use to become a Splunk master (from certification tracks to the company's website, and support portal, and everything in between). The process to obtain a copy of the latest version of Splunk and the default installation of Splunk is also covered.

What you need for this book

If you don't have the time for formal training or to read through gigabytes of help files, but still want to master Splunk, then this book is for you. All you need is a Windows computer, general skills with Windows, and the data that you want to explore.

Who this book is for

Whether you know Splunk basics or not, this book will transform you into a *master Splunker* by providing masterful insights and step-by-step, unusual Splunk solution examples.

Conventions

In this book, you will find a number of styles of text that distinguish between different kinds of information. Here are some examples of these styles, and an explanation of their meaning.

Code words in text, database table names, folder names, filenames, file extensions, pathnames, dummy URLs, user input, and Twitter handles are shown as follows: "The first step is editing the `transforms.conf` configuration file to add the new lookup reference."

A block of code is set as follows:

```
[subsearch]
maxout = 250
maxtime = 120
ttl = 400
```

When we wish to draw your attention to a particular part of a code block, the relevant lines or items are set in bold:

```
lookup BUtoBUName BU as "Business Unit" OUTPUT BUName as "Business
Unit Name" | Table Month, "Business Unit", "Business Unit Name", RFCST
```

Any command-line input or output is written as follows:

```
splunk restart
```

New terms and **important words** are shown in bold. Words that you see on the screen, in menus or dialog boxes for example, appear in the text like this: "Go to **Settings** and then **Indexes**."

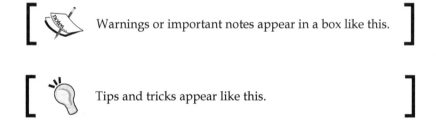

Warnings or important notes appear in a box like this.

Tips and tricks appear like this.

Reader feedback

Feedback from our readers is always welcome. Let us know what you think about this book—what you liked or may have disliked. Reader feedback is important for us to develop titles that you really get the most out of.

To send us general feedback, simply send an e-mail to feedback@packtpub.com, and mention the book title via the subject of your message.

If there is a topic that you have expertise in and you are interested in either writing or contributing to a book, see our author guide on www.packtpub.com/authors.

Customer support

Now that you are the proud owner of a Packt book, we have a number of things to help you to get the most from your purchase.

Downloading the color images of this book

We also provide you with a PDF file that has color images of the screenshots/diagrams used in this book. The color images will help you better understand the changes in the output. You can download this file from `https://www.packtpub.com/sites/default/files/downloads/3830EN_ColoredImages.pdf`.

Errata

Although we have taken every care to ensure the accuracy of our content, mistakes do happen. If you find a mistake in one of our books—maybe a mistake in the text or the code—we would be grateful if you would report this to us. By doing so, you can save other readers from frustration and help us improve subsequent versions of this book. If you find any errata, please report them by visiting `http://www.packtpub.com/submit-errata`, selecting your book, clicking on the **errata submission form** link, and entering the details of your errata. Once your errata are verified, your submission will be accepted and the errata will be uploaded on our website, or added to any list of existing errata, under the Errata section of that title. Any existing errata can be viewed by selecting your title from `http://www.packtpub.com/support`.

Piracy

Piracy of copyright material on the Internet is an ongoing problem across all media. At Packt, we take the protection of our copyright and licenses very seriously. If you come across any illegal copies of our works, in any form, on the Internet, please provide us with the location address or website name immediately so that we can pursue a remedy.

Please contact us at copyright@packtpub.com with a link to the suspected pirated material.

We appreciate your help in protecting our authors, and our ability to bring you valuable content.

Questions

You can contact us at `questions@packtpub.com` if you are having a problem with any aspect of the book, and we will do our best to address it.

The Application of Splunk

1

In this chapter, we will provide an explanation of what Splunk is and how it might fit into an organization's architectural roadmap. The evolution of this technology will also be discussed along with what might be considered standard or typical use cases for the technology. Finally, some more out-of-the-box uses for Splunk will be given.

The following topics will be covered in this chapter:

- The definition of Splunk
- The evolution of Splunk
- The conventional uses of Splunk
- Splunk—outside the box

The definition of Splunk

> "Splunk is an American multinational corporation headquartered in San Francisco, California, which produces software for searching, monitoring, and analyzing machine-generated big data, via a web-style interface."
>
> – http://en.wikipedia.org/wiki/Splunk

The company **Splunk** (which is a reference to cave exploration) was started in 2003 by Michael Baum, Rob Das, and Erik Swan, and was founded to *pursue a disruptive new vision* of making machine-generated data easily accessible, usable, and valuable to everyone.

Machine data (one of the fastest growing segments of big data) is defined as any information that is automatically created without human intervention. This data can be from a wide range of sources, including websites, servers, applications, networks, mobile devices, and so on, and can span multiple environments and can even be Cloud-based.

Splunk (the product) runs from both a standard command line as well as from an interface that is totally web-based (which means that no thick client application needs to be installed to access and use the tool) and performs large-scale, high-speed indexing on both historical and real-time data.

Splunk does not require a *restore* of any of the original data but stores a compressed copy of the original data (along with its indexing information), allowing you to delete or otherwise move (or remove) the original data. Splunk then utilizes this *searchable repository* from which it efficiently creates graphs, reports, alerts, dashboards, and detailed visualizations.

Splunk's main product is **Splunk Enterprise**, or simply **Splunk**, which was developed using C/C++ and Python for maximum performance and which utilizes its own **Search Processing Language** (**SPL**) for maximum functionality and efficiency.

The Splunk documentation describes SPL as follows:

> *"SPL is the search processing language designed by Splunk® for use with Splunk software. SPL encompasses all the search commands and their functions, arguments, and clauses. Its syntax was originally based upon the UNIX pipeline and SQL. The scope of SPL includes data searching, filtering, modification, manipulation, insertion, and deletion."*

Keeping it simple

You can literally install Splunk—on a developer laptop or enterprise server and (almost) everything in between—in minutes using standard installers. It doesn't require any external packages and drops cleanly into its own directory (usually into `c:\Program Files\Splunk`). Once it is installed, you can check out the readme—`splunk.txt`—file (found in that folder) to verify the version number of the build you just installed and where to find the latest online documentation.

Note that at the time of writing this book, simply going to the website `http://docs.splunk.com` will provide you with more than enough documentation to get you started with any of the Splunk products, and all of the information is available to be read online or to be downloaded in the PDF format in order to print or read offline. In addition, it is a good idea to bookmark Splunk's **Splexicon** for further reference. Splexicon is a cool online portal of technical terms that are specific to Splunk, and all the definitions include links to related information from the Splunk documentation.

After installation, Splunk is ready to be used. There are no additional *integration steps* required for Splunk to handle data from particular products. To date, Splunk simply works on almost any kind of data or data source that you might have access to, but should you actually require some assistance, there is a Splunk professional services team that can answer your questions or even deliver specific integration services. This team has reported to have helped customers integrate with technologies such as Tivoli, Netcool, HP OpenView, BMC PATROL, and Nagios.

Single machine deployments of Splunk (where a single instance or the Splunk server handles everything, including data input, indexing, searching, reporting, and so on) are generally used for testing and evaluations. Even when Splunk is to serve a single group or department, it is far more common to distribute functionalities across multiple Splunk servers.

For example, you might have one or more Splunk instance(s) to read input/data, one or more for indexing, and others for searching and reporting. There are many more methodologies for determining the uses and number of Splunk instances implemented such as the following:

- Applicable purpose
- Type of data
- Specific activity focus
- Work team or group to serve
- Group a set of knowledge objects (note that the definition of knowledge objects can vary greatly and is the subject of multiple discussions throughout this book)
- Security
- Environmental uses (testing, developing, and production)

In an enterprise environment, Splunk doesn't have to be (and wouldn't be) deployed directly on a production server. For information's sake, if you do choose to install Splunk on a server to read local files or files from local data sources, the CPU and network footprints are typically the same as if you were tailing those same files and piping the output to **Netcat** (or reading from the same data sources). The Splunk server's memory footprint for just tailing files and forwarding them over the network can be less than 30 MB of the resident memory (to be complete; you should know that there are some installations based on expected usage, perhaps, which will require more resources).

In medium- to large-scale Splunk implementations, it is common to find multiple instances (or servers) of Splunk, perhaps grouped and categorized by a specific purpose or need (as mentioned earlier).

These different deployment configurations of Splunk can completely alter the look, feel, and behavior of that Splunk installation. These deployments or *groups of configurations* might be referred to as Splunk apps; however, one might have the opinion that Splunk apps have much more *ready-to-use configurations* than deployments that you have configured based on your requirements.

Universal file handling

Splunk has the ability to read all kinds of data—in any format—from any device or application. Its power lies in its ability to turn this data into **operational intelligence (OI)**, typically out of the box and without the need for any special parsers or adapters to deal with particular data formats.

Splunk uses internal algorithms to process new data and new data sources automatically and efficiently. Once Splunk is aware of a new data type, you don't have to reintroduce it again, saving time.

Since Splunk can work with both local and remote data, it is almost infinitely scalable. What this means is that the data that you are interested in can be on the same (physical or virtual) machine as the Splunk instance (meaning Splunk's local data) or on an entirely different machine, practically anywhere in the world (meaning it is remote data). Splunk can even take advantage of Cloud-based data.

Generally speaking, when you are thinking about Splunk and data, it is useful to categorize your data into one of the four types of data sources.

In general, one can categorize Splunk data (or input) sources as follows:

- **Files and/or directories**: This is the data that exists as physical files or locations where files will exist (directories or folders).
- **Network events**: This will be the data recorded as part of a machine or environment event.
- **Windows sources**: This will be the data pertaining to MS Windows' specific inputs, including event logs, registry changes, Windows Management Instrumentation, Active Directory, exchange messaging, and performance monitoring information.
- **Other sources**: This data source type covers pretty much everything else, such as mainframe logs, FIFO queues, and scripted inputs to get data from APIs and other remote data interfaces.

Confidentiality and security

Splunk uses a typical *role-based* security model to provide flexible and effective ways to protect all the data indexed by Splunk, by controlling the searches and results in the presentation layer.

More creative methods of implementing access control can also be employed, such as:

- Installing and configuring more than one instance of Splunk, where each is configured for only the data intended for an appropriate audience
- Separating indexes by Splunk role (privileged and public roles as a simple example)
- The use of Splunk apps such as configuring each app appropriately for a specific use, objective, or perhaps for a Splunk security role

More advanced methods of implementing access control are field encryptions, searching exclusion, and field aliasing to censored data. (You might want to research these topics independent of this book's discussions.)

The evolution of Splunk

The term **big data** is used to define information that is so large and complex that it becomes nearly impossible to process using traditional means. Because of the volume and/or unstructured nature of this data, making it useful or turning it into what the industry calls OI is very difficult.

According to the information provided by the **International Data Corporation (IDC)**, unstructured data (generated by machines) might account for more than 90 percent of the data held by organizations today.

This type of data (usually found in massive and ever-growing volumes) chronicles an activity of some sort, a behavior, or a measurement of performance. Today, organizations are missing opportunities that big data can provide them since they are focused on structured data using traditional tools for **business intelligence (BI)** and data warehousing.

Mainstream methods such as relational or multidimensional databases used in an effort to understand an organization's big data are challenging at best.

Approaching big data solution development in this manner requires serious experience and usually results in the delivery of overly complex solutions that seldom allow enough flexibility to ask any questions or get answers to those questions in real time, which is not the requirement and not a *nice-to-have* feature.

The Splunk approach

> *"Splunk software provides a unified way to organize and to extract actionable insights from the massive amounts of machine data generated across diverse sources."*

> – *www.Splunk.com 2014.*

Splunk started with information technology (IT) monitoring servers, messaging queues, websites, and more. Now, Splunk is recognized for its innate ability to solve the specific challenges (and opportunities) of effectively organizing and managing enormous amounts of (virtually any kind) machine-generated big data.

What Splunk does, and does well, is to read all sorts (almost any type, even in real time) of data into what is referred to as Splunk's *internal repository* and add indexes, making it available for immediate analytical analysis and reporting. Users can then easily set up metrics and dashboards (using Splunk) that support basic business intelligence, analytics, and reporting on **key performance indicators** (**KPIs**), and use them to better understand their information and the environment.

Understanding this information requires the ability to quickly search through large amounts of data, sometimes in an unstructured or semi-unstructured way. Conventional query languages (such as SQL or MDX) do not provide the flexibility required for the effective searching of big data.

These query languages depend on schemas. A (database) schema is how the data is to be systematized or structured. This structure is based on the familiarity of the possible applications that will consume the data, the facts or type of information that will be loaded into the database, or the (identified) interests of the potential end users.

A **NoSQL** query approach method is used by Splunk that is reportedly based on the Unix command's pipelining concepts and does not involve or impose any predefined schema. Splunk's **search processing language** (**SPL**) encompasses Splunk's search commands (and their functions, arguments, and clauses).

Search commands tell Splunk what to do with the information retrieved from its indexed data. An example of some Splunk search commands include stats, abstract, accum, crawl, delta, and diff. (Note that there are many more search commands available in Splunk, and the Splunk documentation provides working examples of each!)

> *"You can point Splunk at anything because it doesn't impose a schema when you capture the data; it creates schemas on the fly as you run queries"* explained Sanjay Meta, Splunk's senior director of product marketing.

> – *InformationWeek 1/11/2012.*

The correlation of information

A Splunk search gives the user the ability to effortlessly recognize relationships and patterns in data and data sources based on the following factors:

- Time, proximity, and distance
- Transactions (single or a series)
- Subsearches (searches that actually take the results of one search and then use them as input or to affect other searches)
- Lookups to external data and data sources
- SQL-like joins

Flexible searching and correlating are not Splunk's only magic. Using Splunk, users can also rapidly construct reports and dashboards, and using visualizations (charts, histograms, trend lines, and so on), they can understand and leverage their data without the cost associated with the formal structuring or modeling of the data first.

Conventional use cases

To understand where Splunk has been conventionally leveraged, you'll see that the applicable areas have generally fallen into the categories, as shown in the following screenshot. The areas where Splunk is conventionally used are:

- Investigational searching
- Monitoring and alerting
- Decision support analysis

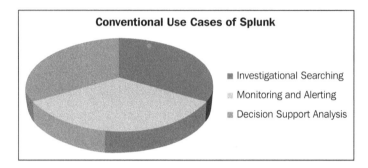

Investigational searching

The practice of investigational searching usually refers to the processes of scrutinizing an environment, infrastructure, or large accumulation of data to look for an occurrence of specific events, errors, or incidents. In addition, this process might include locating information that indicates the potential for an event, error, or incident.

As mentioned, Splunk indexes and makes it possible to search and navigate through data and data sources from any application, server, or network device in real time. This includes logs, configurations, messages, traps and alerts, scripts, and almost any kind of metric, in almost any location.

> *"If a machine can generate it - Splunk can index it…"*
>
> *– www.Splunk.com*

Splunk's powerful searching functionality can be accessed through its **Search & Reporting** app. (This is also the interface that you used to create and edit reports.)

A Splunk app (or application) can be a simple search collecting events, a group of alerts categorized for efficiency (or for many other reasons), or an entire program developed using the Splunk's REST API.

The apps are either:

- Organized collections of configurations
- Sets of objects that contain programs designed to add to or supplement Splunk's basic functionalities
- Completely separate deployments of Splunk itself

The Search & Reporting app provides you with a search bar, time range picker, and a summary of the data previously read into and indexed by Splunk. In addition, there is a dashboard of information that includes quick action icons, a mode selector, event statuses, and several tabs to show various event results.

Splunk search provides you with the ability to:

- Locate the existence of almost anything (not just a short list of predetermined fields)
- Create searches that combine time and terms
- Find errors that cross multiple tiers of an infrastructure (and even access Cloud-based environments)
- Locate and track configuration changes

Users are also allowed to accelerate their searches by shifting search modes:

- They can use the fast mode to quickly locate just the search pattern
- They can use the verbose mode to locate the search pattern and also return related pertinent information to help with problem resolution
- The smart mode (more on this mode later)

A more advanced feature of Splunk is its ability to create and run automated searches through the **command-line interface (CLI)** and the even more advanced, Splunk's REST API.

Splunk searches initiated using these advanced features do not go through Splunk Web; therefore, they are much more efficient (more efficient because in these search types, Splunk does not calculate or generate the event timeline, which saves processing time).

Searching with pivot

In addition to the previously mentioned searching options, Splunk's pivot tool is a drag-and-drop interface that enables you to report on a specific dataset without using SPL (mentioned earlier in this chapter).

The pivot tool uses data model objects (designed and built using the data model editor (which is, discussed later in this book) to arrange and filter the data into more manageable segments, allowing more focused analysis and reporting.

The event timeline

The Splunk event timeline is a visual representation of the number of events that occur at each point in time; it is used to highlight the patterns of events or investigate the highs and lows in event activity.

Calculating the Splunk search event timeline can be very resource expensive and intensive because it needs to create links and folders in order to keep the statistics for the events referenced in the search in a dispatch directory such that this information is available when the user clicks on a bar in the timeline.

 Splunk search makes it possible for an organization to efficiently identify and resolve issues faster than with most other search tools and simply obsoletes any form of manual research of this information.

Monitoring

Monitoring numerous applications and environments is a typical requirement of any organization's data or support center. The ability to monitor any infrastructure in real time is essential to identify issues, problems, and attacks before they can impact customers, services, and ultimately profitability.

With Splunk's monitoring abilities, specific patterns, trends and thresholds, and so on can be established as events for Splunk to keep an alert for, so that specific individuals don't have to.

Splunk can also trigger notifications (discussed later in this chapter) in real time so that appropriate actions can be taken to follow up on an event or even avoid it as well as avoid the downtime and the expense potentially caused by an event.

Splunk also has the power to execute actions based on certain events or conditions. These actions can include activities such as:

- Sending an e-mail
- Running a program or script
- Creating an organizational support or action ticket

For all events, all of this event information is tracked by Splunk in the form of its internal (Splunk) tickets that can be easily reported at a future date.

Typical Splunk monitoring marks might include the following:

- **Active Directory**: Splunk can watch for changes to an Active Directory environment and collect user and machine metadata.

- **MS Windows event logs and Windows printer information**: Splunk has the ability to locate problems within MS Windows systems and printers located anywhere within the infrastructure.

- **Files and directories**: With Splunk, you can literally monitor all your data sources within your infrastructure, including viewing new data when it arrives.

- **Windows performance**: Windows generates enormous amounts of data that indicates a system's health. A proper analysis of this data can make the difference between a healthy, well-functioning system and a system that suffers from poor performance or downtime. Splunk supports the monitoring of all the Windows performance counters available to the system in real time, and it includes support for both local and remote collections of performance data.

- **WMI-based data**: You can pull event logs from all the Windows servers and desktops in your environment without having to install anything on those machines.

- **Windows registry information**: A registry's health is also very important. Splunk not only tells you when changes to the registry are made but also tells you whether or not those changes were successful.

Alerting

In addition to searching and monitoring your big data, Splunk can be configured to alert anyone within an organization as to when an event occurs or when a search result meets specific circumstances. You can have both your real-time and historical searches run automatically on a regular schedule for a variety of alerting scenarios.

You can base your Splunk alerts on a wide range of threshold and trend-based situations, for example:

- Empty or null conditions
- About to exceed conditions
- Events that might precede environmental attacks
- Server or application errors
- Utilizations

All alerts in Splunk are based on timing, meaning that you can configure an alert as:

- **Real-time alerts**: These are alerts that are triggered every time a search returns a specific result, such as when the available disk space reaches a certain level. This kind of alert will give an administrator time to react to the situation before the available space reaches its capacity.

- **Historical alerts**: These are alerts based on scheduled searches to run on a regular basis. These alerts are triggered when the number of events of a certain kind exceed a certain threshold. For example, if a particular application logs errors that exceed a predetermined average.

- **Rolling time-frame alerts**: These alerts can be configured to alert you when a specific condition occurs within a moving time frame. For example, if the number of acceptable failed login attempts exceed 3 in the last 10 minutes (the last 10 minutes based on the time for which a search runs).

Splunk also allows you to create scheduled reports that trigger alerts to perform an action each time the report runs and completes. The alert can be in the form of a message or provide someone with the actual results of the report. (These alert reports might also be set up to alert individuals regardless of whether they are actually set up to receive the actual reports!)

Reporting

Alerts create records when they are triggered (by the designated event occurrence or when the search result meets the specific circumstances). Alert trigger records can be reviewed easily in Splunk, using the Splunk alert manager (if they have been enabled to take advantage of this feature).

The Splunk alert manager can be used to filter trigger records (alert results) by application, the alert severity, and the alert type. You can also search for specific keywords within the alert output. Alert/trigger records can be set up to automatically expire, or you can use the alert manager to manually delete individual alert records as desired.

Reports can also be created when you create a search (or a pivot) that you would like to run in the future (or share with another Splunk user).

Visibility in the operational world

In the world of IT **service-level agreement** (**SLA**), a support organization's ability to visualize operational data in real time is vital. This visibility needs to be present across every component of their application's architecture.

IT environments generate overwhelming amounts of information based on:

- Configuration changes
- User activities
- User requests
- Operational events
- Incidents
- Deployments
- Streaming events

Additionally, as the world digitizes the volume, the velocity and variety of additional types of data becoming available for analysis increases.

The ability to actually gain (and maintain) visibility in this operationally vital information is referred to as gaining operational intelligence.

Operational intelligence

Operational intelligence (OI) is a category of real-time, dynamic, business analytics that can deliver key insights and actually drive (manual or automated) actions (specific operational instructions) from the information consumed.

A great majority of IT operations struggle today to access and view operational data, especially in a timely and cost-efficient manner.

Today, the industry has established an organization's ability to evaluate and visualize (the volumes of operational information) in real time as the key metric (or KPI) to evaluate an organization's operational ability to monitor, support, and sustain itself.

At all levels of business and information technology, professionals have begun to realize how IT service quality can impact their revenue and profitability; therefore, they are looking for OI solutions that can run realistic queries against this information to view their operational data and understand what is occurring or is about to occur, in real time.

Having the ability to access and understand this information, operations can:

- Automate the validation of a release or deployment
- Identify changes when an incident occurs
- Quickly identify the root cause of an incident
- Automate environment consistency checking
- Monitor user transactions
- Empower support staff to find answers (significantly reducing escalations)
- Give developers self-service to access application or server logs
- Create real-time views of data, highlighting the key application performance metrics
- Leverage user preferences and usage trends
- Identify security breaches
- Measure performance

Traditional monitoring tools are inadequate to monitor large-scale distributed custom applications, because they typically don't span all the technologies in an organization's infrastructure and cannot serve the multiple analytic needs effectively. These tools are usually more focused on a particular technology and/or a particular metric and don't provide a complete picture that integrates the data across all application components and infrastructures.

A technology-agnostic approach

Splunk can index and harness all the operational data of an organization and deliver true service-level reporting, providing a centralized view across all of the interconnected application components and the infrastructures—all without spending millions of dollars in instrumenting the infrastructure with multiple technologies and/or tools (and having to support and maintain them).

No matter how increasingly complex, modular, or distributed and dynamic systems have become, the Splunk technology continues to make it possible to understand these system topologies and to visualize how these systems change in response to changes in the environment or the isolated (related) actions of users or events.

Splunk can be used to link events or transactions (even across multiple technology tiers), put together the entire picture, track performance, visualize usage trends, support better planning for capacity, spot SLA infractions, and even track how the support team is doing, based on how they are being measured.

Splunk enables new levels of visibility with actionable insights to an organization's operational information, which helps in making better decisions.

Decision support – analysis in real time

How will an organization do its analysis? The difference between profits and loss (or even survival and extinction) might depend on an organization's ability to make good decisions.

A **Decision Support System (DSS)** can support an organization's key individuals (management, operations, planners, and so on) to effectively measure the predictors (which can be rapidly fluctuating and not easily specified in advance) and make the best decisions, decreasing the risk.

There are numerous advantages to successfully implemented organizational decision support systems (those that are successfully implemented). Some of them include:

- Increased productivity
- Higher efficiency
- Better communication
- Cost reduction
- Time savings
- Gaining operational intelligence (described earlier in this chapter)
- Supportive education

- Enhancing the ability to control processes and processing
- Trend/pattern identification
- Measuring the results of services by channel, location, season, demographic, or a number of other parameters
- The reconciliation of fees
- Finding the heaviest users (or abusers)
- Many more...

Can you use Splunk as a real-time decision support system? Of course, you can! Splunk becomes your DSS by providing the following abilities for users:

- Splunk is adaptable, flexible, interactive, and easy to learn and use
- Splunk can be used to answer both structured and unstructured questions based on data
- Splunk can produce responses efficiently and quickly
- Splunk supports individuals and groups at all levels within an organization
- Splunk permits a scheduled-control of developed processes
- Splunk supports the development of Splunk configurations, apps, and so on (by all the levels of end users)
- Splunk provides access to all forms of data in a universal fashion
- Splunk is available in both standalone and web-based integrations
- Splunk possess the ability to collect real-time data with details of this data (collected in an organization's master or other data) and so much more

ETL analytics and preconceptions

Typically, your average analytical project will begin with requirements: a predetermined set of questions to be answered based on the available data. Requirements will then evolve into a data modeling effort, with the objective of producing a model developed specifically to allow users to answer defined questions, over and over again (based on different parameters, such as customer, period, or product).

Limitations (of this approach to analytics) are imposed to analytics because the use of formal data models requires structured schemas to use (access or query) the data. However, the data indexed in Splunk doesn't have these limitations because the schema is applied at the time of searching, allowing you to come up with and ask different questions while they continue to explore and get to know the data.

Another significant feature of Splunk is that it does not require data to be specifically extracted, transformed, and then (re)loaded (ETL'ed) into an accessible model for Splunk to get started. Splunk just needs to be pointed to the data for it to index the data and be ready to go.

These capabilities (along with the ability to easily create dashboards and applications based on specific objectives), empower the Splunk user (and the business) with key insights — all in real time.

The complements of Splunk

Today, organizations have implemented analytical BI tools and (in some cases) even **enterprise data warehouses (EDW)**.

You might think that Splunk will have to compete with these tools, but Splunk's goal is to not replace the existing tools and work with the existing tools, essentially *complimenting* them by giving users the ability to integrate understandings from available machine data sources with any of their organized or structured data. This kind of integrated intelligence can be established quickly (usually in a matter of hours, not days or months).

Using the compliment (not to replace) methodology:

- Data architects can expand the scope of the data being used in their other analytical tools
- Developers can use **software development kits (SDKs)** and **application program interfaces (APIs)** to directly access Splunk data from within their applications (making it available in the existing data visualization tools)
- Business analysts can take advantage of Splunk's easy-to-use interface in order to create a wide range of searches and alerts, dashboards, and perform in-depth data analytics

Splunk can also be the *engine* behind applications by exploiting the Splunk ODBC connector to connect to and access any data already read into and indexed by Splunk, harnessing the power and capabilities of the data, perhaps through an interface more familiar to a business analyst and not requiring specific programming to access the data.

ODBC

An analyst can leverage expertise in technologies such as MS Excel or Tableau to perform actions that might otherwise require a Splunk administrator using the Splunk ODBC driver to connect to Splunk data. The analyst can then create specific queries on the Splunk-indexed data, using the interface (for example, the query wizard in Excel), and then the Splunk ODBC driver will transform these requests into effectual Splunk searches (behind the scenes).

Splunk – outside the box

Splunk has been emerging as a definitive leader to collect, analyze, and visualize machine big data. Its universal method of organizing and extracting information from massive amounts of data, from virtually any source of data, has opened up and will continue to open up new opportunities for itself in unconventional areas.

Once data is in Splunk, the *sky is the limit*. The Splunk software is scalable (datacenters, Cloud infrastructures, and even commodity hardware) to do the following:

> "*Collect and index terabytes of data, across multi-geography, multi-datacenter and hybrid cloud infrastructures*"

> *– Splunk.com*

From a development perspective, Splunk includes a built-in software REST API as well as development kits (or SDKs) for JavaScript and JSON, with additional downloadable SDKs for Java, Python, PHP, C#, and Ruby and JavaScript. This supports the development of custom "big apps" for big data by making the power of Splunk the "engine" of a developed custom application.

The following areas might be considered as perhaps unconventional candidates to leverage Splunk technologies and applications due to their need to work with enormous amounts of unstructured or otherwise unconventional data.

Customer Relationship Management

Customer Relationship Management (CRM) is a method to manage a company's interactions with current and future customers. It involves using technology to organize, automate, and synchronize sales, marketing, customer service, and technical support information—all ever-changing and evolving—in real time.

Emerging technologies

Emerging technologies include the technical innovations that represent progressive developments within a field such as agriculture, biomed, electronic, energy, manufacturing, and materials science to name a few. All these areas typically deal with a large amount of research and/or test data.

Knowledge discovery and data mining

Knowledge discovery and data mining is the process of collecting, searching, and analyzing a large amount of data in a database (or elsewhere) to identify patterns or relationships in order to drive better decision making or new discoveries.

Disaster recovery

Disaster recovery (**DR**) refers to the process, policies, and procedures that are related to preparing for recovery or the continuation of technology infrastructure, which are vital to an organization after a natural or human-induced disaster. All types of information is continually examined to help put control measures in place, which can reduce or eliminate various threats for organizations. Different types of data measures can be included in disaster recovery, control measures, and strategies.

Virus protection

The business of virus protection involves the ability to detect known threats and identify new and unknown threats through the analysis of massive volumes of activity data. In addition, it is important to strive to keep up with the ever-evolving security threats by identifying new attacks or threat profiles before conventional methods can.

The enhancement of structured data

As discussed earlier in this chapter, this is the concept of connecting machine generated big data with an organization's enterprise or master data. Connecting this data can have the effect of adding context to the information mined from machine data, making it even more valuable. This "information in context" helps you to establish an informational framework and can also mean the presentation of a "latest image" (from real-time machine data) and the historic value of that image (from historic data sources) at meaningful intervals.

There are virtually limitless opportunities for the investment of enrichment of data by connecting it to a machine or other big data, such as data warehouses, general ledger systems, point of sale, transactional communications, and so on.

Project management

Project management is another area that is always ripe for improvement by accessing project specifics across all the projects in all genres. Information generated by popular project management software systems (such as MS Project or JIRA, for example) can be accessed to predict project bottlenecks or failure points, risk areas, success factors, and profitability or to assist in resource planning as well as in sales and marketing programs.

The entire product development life cycle can be made more efficient, from monitoring code checkins and build servers to pinpointing production issues in real time and gaining a valuable awareness of application usage and user preferences.

Firewall applications

Software solutions that are firewall applications will be required to pour through the volumes of firewall-generated data to report on the top blocks and accesses (sources, services, and ports) and active firewall rules and to generally show traffic patterns and trends over time.

Enterprise wireless solutions

Enterprise wireless solutions refer to the process of monitoring all wireless activity within an organization for the maintenance and support of the wireless equipment as well as policy control, threat protection, and performance optimization.

Hadoop technologies

What is Hadoop anyway? The Hadoop technology is designed to be installed and run on a (sometimes) large number of machines (that is, in a cluster) that do not have to be high-end and share memory or storage.

The object is the distributed processing of large data sets across many severing Hadoop machines. This means that virtually unlimited amounts of big data can be loaded into Hadoop because it breaks up the data into segments or pieces and spreads it across the different Hadoop servers in the cluster.

There is no central entry point to the data; Hadoop keeps track of where the data resides. Because there are multiple copy stores, the data stored on a server that goes offline can be automatically replicated from a known good copy.

So, where does Splunk fit in with Hadoop? Splunk supports the searching of data stored in the **Hadoop Distributed File System** (**HDFS**) with **Hunk** (a Splunk app). Organizations can use this to enable Splunk to work with existing big data investments.

Media measurement

This is an exciting area. Media measurement can refer to the ability to measure program popularity or mouse clicks, views, and plays by device and over a period of time. An example of this is the ever-improving recommendations that are made based on individual interests—derived from automated big data analysis and relationship identification.

Social media

Today's social media technologies are vast and include ever-changing content. This media is beginning to be actively monitored for specific information or search criteria.

This supports the ability to extract insights, measure performance, identify opportunities and infractions, and assess competitor activities or the ability to be alerted to impending crises or conditions. The results of this effort serve market researchers, PR staff, marketing teams, social engagement and community staff, agencies, and sales teams.

Splunk can be the tool to facilitate the monitoring and organizing of this data into valuable intelligence.

Geographical Information Systems

Geographical Information Systems (**GIS**) are designed to capture, store, manipulate, analyze, manage, and present all types of geographical data intended to support analysis and decision making. A GIS application requires the ability to create real-time queries (user-created searches), analyze spatial data in maps, and present the results of all these operations in an organized manner.

Mobile Device Management

Mobile devices are commonplace in our world today. The term mobile device management typically refers to the monitoring and controlling of all wireless activities, such as the distribution of applications, data, and configuration settings for all types of mobile devices, including smart phones, tablet computers, ruggedized mobile computers, mobile printers, mobile POS devices, and so on. By controlling and protecting this big data for all mobile devices in the network, **Mobile Device Management** (**MDM**) can reduce support costs and risks to the organization and the individual consumer. The intent of using MDM is to optimize the functionality and security of a mobile communications network while minimizing cost and downtime.

Splunk in action

Today, it is reported that over 6,400 customers across the world rely on the Splunk technology in some way to support their operational intelligence initiatives. They have learned that big data can provide them with a real-time, *360-degree view* of their business environments.

Summary

In this chapter, we provided you with an explanation of what Splunk is, where it was started, and what its initial focus was. We also discussed the evolution of the technology, giving the conventional use cases as well as some more advanced, forward-thinking, or out-of-the-box type opportunities to leverage the technology in the future.

In the next chapter, we will explore advanced searching topics and provide practical examples.

2
Advanced Searching

In this chapter, we will demonstrate advanced searching topics and techniques, providing meaningful examples as we go along. The following topics will be covered:

- Searching for operators, command formats, and tags
- Subsearching
- Searching with parameters
- Efficient searching with macros
- Search results

Searching in Splunk

It would be negligent for a book on mastering Splunk searching to not mention the dashboard of version 6.0.

The search dashboard

If you take a look at the Splunk search dashboard (and you should), you can break it down into four general areas. They are given as follows:

- **The search bar**: The search bar is a long textbox into which you can enter your searches when you use Splunk Web.
- **Range picker**: Using the (time) range picker, you can set the period over which to apply your search. You are provided with a good supply of preset time ranges that you can select from, but you can also enter a custom time range.
- **How-To** (panel): This is a Splunk panel that contains links that you can use to access the **Search Tutorial** and **Search Manual** pages.
- **What-To** (panel): This is another Splunk panel that displays a summary of the data that is installed on the current Splunk instance.

The new search dashboard

After you run a new search, you're taken to the **New Search** page. The search bar and time range picker are still available in this view, but the dashboard updates many more elements, including search action buttons, a search mode selector, counts of events, a job status bar, and the results tabs for events, statistics, and visualizations.

The Splunk search mechanism

All searches in Splunk take advantage of the *indexes* that are set up on the data that you are searching. Indexes exist in every database, and Splunk is not an exception. Database indexes and Splunk indexes might differ physically, but in concept, they are the same—both are used to optimize performance. Splunk's indexes organize words or phrases in the data over time. Successful Splunk searches (those that yield results) return records (events) that meet your search criteria. The more matches you find in your data, the more events returned by Splunk. This will impact the overall searching performance, so it is important to be as specific in your searches as you can.

Before we start, the following are a few things that you need to keep in mind:

- Search terms are *case insensitive*
- Search terms are *additive*
- Only the specified time frame is queried

The Splunk quick reference guide

To all of us future Splunk masters, Splunk has a *Splunk Language Quick Reference Guide* (updated for version 6.0) available for download in the PDF format from the company's website at `http://www.splunk.com/web_assets/pdfs/secure/Splunk_Quick_Reference_Guide.pdf`. I recommend that you take a look.

Please assist me, let me go

To master Splunk, you need to master Splunk's search language, which includes an almost endless array of commands, arguments, and functions. To help you with this, Splunk offers a search assistant.

The Splunk searching assistant uses *typeahead* to suggest search commands and arguments as you type into the search bar. These suggestions are based on the content of the datasource you are searching and are updated as you continue to type. In addition, the search assistant will also display the number of matches for the search term, giving you an idea of how many search results Splunk will return.

The screenshot in the next section shows the Splunk search assistant in action. I've typed TM1 into the search bar, and Splunk has displayed every occurrence of these letters that it found within my datasource (various Cognos TM1 server logs) along with the hit count.

Some information for future reference: the search assistant uses Python to perform a reverse URL lookup in order to return the description and syntax information as you type.

 You can control the behavior of the search assistant with UI settings in the **SearchBar** module, but it is recommended that (if possible) you keep the default settings and use the search assistant as a reference. Keep in mind that this *assistance* might impact the performance in some environments (typically in those environments that include excessive volumes of raw data).

Basic optimization

Searching in Splunk can be done from Splunk Web, the command-line interface (CLI), or the REST API. When you are searching using the web interface, you can (and should) optimize the search by setting the search mode (fast, verbose, or smart). The search mode selector is in the upper right-hand corner of the search bar. The available modes are smart (default), fast, and verbose. This is shown in the following screenshot:

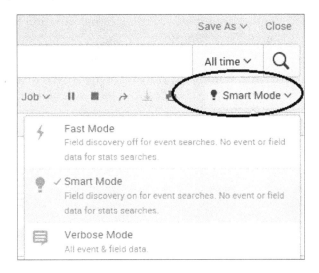

Depending on the search mode, Splunk automatically discovers and extracts fields other than the default fields, returns results as an events list or table, and runs the calculations required to generate the event timeline. This "additional work" can affect the performance; therefore, the recommended approach will be to utilize Splunk's fast mode during which you can conduct your initial search discovery (with the help of the search assistant), after which you can move to either the verbose or the smart mode (depending on specific requirements and the outcome of your search discovery).

Fast, verbose, or smart?

Splunk adjusts the search method it uses based on the selected search mode. At a high-level, the fast mode is, as the name suggests, fast (typically, the fastest method) because it tells Splunk to disable field discovery and just use its default fields, while the verbose mode will take the time to discover all the fields it can. The smart mode will take an approach (enable or disable field discovery) based on the search command's specifics.

The breakdown of commands

Some Splunk **search processing language** (**SPL**) searching commands have specific functions, arguments, and clauses associated with them. These specify how your search commands will act on search results and/or which fields they act on. In addition, search commands fall into one of the three forms, as follows:

- **Streaming**: Streaming commands apply a transformation to each event returned by a search. For example, when the `regex` command is streaming, it extracts fields and adds them to events at search time.

- **Reporting**: Reporting commands transform the search result's data into the data structures required for visualizations such as columns, bars, lines, area, and pie charts.

- **Nonstreaming**: Nonstreaming commands analyze the entire set of data available at a given level, and then derive the search result's output from that set.

Understanding the difference between sparse and dense

Always consider what you are asking Splunk to do. Based on your search objectives, you need to consider whether what you are searching for is *sparse* or *dense*. Searches that attempt to analyze large volumes of data with the expectation of yielding a few events or a single event are considered to be sparse searches. Searches that intend to summarize many occurrences of events are dense searches.

With an understanding of what type of search you are interested in performing and how Splunk will process the search, you can consider various means of **knowledgeable optimizations (KO)**.

Knowledgeable optimizations can include a simple recoding of the **search pipeline** (the structure of a Splunk search in which consecutive commands are chained together using a pipe character [|]), using more relevant search commands or operators, applying simplified logic, or configuring Splunk to recognize certain key information that you identify within your search results as you index new data.

Searching for operators, command formats, and tags

Every Splunk search will begin with search terms. These are keywords, phrases, Boolean expressions, key-value pairs, and so on, that specify which events you want to retrieve with the search.

Splunk commands can be *stacked* by delimiting them with the pipe character (|). When you stack commands in this way, Splunk will use the results (or the output) of the command on the left as an input to the command on the right, further filtering or refining the final result.

A simple example of *command stacking* might be to use commands in order to further filter retrieved events, unwanted information, extract additional event information, evaluate new fields, calculate statistics, sort results, or create a visualization (such as a chart).

The search example in the next section examines Cognos TM1 server log files for the phrase Shutdown in an attempt to determine how many times the TM1 server was shut down. Next, I've added a search field to only see the matching events that occurred (so far) in the year 2014. Finally, I want to produce a visualization of the results (to show on which days the server was shut down and how many times), so I stack the search command using the pipe delimiter to feed the results of my search into the Splunk chart command (along with the arguments I need to create a "count by day" chart).

The process flow

Before creating more complex Splunk queries or attempting any knowledgeable optimizations, it is important to understand the separate steps that occur when Splunk processes your search command pipeline. The concept of separate steps (rather than a single large query) allows Splunk to be efficient in processing your request, in much the same way as separate, smaller-sized SQL queries are more efficient than one large complicated query.

Consider the following search query example:

```
Shutdown date_year=2014 | chart count by date_mday
```

The following process will occur:

- All the indexed data (for this installation of Splunk and which version the user is configured for) is used as an input for the Splunk search
- An intermediate result table is created, containing all the events in the data that matched the search criteria (the term Shutdown is found in an event that occurs in the year 2014)
- The intermediate result table is then read into the chart command, and a visualization is created by summarizing the matching events into a count by day

Boolean expressions

The Boolean data type (a data type with only two possible values: true and false) is supported within Splunk search. The following operators are currently supported:

- AND
- OR
- NOT

Splunk Boolean searches can be simple or compound, meaning that you can have a single Boolean expression, such as the following:

```
Shutdown OR Closing
```

You can also have a compound Boolean expression, such as the following:

```
(shutdown OR Closing) AND (date_mday=3 OR date_mday=4)
```

Splunk, like any programming language, evaluates Boolean expressions using a predetermined precedence. What this means is that your Splunk search will be evaluated as follows:

1. Evaluate the expressions within the parentheses.
2. Evaluate the OR clauses.
3. Evaluate the AND or NOT clauses.

As a Splunk master, the following are some key points that you need to remember when designing your Splunk searches:

- All Boolean operators *must* be capitalized (or Splunk will not evaluate them as an operator)
- The AND operator is always implied between terms, that is, `shutdownclosing` is the same as `shutdown AND closing`
- You should always use parentheses to group your Boolean expressions (this helps with readability, among other things)
- Do not write searches based on exclusion, rather strive for inclusion (`error` instead of NOT `successful`)

You can quote me, I'm escaping

All but the simplest search commands will include white spaces, commas, pipes, quotes, and/or brackets. In addition, in most use cases, you won't want to search for the actual meaning of Splunk keywords and phrases.

To make sure that Splunk interprets your search pipelines correctly, you will need to use **quotes** and **escapes**.

Generally, you should always use quotes to ensure that your searches are interpreted correctly, both by Splunk as well as by other readers. Keep in mind that the following Splunk searches are completely different searches:

```
Server shutdown
"Server shutdown"
```

In the first search, Splunk *implies* the Boolean operator AND, so events with the words Server and shutdown in them will be returned. In the second search, only those events that have an occurrence of the phrase Server shutdown will be returned, obviously yielding potentially different results.

Furthermore, if you do want to search for events that contain the actual (raw) values of Splunk keywords or operators, you'll need to wrap the events in quotes. The rules for using quotes in Splunk search pipelines are given as follows:

- Use quotes around phrases and field values that include white spaces, commas, pipes, quotes, and/or brackets
- Quotes must be balanced (an opening quote must be followed by an unescaped closing quote)
- Use quotes around keywords and phrases if you don't want to search for their default meaning, such as Boolean operators and field-value pairs

As the quote character is used to correctly qualify your search logic, this makes it difficult to search for the actual value of a quote. To resolve this issue, you need to use the backslash character (\) to create an escape sequence.

The backslash character (\) can be used to escape quotes, pipes, and itself. Backslash escape sequences are still expanded inside quotes.

Consider the following examples:

- The sequence \| as part of a search will send a pipe character to the command, instead of having the pipe split between commands
- The sequence \" will send a literal quote to the command, for example, searching for a literal quotation mark or inserting a literal quotation mark into a field using the rex command
- The \\ sequence will be available as a literal backslash in the command

A simple example would be if you wanted to look for events that actually contain a quote character. If you use the simple search of a single quote or even wrap a quote within quotes, you will receive a syntax error.

If you use a backslash to escape the quote, you'll get better results.

One more thing to make a note of: asterisks, *, cannot be searched for using a backslash to escape the character. Splunk treats the asterisk character as a major breaker (more on this later).

Tag me Splunk!

Based on the search pipeline you construct, Splunk will effectively dissect and search through all of its indexed data. Having said that, there might be occasions where you would want to add additional intelligence to the searching—things that you know, but Splunk might not. This might be relevant information about how your organization is structured or a specific way in which you use areas of data. Examples might be host names or server names. Instead of requiring your users to retype this information (into the search pipeline each time), you can create a knowledge object in the form of a Splunk search tag.

Assigning a search tag

To assist your users (hopefully, to make searching more effective) with particular groups of event data, you can assign tags (one or multiple) to any field/value combinations (including `eventtype`, `host`, `source`, or `sourcetype`) and then perform your searches based on those tags.

Tagging field-value pairs

Let's take a look at an example. Wherever I go, it seems that Cognos TM1 servers are logging message data. This (machine-generated) data can be monitored and inputted by a Splunk server, where it will be indexed and made available for searching. This data is made up of logs generated from multiple Cognos TM1 admin servers and indexed by a single Splunk server.

If I wanted to have the capacity to search an individual server source, without having to qualify it in each of my searches, I could create a tag for this server.

So, in a typical search result (using Splunk Web), you can locate an event (that has the field value pair that you want to tag) and then perform the following steps:

1. First, locate the arrow graphic (next to the event) and click on it.
2. Again, locate the arrow graphic, this time under **Actions**, and click on it (next to your field value).
3. Select **Edit Tags**.
4. Now, you can construct your tag and click on **Save** (to actually add this tag).

In this example, a tag named `TM1-2` was created to specify an individual Cognos TM1 server source. Now, in the future, this tag can be used to narrow down searches and separate events that occurred only in that server log.

The syntax to narrow down a search (as shown in the preceding example) is as follows:

```
tag=<tagname>
```

Taking this a bit further, you can narrow down a search by associating a tag with a specific field using the following syntax:

```
tag::<field>=<tagname>
```

Wild tags!

You, as a Splunk master, can use the asterisk (*) as a wildcard when you are searching using Splunk tags. For example, if you have multiple `sourcetype` tags for various types of TM1 servers, such as TM1-1 all the way through TM1-99, you have the ability to search for all of them simply using the following code:

```
tag::eventtype=TM1-*
```

What if you wanted to locate all the hosts whose tags contain 44? No problem, you can search for the tag as follows:

```
tag::host=*44*
```

Although you'll find the following example in several places in the Splunk documentation, I have yet to find a way to use it. If you want to search for all the events with event types that have no tags associated with them, you can search for the Boolean expression as follows:

```
NOT tag::eventtype=*
```

Wildcards – generally speaking

Yes, Splunk does support wildcards, and this extends the flexibility of your search efforts. It is, however, vital to recognize that the *more flexible* (or less specific) your Splunk searches are, the less efficient they will be. Proceed with caution when implementing wildcards within your searches (especially complex or clever ones).

Disabling and deleting tags

Once you have established a tag, you can manage it—delete it or disable it—by going to **Settings** and then selecting **Tags**.

From there, you can select all unique tag objects to view your tags (some tags might not be public). Finally, from there, you can change the status (to disable) or select the action to be deleted.

Transactional searching

"A transaction comprises a "unit of work" treated in a coherent and reliable way independent of other data."

– Wikipedia, 2014.

In Splunk, you can (either using Splunk Web or the CLI) search for and identify *related raw events* and group them into *one single event*, which we will then refer to as a *transaction*.

These events can be linked together by the fields that they have in common. In addition, transactions can be saved as transactional types for later reuse.

Transactions can include the following:

- Different events from the same source/host
- Different events from different sources / same host
- Similar events from different hosts/sources

It's important to understand the power of Splunk transactional searches, so let's consider a few conceptual examples for its use:

- A particular server error triggers several events to be logged
- All events that occur within a precise period of time of each other
- Events that share the same host or cookie value
- Password change attempts that occurred near unsuccessful logins
- All of the web addresses that a particular IP address viewed over a specific range of time

To use Splunk transactions, you can either *call a transaction type* (which you configured via the `transactiontypes.conf` file) or *define transaction constraints within your search* (by setting the search options of the transaction command).

The following is the transaction command's syntax:

```
transaction [<field-list>] [name=<transaction-name>] <txn_definition-
opt>* <memcontrol-opt>* <rendering-opt>*
```

A Splunk transaction is made up of two key arguments: a field name (or a list of field names, delimited by a comma) and a name for the transaction, and several other optional arguments:

- **The field list**: The field list will be a string value made up of one or more field names that you want Splunk to use the values of in order to group events into transactions.

- **The transaction name**: This will be the ID (name) that will be referred to in your transaction or the name of a transaction type from the `transactiontypes.conf` file.

- **The optional arguments**: If other configuration arguments (such as `maxspan`) are provided in your Splunk search, they overrule the values of the parameter that is specified in the transaction definition (within the `transactiontypes.conf` file). If these parameters are not specified in the file, Splunk Enterprise uses the default value.

Knowledge management

As mentioned, you can define or create Splunk transactional types for later use by yourself or for other Splunk users by utilizing the `transactiontypes.conf` file. A lot of thought should go into a Splunk knowledge management strategy. You will find more on this topic later in this book, but for now, here are the basics you can use to define some Splunk transactions:

1. If it doesn't already exist, you can use a text editor to create a `transactiontypes.conf` file in `$SPLUNK_HOME/etc/system/local/` or your own custom app directory in `$SPLUNK_HOME/etc/apps/`.

2. Next, define transactions using the following arguments:

```
[<transactiontype>]
maxspan =  [<integer> s|m|h|d|-1]
maxpause = [<integer> s|m|h|d|-1]
fields = <comma-separated list of fields>
startswith = <transam-filter-string>
endswith=<transam-filter-string>
```

Let's discover the functions of the code terms in the preceding example:

- `transactiontype`: This is the name of the transaction type
- `maxspan`: This sets the maximum time span for the transaction
- `maxpause`: This sets the maximum pause between events in a transaction
- `maxevents`: This sets the maximum number of events in a transaction

- `fields`: This is a comma-separated list of fields
- `startswith`: This marks the beginning of a new transaction
- `endswith`: This marks the end of a transaction

For example, I can edit the Splunk `transactiontypes.conf` file to include a new Splunk transactional type named `TM1-2`. This tag can be used to look for the possibilities that a TM1 admin server was shut down and restarted (or restarted and then shut down) within a one-hour time span and the events occurred no longer than 15 minutes between each other.

For ever after or until the Splunk `transactiontypes.conf` file is changed, this transaction can be searched by typing the following:

```
sourcetype=tm1* | transaction TM1-2
```

Some working examples

Here is an example of knowledge management:

```
http | transaction maxpause=2s
```

Results will be all the transactions defined as events with the string `http` in them that occurred within two seconds of each other. Consider the following:

```
sourcetype=access_* | transaction clientip maxspan=30s maxpause=5s
```

This defines a transaction based on web access events that share the same IP address. The first and last events in the transaction should be no more than 30 seconds apart, and each event should not be longer than 5 seconds apart. Consider the following:

```
... | transaction from maxspan=90s maxpause=5s
```

This defines a transaction that groups search results that have the same value of `from`, with a maximum span of 90 seconds, and a pause between events no greater than 5 seconds into a transaction.

Subsearching

A subsearch is a Splunk search that uses a search pipeline as the argument. Subsearches in Splunk are contained in square brackets and evaluated first. Think of a subsearch as being similar to a SQL subquery (a subquery is a SQL query nested inside a larger query).

Subsearches are mainly used for three purposes:

- To parameterize one search using the output of another search
- To run a separate search but to stitch the output to the first search using the `append` command
- To create a conditional search where you only see the results of your search if the result meets the criteria or perhaps the threshold of the subsearch

Generally, you use a subsearch to take the results of one search and use them in another search, all in a single Splunk search pipeline. Because of how this works, the second search must be able to accept arguments, such as with the `append` command (as mentioned earlier).

Some examples of subsearching are as follows:

- **Parameterization**: Consider the following code:

  ```
  sourcetype=TM1* ERROR[search earliest=-30d | top limit=1 date_
  mday| fields + date_mday]
  ```

  The preceding Splunk search utilizes a subsearch as a parameterized search of all TM1 logs indexed within the Splunk instance that have error events. The subsearch (enclosed in square brackets) filters the search (looking for the `ERROR` character string in all the data of the sourcetype `TM1*`) to the past 30 days and then the top event in a single day.

- **Appending**: Splunk's `append` command can be used to append the results of a subsearch to the results of a current search:

  ```
  sourcetype=TM1* ERROR | stats dc(date_year), count by sourcetype |
  append [search sourcetype=TM1* | top 1 sourcetype by date_year]
  ```

  The preceding Splunk search utilizes a subsearch with an `append` command to combine 22 TM1 server log searches. The main search looks through all the indexed TM1 sources for "error" events; the subsequent search yields a count of the events by TM1 source by year, and the next subsearch returns the top (or the most active) TM1 source by year. The results of the two searches are then appended.

- **Conditions**: Consider the following code:

```
sourcetype=access_* | stats dc(clientip), count by method | append
[search sourcetype=access_* clientip where action = 'addtocart' by
method]
```

The preceding Splunk search counts the number of different IP addresses
that accessed the web server and also the user that accessed the web server
the most for each type of page request (method); it was modified with
the `where` clause to limit the counts to only those that are the `addtocart`
actions (in other words, which user added the most to their online shopping
cart—whether they actually purchased anything or not).

To understand the preceding search command better, we can dissect it into smaller
sections as follows:

Search command section	Purpose
`sourcetype=access_*`	This searches the web server logs indexed under the `access_*` source type
`stats dc(clientip) count by method`	This counts the number of events by method for each client IP
`[search sourcetype=access_* clientip where action = 'addtocart' by method]`	This looks for only the `addtocart` events

Output settings for subsearches

When performing a Splunk subsearch, you will often utilize the `format` command,
which takes the results of a subsearch and formats them into a **single result**.

Depending on the search pipeline, the results returned might be numerous, which
will impact the performance of your search. To remedy this, you can change the
number of results that the `format` command operates over in line with your search
by appending the following to the end of your subsearch:

```
| format maxresults = <integer>.
```

More aligned to the Splunk master perspective, it is recommended that you take a
more conservative approach and utilize Splunk's `limits.conf` file to enforce limits
on your subsearches.

This file exists in the `$SPLUNK_HOME/etc/system/default/` folder (for global settings), or for localized control, you might find (or create) a copy in the `$SPLUNK_HOME/etc/system/local/` folder. The file controls all Splunk searches (provided it is coded correctly, based on your environment), but also contains a section specific to Splunk subsearches, titled `subsearch`. Within this section, there are three important subsections:

- `maxout`: This is the maximum number of results to be returned from a subsearch. The default is 100.
- `maxtime`: This is the maximum number of seconds to run a subsearch for before finalizing. This defaults to 60.
- `ttl`: This is the time to cache a given subsearch's results. This defaults to 300.

The following is a sample subsearch section from a `limits.conf` file:

```
[subsearch]
maxout = 250
maxtime = 120
ttl = 400
```

Search Job Inspector

After running a Splunk search, you can click on the **Job** menu and select **Inspect Job** to open the **Search Job Inspector** dialog.

Within the **Search Job Inspector** dialog, you can view a summary of the returned events and (search) execution costs; also, under **Search job properties**, you can scroll down to the **remoteSearch** component and take a look at the actual Splunk search query that resulted from your subsearch.

The Splunk search job inspector can help you determine performance bottlenecks within your Splunk search pipeline, such as which search has the greatest "cost" (takes the most time). It dissects the behavior of your searches so that you better understand how to optimize them.

Searching with parameters

In Splunk, searches can be initiated in both Splunk Web as well as in the Splunk command-line interface or CLI (for information on how to access the CLI and find help for it, refer to the *SplunkAdmin* manual).

Your searches in CLI work the same way as searches in Splunk Web, except that there is no timeline given with the search results and there is no default time range. Instead, the results are displayed as a raw events list or a table, depending on the type of your search. Searching parameters (such as batch, header, and wrap) are options that control the way the CLI search is run or the way the search results are displayed.

 In addition to Splunk Web and Splunk CLI, there is an **applications programming interface (API)** available, which Splunk programmers can use to perform searches and manage Splunk configurations and objects.

Searching with the CLI will not be covered in this book, so our discussion on searching with parameters will focus on the (advanced) searching idea of parameterizing portions of a Splunk search, using statements such as `eval` and also segue into our next section, *Splunk macros*.

In Splunk searches, you have the ability to parameterize a search through the use of the `eval` statement. This means that a search can be written to take as its search criteria the current value of the following:

- A single field
- A portion of a field or fields
- Multiple fields
- A calculated value
- A logically built value

The eval statement

The Splunk `eval` statement will evaluate (almost) any expression and put the resulting value into a (required) field that can be used (as a parameter) by a Splunk search. Its syntax is simple:

```
eval <eval-field>=<eval-expression>
```

It has the following parameters:

- `eval-field`: This is the destination (string) field name for the resulting value
- `eval-expression`: This is a combination of values, variables, operators, and functions that represent the value of the `eval` destination field

The `eval` statement can include arithmetic, concatenation, and Boolean operators as well as a number of Splunk functions (such as `ifnull`, `tostring`, and `upper`, to name a few).

A simple example

Let's see a simple `eval` example:

```
sourcetype=TM1* error | EVAL event_date =  date_month  + "/" + date_
mday + "/" + date_year | where event_date = "october/24/2007"
```

The preceding Splunk search uses the `eval` statement to create a new field named `event_date` by concatenating the `date_month`, `date_mday`, and `date_year` fields and then uses this field in the search to locate only the events that occurred on a particular date. Consider the following:

```
sourcetype=TM1* error   | eval status = if(date_wday == "sunday",
"Error", "OK")| search status=Error
```

The preceding Splunk search uses the `eval` statement to update the field status using some logic. In this case, if errors are found in the TM1 server logs that occurred on a Sunday, then they are truly errors and Splunk should return those events for review, otherwise (if the error occurred on any other day), the events are ignored (not returned).

Splunk macros

A Splunk macro can be thought of as a (hopefully, previously tested and otherwise validated) reusable assembly of Splunk (or business) logic – basically, any part or even all of a Splunk search that you don't want to type in again. Saved macros can even be defined to receive arguments when reused. Splunk macros are an integral part of knowledge management.

To understand how macros might be defined, saved, and reused, let's take a look at the previous example using the previously defined `eval` statement. In the following search, we defined a new field to be evaluated and searched on, named `event_date`:

```
sourcetype=TM1* error | EVAL event_date =  date_month  + "/" + date_
mday + "/" + date_year | where event_date = "october/24/2007"
```

The `event_date` field is made up of the `date_month`, `date_mday`, and `date_year` fields. Since we will perhaps want to perform multiple searches in the future, searching for events that occurred on different dates and we don't want to retype the `eval` statement, we can save our definition of `event_date` as a macro, which we can call in our future search pipelines.

Creating your own macro

The easiest way to create a Splunk search macro is through Splunk Web. Under **Settings**, select **Advanced Search** and then click on **Search macros**.

In the **Search macros** page, you will see previously defined macros. You can then click on **New** to define the new search macro on the **Add new** page.

In the **Add new** page, you'll see the following fields:

- **Destination app**: This is the name of the Splunk app you want to restrict your search macro to; by default, your search macros are restricted to the search app.

- **Name**: This is the name of your search macro (in our example, we'll use TM1_Event_Date). If you want your search macro to take an argument, you will need to indicate this by appending the number of arguments to the name; for example, if TM1_Event_Date requires two arguments, it should be named TM1_Event_Date(2).

- **Definition**: This is the string that your search macro expands to when referenced in another search. If your search macro requires the user to type arguments, you will indicate this by wrapping dollar signs around the arguments; for example, $arg1$. The arguments' values are then specified when the search macro is invoked.

For your example, you can type the following eval statement to define your new search field into the **Definition** area in the **Add new** page:

```
EVAL event_date =  date_month  + "/" + date_mday + "/" + date_year
```

Using your macros

To include a saved Splunk search macro in a search, you need to use the left quote (also known as a grave accent) character. Note that this is *not* the straight quote character that appears on the same key as the double quote (").

Consider the following example:

```
sourcetype=TM1* error  |  `TM1_Event_Date`  |  where event_date =
"october/24/2007"
```

In this example, I created a macro to avoid redefining my search field, event_date. What if I build on this idea—the idea is that if I regularly search for (in this case) TM1 error events that occurred on a specific date (that is, month/day/year), then why not just save the entire search as a Splunk macro that receives a date at search time? To do this, I can create a new macro, named TM1Events(1). Remember that the naming convention that Splunk understands is to include (in parentheses) the number of arguments that will be supplied at search time; so, in this case it will be 1. The following screenshot shows my macro definition (notice that I added my argument wrapped in dollar signs, $argme$) to the **Definition** area and named by a single argument (argme) in the **Arguments** area:

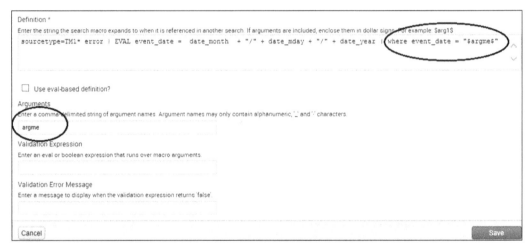

My macro definition

Now, we can use the following to run the Splunk search (to call my macro):

```
`TM1Events("october/24/2007")`
```

The limitations of Splunk

There really isn't any limit to the number of macros you can define or to the number that can be included in a single search; just keep in mind that when you read the preceding Splunk search example, one doesn't inherently know how TM1_Event_Date is defined. This is another area where a robust knowledge management strategy is critical.

Search results

When you run a Splunk search, you'll see that not all of the Splunk Web search results tabs (**Events**, **Statistics**, and **Visualization**) will be populated.

- **Event searches**: If your search returns only events, only the **Events** results tab is populated
- **Transformational searches**: If your search includes transforming commands, you can view the results in the **Statistics** and **Visualization** tabs (as well as in the **Events** tab)
- **Transformational commands**: Transformational commands transform the event results into numerical values that Splunk can use for statistical purposes, that is, creating charts, tables, and graphs

Transforming commands include the following:

- `chart`
- `timechart`
- `stats`
- `top`
- `rare`
- `contingency`

Some basic Splunk search examples

To illustrate the differences in the results tabs, let's use an earlier search example. You might recall the following search (using a macro that we created):

```
`TM1Events("october/24/2007")`
```

This search is a simple events search and will only populate the **Events** results tab. However, the **Statistics** and **Visualization** results tabs are not populated.

Now, we can add a transformation command (in this case, I've chosen to add the `timechart` command to break up our results from the search day as "events per second") to our search, as follows:

```
`TM1Events("october/24/2007")` | timechart per_second(date_second)
```

Now, *all* the result tabs are populated.

Additional formatting

Splunk also provides several commands to improve the look of your search results. These include the following:

- `abstract`: This shows a summary of up to five lines for each search result.
- `diff`: This compares values between search results and shows the differences between the two.
- `highlight`: This highlights specified terms.
- `iconify`: This displays a different icon for each event type.
- `outputtext`: This outputs the `_raw` field of your current search into `_xml`.
- `scrub`: This anonymizes the current search results.
- `xmlunescape`: This unescapes all XML characters.
- `append`: This is not a typical formatting command, but it is worth mentioning. This appends the current results to the tabular results of another search result.

Summary

In this chapter, we provided the reader with an exploration of some of the Splunk advanced search topics, such as some simple (search commands) optimization strategies based on the search command objectives. In addition, we took a look at search operators, tagging, transactional searches, subsearches, and macros. We used working examples in some cases, leveraging some of the most-used Splunk search commands (`chart`, `eval`, `timechart`, `top`, `transaction`, and `where`).

In the next chapter, we will review advanced tables, charts, and field topics and provide practical examples.

3
Mastering Tables, Charts, and Fields

This chapter will provide you with in-depth methods for leveraging Splunk tables, charts, and fields and also provide some working examples. The topics that will be covered in this chapter are:

- Tables, charts, and fields
- Drilldowns
- Pivots
- Sparklines

Tables, charts, and fields

After reading *Chapter 2*, *Advanced Searching*, you should know that when you run a Splunk search, your command pipeline determines which search result's tab (or tabs) will get populated. We know that if you are concentrating on retrieving events, your results will be returned in the **Events** tab, while event transformations will be visible in the **Statistics** and **Visualization** tabs.

In this chapter, we will cover the transformation of event data, and therefore, the **Statistics** and **Visualization** tabs.

Splunking into tables

Splunking your search results into a table might be the easiest and most straightforward method of transforming your search results into a more readable form. Rather than looking at raw event data, you can use Splunk commands to reduce the noise of the raw events into the Splunk **Statistics** tab, presented as a table in the tab.

You can utilize Splunk's `fields` command to improve the level of readability of the **Statistics** tab by keeping or removing a field (or multiple fields) from your Splunk search results:

- Use + to keep only the fields that match one of the fields in the (fields) list
- Use – to remove the field(s) that matches the (fields) list

It's common practice to be specific in what you want your Splunk search results to return. The `fields` command allows you to do this. Splunk's `table` command is (somewhat) similar to the `fields` command (discussed later in this chapter). The `table` command enables you to specify (limit) the fields that you want to keep in your results (in your table). However, keep in mind that Splunk requires certain *internal* fields to be present in a search to perform some commands (such as the `chart` command), and the `table` command (by default) might pull these fields out of the search results. As a rule, the best approach for limiting results is to use the `fields` command (because it always retains all the internal fields).

The table command

The `table` command is simply the command "table" and a (required) "field list." A table is created using only the fields you named. Wildcards can be used as part of the field list. Columns are displayed in the same order in which the fields are specified.

Please note the following cases:

- Column headers = field names
- Rows = field values
- Each row = 1 event

The following example uses the `table` command to create a three-column table, `date_year`, `date_month`, and `date_wday`, as shown in the following screenshot:

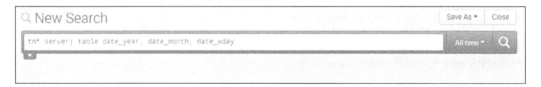

The result looks like the following screenshot:

Search results

Splunk's `table` command does not allow you to rename the Splunk fields. You can only rename the fields that you specify and want to show in your results table. You need to use the `rename` command if you want to rename a field.

The Splunk rename command

You can use Splunk's `rename` command to rename a specific field or multiple fields. With this command, you can give your fields more meaningful names, such as `month` instead of `date_month`. To rename multiple fields, you can use wildcards. If you want to use a phrase (if there are spaces in your new field name), you need to wrap the phrase within quotes. The syntax is simple, as follows:

```
rename old-field-name as new-field-name
```

To rename a field to a text phrase, you can use quotes as shown in the following syntax:

```
... | rename SESSIONID AS "The Session"
```

You can also use wildcards to rename multiple fields:

```
... | rename *ip AS IPaddress_*
```

In the following example, I've used the `rename` command to rename all the three fields to what I want and then I've used those names in my `table` command:

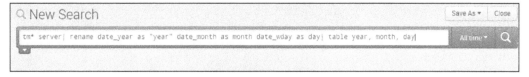

The rename command

The results of the search, using the `rename` command, look like the following screenshot:

Search result of the rename command

Another example of using the Splunk `table` command to transform your search results is explained here. In this case, the Splunk server has indexed a raw CSV file exported from a Cognos TM1 model. Because there are no headings in the file, Splunk has interpreted the data as field names. In addition, Splunk interpreted each record's forecast amount as a string. I've utilized Splunk's `rename` command to rename the fields with names that are more meaningful, such as:

- May as `Month`
- Actual as `Version`
- FY 2012 as `Year`
- Many others

In addition, I've used Splunk's `eval` command to create a rounded forecast amount:

```
Eval = RFCST= round(FCST)
```

Finally, I used the `table` command to present my search results in a more readable fashion:

```
sourcetype=csv 2014 "Current Forecast" "Direct"  "513500" |  rename
May as "Month" Actual as "Version" "FY 2012" as Year 650693NLR001
as "Business Unit" 100000 as "FCST" "09997_Eliminations Co 2" as
"Account" "451200" as "Activity" | eval RFCST= round(FCST) | Table
Month, "Business Unit", Activity, Account, RFCST, FCST
```

After running the (preceding) Splunk search pipeline, the following results are obtained:

Month	Business Unit	Activity	Account	RFCST	FCST
June	999999	513500	42000-S2S GLOBAL	3049034	3049033.736
May	999999	513500	42000-S2S GLOBAL	3049034	3049033.736
April	999999	513500	42000-S2S GLOBAL	3049034	3049033.736
March	999999	513500	42000-S2S GLOBAL	3048728	3048728.3670000001
February	999999	513500	42000-S2S GLOBAL	3225361	3225361.287

Search results of the table command

Limits

As you might know by now, Splunk uses configuration (or conf) files to allow you to override its default attributes, parameters, and thresholds. The `limits.conf` file contains possible attribute-value pairs for configuring *limits for search commands*. Note that there is a `limits.conf` file at the following location:

`$SPLUNK_HOME/etc/system/default/`.

> Note that the changes to the `limits.conf` file should be made to the file located in your Splunk `local` directory, not in the Splunk `home` directory.

In a default installation, the Splunk `table` command will shorten the total number of results returned if the `truncate_report` parameter in the Splunk configuration file, `limits.conf`, is set to `1`.

Fields

When Splunk indexes your data, it labels each event with a number of fields. These fields become a part of the index's event data and are returned as part of the search results. Splunk also adds some data a number of default fields that serve particular purposes within Splunk's internal processing. The following are some of Splunk's default fields along with their purposes (you can refer to the product's documentation for a complete list):

- `index`: This identifies the index in which the event is located
- `linecount`: This describes the number of lines that the event contains

Once the data has been indexed, you can use these default fields in your Splunk searches. If you don't need them, you might want to consider removing them from your search results to improve performance and possibly the readability of your results. You can use the Splunk `fields` command to tell Splunk to keep or remove a field (or fields) from your search results.

 Keep in mind, though, that some default fields might be needed by Splunk internally based on your search pipeline. For example, most statistical commands require the default `_time` field.

The `fields` command is simple:

```
fields [+|-] <field-list>
```

The field list is a comma-delimited list of fields to keep (+) or remove (-) a field and can include wildcards. A leading + sign will keep the field list, while - will remove the fields listed. Note that if you do not include + or -, Splunk assumes the value to be +.

An example of the fields command

Consider the following code, which we used earlier to present the search results:

```
sourcetype=csv 2014 "Current Forecast" "Direct"  "513500" | rename
May as "Month" Actual as "Version" "FY 2012" as Year 650693NLR001
as "Business Unit" 100000 as "FCST" "09997_Eliminations Co 2" as
"Account" "451200" as "Activity" | eval RFCST= round(FCST) | Table
Month, "Business Unit", Activity, Account, RFCST, FCST
```

The result that we obtained using the preceding code is shown as follows:

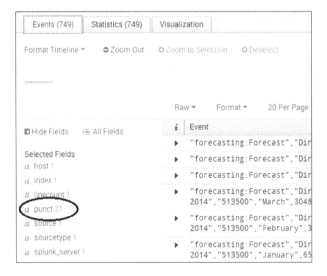

We'll now take a look at the same code (used previously), using the
`fields` command:

```
sourcetype=csv 2014 "Current Forecast" "Direct"  "513500" | fields -
punct |  rename May as "Month" Actual as "Version" "FY 2012" as Year
650693NLR001 as "Business Unit" 100000 as "FCST" "09997_Eliminations
Co 2" as "Account" "451200" as "Activity" | eval RFCST= round(FCST) |
Table Month, "Business Unit", Activity, Account, RFCST, FCST
```

The result obtained (using the `fields` command to remove the field named `punct`)
is as follows:

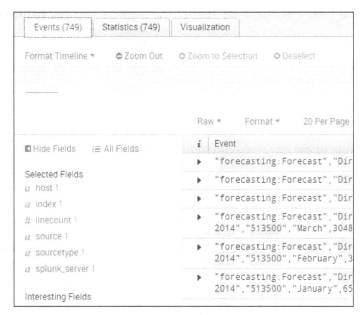

Search result of the fields command

Returning search results as charts

We've covered the **Events** and **Statistics** tabs until this point, so now we will take a
look at the **Visualizations** tab.

Basically, Splunk delivers the simple "list of events" visualization as the standard
search result option. In addition, other options (covered in this chapter) include
tables and charts such as column, line, area, and pie chart (which are displayed on
the Splunk **Visualizations** tab).

Splunk's `chart` command is a reporting command that returns your search results
in a data structure (described in a tabular output) that supports visualization such
as a chart.

The chart command

The `chart` command is a bit more complex than the Splunk `table` command. It has both required and optional arguments. Charted fields are converted automatically to numerical quantities as required by Splunk. With the `chart` command (as opposed to the somewhat similar `timechart` command that always generates a `_time` x-axis as is discussed later in this chapter), you are able to set your own x-axis for your chart visualization.

The required arguments for the `chart` command are `aggregator`, `sparkline-agg-term`, and `eval-expression`, which are explained as follows (note that if you don't use sparklines in your visualization, `sparkline-agg-term` is not required.):

- `aggregator`: This argument specifies an aggregator or function
- `sparkline-agg-term`: This argument is the sparkline (sparklines are discussed later in this chapter) specifier
- `eval-expression`: This argument is a combination of literals, fields, operators, and functions that represent the value of your destination field

A simple example of the `chart` command is shown as follows:

```
sourcetype=csv "Current Forecast" "Direct"  "513500" | rename 100000
as "FCST", "FY 2012" as "Year"| eval RFCST= round(FCST) | chart
avg(RFCST) by Year
```

In this example (using a Cognos TM1 exported CSV file as the source), I use a common Splunk statistics function, `avg`, as the aggregator and specify the x-axis of the chart as `year` using `by` (the `over` command will work here as well). I've also created a value named `FCST` using the `rename` command, which I then use as `eval-expression` of this search. I don't need sparklines in this visualization, so there is no `sparkline-agg-term` used in the command.

The `search` command shown in Splunk Web is as follows:

The search command

The result obtained by running the previous `search` command is as follows:

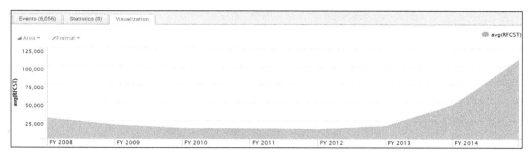

Result of the search command

The split-by fields

When using Splunk's `chart` command, you have the ability to designate a "split-by field." This means that your Splunk search output will be a table where each column represents a distinct value of the split-by field, as shown here:

```
sourcetype=csv "2014" "Current Forecast" "Direct" "513500" | rename
100000 as "FCST", "May" as "Month" | eval RFCST= round(FCST) | sort
by Month | chart sum(FCST) by FCST, Month
```

In the preceding example, we have `chart sum(FCST) by FCST, Month`; so, the first field after `by FCST` ends up being represented as one-field-per-row (Splunk refers to this as `group by`). The second field after `by Month` ends up being represented as one-field-per-column (this is the `split-by` field). The resulting visualization is different, as shown here:

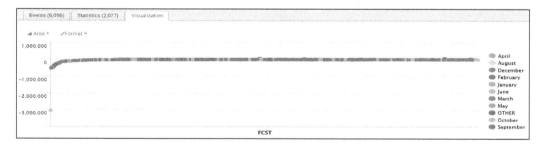

The where clause

You can think of the Splunk `where` clause as being similar to the `where` clause in a SQL query. The "where" specifies the criteria for including (or excluding) particular data within a Splunk search pipeline. For example, consider the following search:

```
sourcetype=csv "2014" "Direct" "513500" ("Current Forecast" OR
"Budget") | rename 100000 as "FCST", "May" as "Month", Actual as
"Version" | eval RFCST= round(FCST) | chart var(FCST) over Month by
Version
```

The preceding search generates the following output:

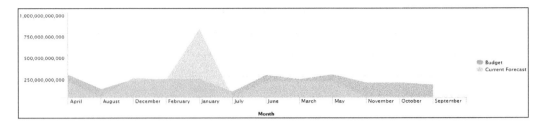

The previous code can be changed as follows using the `where` clause:

```
sourcetype=csv "2014"  "Direct"  "513500" ("Current Forecast" OR
"Budget")  | rename 100000 as "FCST", "May" as "Month", Actual as
"Version" | eval RFCST= round(FCST)  |  where FCST > 99999 | chart
var(FCST) over Month by Version
```

The given code will generate the following output:

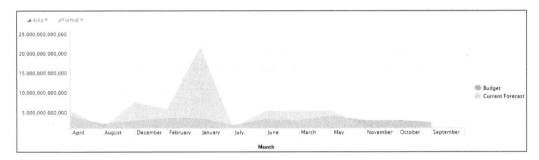

More visualization examples

In the following example, we're interested in events returned by a Cognos TM1 transaction log with the mention of the TM1 control dimension named `}clients`. We want to see this information visualized by the hour, over weekdays, and then month:

```
tm1* }Clients| chart count(date_hour) over date_wday by date_month  |
sort by date_wday
```

The chart obtained after running this code is as follows:

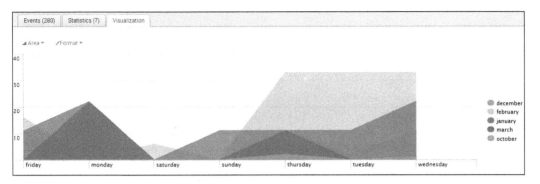

This example visualizes the earliest hour by week day when a Cognos TM1 "Error" occurred, using the earliest command, as shown here:

```
tm1* "Error" | chart earliest(date_hour) over date_wday
```

This command generates the following output:

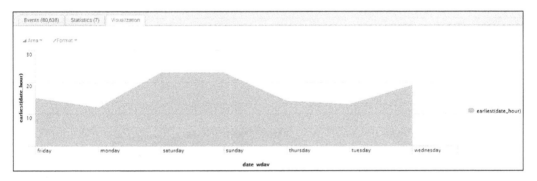

In the next example, we will visualize the median of the FCST value by month for each version of the data (actual, budget, current, and prior forecast) by using the median command (along with over and by):

```
sourcetype=csv "2014"  "Direct"  "513500" |  rename 100000 as "FCST",
"May" as "Month", Actual as "Version" | eval RFCST= round(FCST) |
chart Median(FCST) over Month by Version
```

The preceding search command generates the following output:

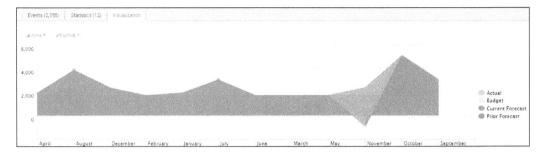

In the following example, we visualize the sample variance of the FCST value by month for the versions of the data Budget and Current Forecast by using the var command (and over and by):

```
sourcetype=csv "2014" "Direct" "513500" ("Current Forecast" OR
"Budget") | rename 100000 as "FCST", "May" as "Month", Actual as
"Version" | eval RFCST= round(FCST) | chart var(FCST) over Month by
Version
```

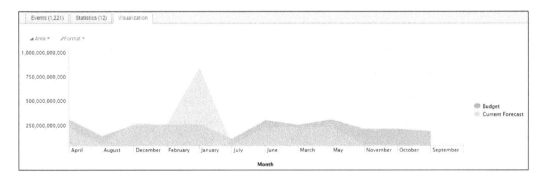

Some additional functions

When using the chart command, there is a list of powerful functions that you should be aware of.

These include avg, C or Count, dc or distinct_count, earliest, estdc, estdc_ error, First, Last, latest, List, max, Median, Min, Mode, Range, Stdev, Stdevp, sum, sumsq, Values, Var, and varp.

You can refer to the product documentation for the purpose and syntax of each of these commands.

Splunk bucketing

The Splunk bucketing option allows you to group events into discreet buckets of information for better analysis. For example, the number of events returned from the indexed data might be overwhelming, so it makes more sense to group or bucket them by a span (or a time range) of time (seconds, minutes, hours, days, months, or even subseconds).

We can use the following example to illustrate this point:

```
tm1* error | stats count(_raw) by _time source
```

Notice the generated output:

Here is an additional example:

```
tm1* error | bucket _time span=5d | stats count(_raw) by _time source
```

The output obtained is as follows:

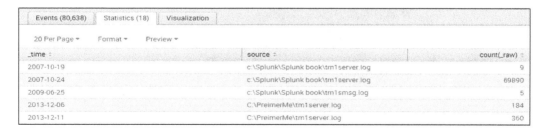

Reporting using the timechart command

Similar to the `chart` command, `timechart` is a reporting command for creating time series charts with a corresponding table of statistics. As discussed earlier, `timechart` always generates a `_time` x-axis (while with `chart`, you are able to set your own x-axis for your chart visualization). This is an important difference as the following commands appear to be identical (they just use different reporting commands) but yield very different results:

```
tm1* rule |   chart count(date_hour) by date_wday
tm1* rule |   timechart count(date_hour) by date_wday
```

The `chart` command displays the following visualization:

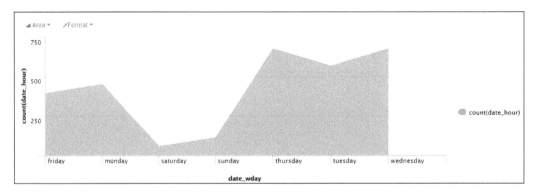

The `timechart` command displays the following version of the visualization:

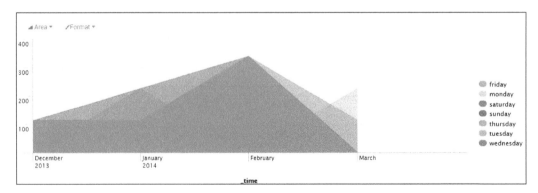

Arguments required by the timechart command

When you use the Splunk `timechart` command, a single aggregation or an `eval` expression must be supplied, as follows:

- **Single aggregation**: This is an aggregation applied to a single field
- **Eval expression**: This is a combination of literals, fields, operators, and functions that represent the value of your destination field

Bucket time spans versus per_* functions

The `per_day()`, `per_hour()`, `per_minute()`, and `per_second()` functions are the aggregator functions to be used with `timechart` in order to get a consistent scale for your data (when an explicit span (a time range) is not provided). The functions are described as follows:

- `per_day()`: This function returns the values of the field X per day
- `per_hour()`: This function returns the values of the field X per hour
- `per_minute()`: This function returns the values of the field X per minute
- `per_second()`: This function returns the values of the field X per second

In the following example, we've used the `per_day` function with `timechart` (to calculate the per day total of the `other` field):

```
sourcetype=access_* action=purchase | timechart per_day(other) by file
usenull=f
```

The preceding code generates the following output:

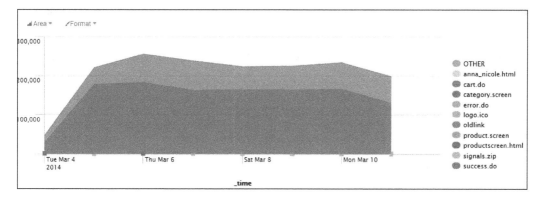

The same search command, written using `span` and `sum` is shown as follows:

```
sourcetype=access_* action=purchase | timechart span=1d sum(other) by
file usenull=f
```

This search generates the following chart:

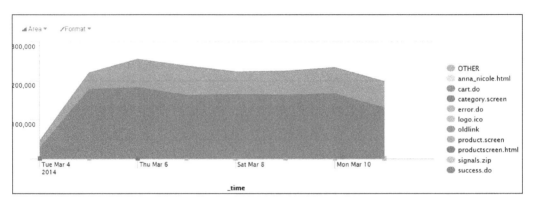

Drilldowns

According to *webopedia*, in information technology, a drilldown can be defined as follows:

> "*To move from summary information to detailed data by focusing in on something.*"
>
> *– webopedia 2014*

Splunk offers the ability to initiate a search by clicking on a (row in a) table or (a bar in) a chart. This search will be based on the information that you clicked on in the table or chart. This search that dives deeper into the details of a selection is known as a drilldown and is displayed in a separate window from the original search results.

As an example, we can use one of our earlier Splunk search examples (shown next):

```
sourcetype=csv 2014 "Current Forecast" "Direct"  "513500" |  rename
May as "Month" Actual as "Version" "FY 2012" as Year 650693NLR001
as "Business Unit" 100000 as "FCST" "09997_Eliminations Co 2" as
"Account" "451200" as "Activity" | eval RFCST= round(FCST) | Table
"Business Unit", Activity, Account, RFCST, FCST
```

From this search, we can get the following table visualization:

Business Unit ⇵	Activity ⇵	Account ⇵	RFCST ⇵	FCST
999999	513500	42000-S2S GLOBAL	3049034	3049033.73
999999	513500	42000-S2S GLOBAL	3049034	3049033.73
999999	513500	42000-S2S GLOBAL	3049034	3049033.73
999999	513500	42000-S2S GLOBAL	3048728	3048728.367000000
999999	513500	42000-S2S GLOBAL	3225361	3225361.28
999999	513500	42000-S2S GLOBAL	6567749	6567748.696999999
999999	513500	42000-S2S GLOBAL	3726281	3726281.206999999

Events (749) Statistics (749) Visualization

20 Per Page ▾   Format ▾   Preview ▾   ◀ Prev 1 2 3 4 5 ... Next ▶

If this table is set up for a row drilldown (more on this in a minute), Splunk will move to the **Search** view and run the following search when you click on the first row of the panel:

```
sourcetype=csv 2014 "Current Forecast" "Direct"  "513500"  | rename
May as "Month" Actual as "Version" "FY 2012" as Year 650693NLR001
as "Business Unit" 100000 as "FCST" "09997_Eliminations Co 2" as
"Account" "451200" as "Activity" | search "Business Unit"=999999
Activity=513500 Account="42000-S2S GLOBAL" FCST="3049033.736" | eval
RFCST= round(FCST) | search RFCST=3049034
```

The preceding search then provides detailed event information based on the row selected in your original search. Note that the original transformation command (table) is removed from this detailed search, so there are no results displayed on the **Statistics** or **Visualization** tabs, as shown here:

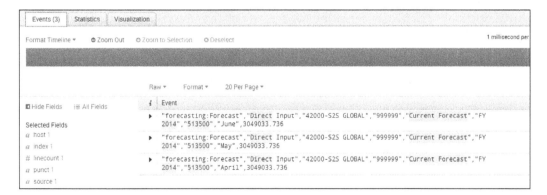

The drilldown options

In the preceding example, I knew that the row drilldown was enabled. To view your table results' drilldown options (or change them), after you run your search, you can click on the **Format** menu under the **Statistics** tab:

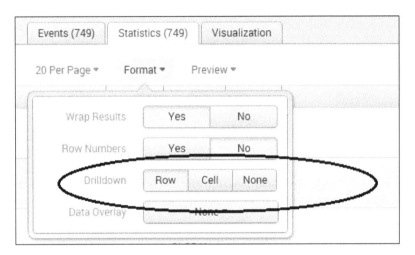

Table visualizations have three drilldown options. They are:

- **Row**: A click on a row sets off a search across the x-axis value represented by that row

- **Cell**: A click on a cell launches a drill down search on both the x-axis and y-axis values represented in that cell

- **None (off)**: This option turns off the drill down functionality for the table

Chart visualizations such as bar, column, line, area, and pie charts have two drill down options. Let's take another look at one of our previous Splunk search examples that include the chart command as shown next:

```
tm1* rule | chart count(date_hour) by date_wday
```

We can then click on the **Format** menu under the **Visualizations** tab, as shown in the following screenshot:

You can see that the two drilldown options here are:

- **Yes**: This option enables the drilldown functionality for the visualization. This lets you drill down on a particular part of a chart or legend by clicking on it.
- **No**: This option turns off the drilldown functionality for the visualization.

The basic drilldown functionality

In general, when a Splunk search involved in the creation of a table or chart uses transforming commands, the drilldown functionality removes the final transforming command and replaces it with arguments that drill down on the specific x-axis value or a combination of the values of the x and y axes caught by the click.

Row drilldowns

As shown earlier, when a table has the drilldown value of a row, you can initiate drilldown searches along all the rows by clicking on them. Let's take a look at a simple example using the following search:

```
sourcetype=csv 2014 "Current Forecast" "Direct"  |   rename May
as "Month" Actual as "Version" "FY 2012" as Year 650693NLR001
as "Business Unit" 100000 as "FCST" "09997_Eliminations Co 2"
as "Account" "451200" as "Activity" | eval RFCST= round(FCST) |
eventstats sum(RFCST) as total_RFCST| Table Activity, Account, total_
RFCST
```

In this table, a row click drilldown search will concentrate on the x-axis value of the selected row, which in this case will be a value of the `Activity`, `Account`, and `total_RFCST` fields:

This row click sets off the following search, which finds 11 results:

```
sourcetype=csv 2014 "Current Forecast" "Direct"    | rename May
as "Month" Actual as "Version" "FY 2012" as Year 650693NLR001 as
"Business Unit" 100000 as "FCST" "09997_Eliminations Co 2" as
"Account" "451200" as "Activity"    | eval RFCST= round(FCST)    |
eventstats sum(RFCST) as total_RFCST| search Activity=516550
Account="09996-ELIM CO 20 REV/COS" total_RFCST=1335725390
```

These 11 results are as shown in the following screenshot:

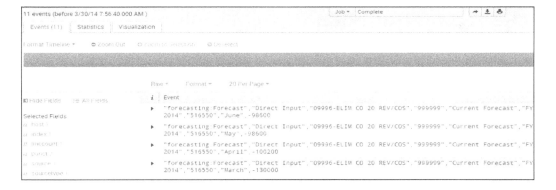

Notice that Splunk added the search at the end for
`Activity=516550 Account="09996ELIM CO 20 REV/COS"`
`total_RFCST=1335725390` and removed the transformations
`Table Activity, Account,` and `total_RFCST`.

Cell drilldowns

When a table has the drilldown value of a cell, you can initiate drilldown searches for specific cells by clicking on them. As an example, we'll use a search similar to the search from the earlier command:

```
sourcetype=csv 2014 "Current Forecast" "Direct"    |   rename May
as "Month" Actual as "Version" "FY 2012" as Year 650693NLR001
as "Business Unit" 100000 as "FCST" "09997_Eliminations Co 2"
as "Account" "451200" as "Activity" | eval RFCST= round(FCST) |
eventstats sum(RFCST) as total_RFCST| Table Activity, Account,
Version, total_RFCST
```

In this table, a cell click drilldown search will concentrate on a combination of the x-axis value (the value in the first column for the cell's row — in this case, 516550) and the y-axis value (the value of the cell's column we clicked on — in this case, Current Forecast):

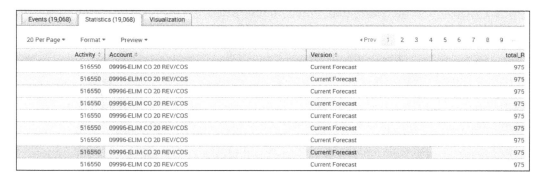

The Splunk drilldown removes the transforming commands again (Table Activity, Account, Version, total_RFCST) and adds the new search parameters (search Activity=516550 Version="Current Forecast"):

```
sourcetype=csv 2014 "Current Forecast" "Direct"    | rename May
as "Month" Actual as "Version" "FY 2012" as Year 650693NLR001 as
"Business Unit" 100000 as "FCST" "09997_Eliminations Co 2" as
"Account" "451200" as "Activity"  | eval RFCST= round(FCST)   |
eventstats sum(RFCST) as total_RFCST| search Activity=516550
Version="Current Forecast"
```

This command yields 22 results:

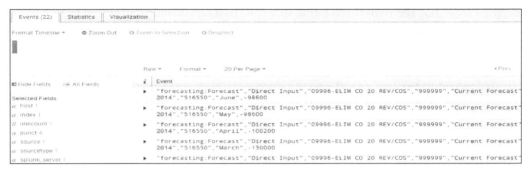

The 22 search results in the Events tab

Chart drilldowns

Drilldown searches on charts (bar, column, line, area, and pie) behave differently depending on whether you click in the body of the chart (for a pie chart, you can also click on the label pointing to a slice in the pie) or in the chart legend (if a legend is displayed).

As with tables, drilldowns from charts create a (drilldown) search that is identical to the original search but without transforming commands and with an additional search term based on the x-axis value that you select in the chart.

Let's use an earlier example of a bar chart based on the following search of Cognos TM1 logs:

```
tm1* rule | chart count(date_hour) by date_wday
```

In this chart, the y-axis is the day of the week (date_wday) value, while the x-axis is the total count per hour (count(date_hour)):

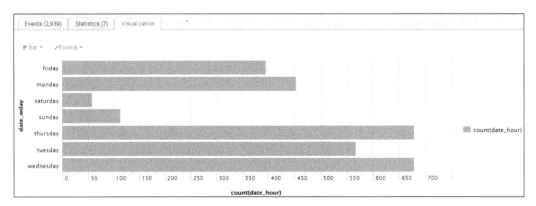

If you click in the body of the chart, the drilldown search drills down on the x-axis value represented by that bar:

```
tm1* rule date_wday=Monday
```

As with the earlier table drilldown examples, this drilldown search is identical to the original search, except that the final set of transforming commands have been removed and a focus has been added on the aggregator value of date_wday.

Legends

Drilldown searches for chart legends only work when there is a split-by (or y-axis) field in the chart. For example, sometimes the legend element is something that can't really be drilled down into, and then clicks on such legend items will return an error message.

Pivot

You can create your Splunk reports without having to use the Splunk Enterprise **Search Processing Language** (**SPL**) by utilizing the Splunk pivot tool.

Splunk pivot is a simple drag-and-drop interface that uses (predefined) data models and data model objects. These data models (designed by the knowledge managers in an organization and discussed later in this book) are used by the pivot tool to define, subdivide, and set attributes for the event data you are interested in.

You can create a Splunk pivot table by following these steps:

1. Go to the Splunk Home page and click on **Pivot** for the app workspace you want to use:

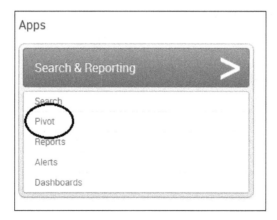

2. Next, from the **Select a Data Model** page, you can then choose a specific data model (by identifying which dataset to work with):

3. Once you select a data model, you can select the list of objects (which can be an object type of event, transaction, search, or child, and can represent a specific view or a slice of a Splunk search result) within that data model (or click on **edit objects** to edit or add to the objects within the data model) to work with:

4. After you select a specific object, Splunk will take you to the pivot editor, where you can create your pivot:

The pivot editor

Splunk will start the pivot editor in what is referred to as the pivot table mode.

In the pivot table mode, the editor displays only one row that represents the object's total result count over all the time spans, based on the type of object you've selected:

- `event type`: This is the total number of events (selected by the object)
- `transaction type`: This is the total number of transactions (identified by the object)
- `search type`: This is the total number of table rows (returned by the base search in the object)

Pivot tables are defined by you using Splunk pivot elements, which are of four basic pivot element categories: filters, split rows, split columns, and column values.

Only two pivot elements will be defined when you start a **Filter** element (always set to **All time**) and a **Column Values** element (always set to **Count of Prior For** (based on the object type) of your selected object), as shown in the following screenshot:

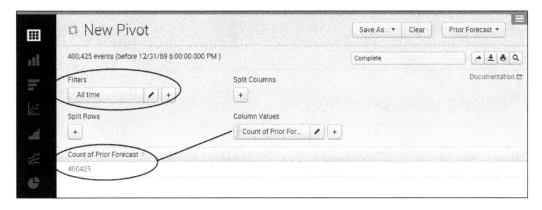

Using the editor, you can add, define, and remove multiple pivot elements from each pivot element category to define your pivot table:

- **Filters**: This category is used to reduce the result count for the object
- **Split Rows**: This category is used to split up the pivot results by rows
- **Split Columns**: This category is used to break up field values by columns
- **Column Values**: This category is used to show the aggregate results, such as counts, sums, and averages

Working with pivot elements

Within the pivot editor, all pivot element categories can be managed in the same way:

1. Click on the **+** icon to open the element dialog, where you choose an attribute and then define how the element uses this attribute.

2. Click on the pencil icon on the element to open the element dialog in order to edit how a pivot element is defined.

3. Drag-and-drop elements within their pivot element categories to reorder them.

4. Drag-and-drop the elements between pivot element categories to transfer the element to the desired pivot category (with transfers, there are some restrictions on what can and cannot be transferred by drag-and-drop).

5. Click on the pencil icon on the element to open the element dialog and click on **Remove** to remove the element (or you can click on the element and shake it up and down until it turns red and then drop it—my favorite method).

The management of the pivot elements is done using the pivot element dialog. The element dialog is broken up into two steps: choose (or change) the element, and configure the element (configuration). We'll look at each category in the following sections.

Filtering your pivots

Splunk pivots can be filtered using filter elements.

Splunk supports three kinds of filter elements that can be used with pivots. It's important to understand each one of them:

- **Time**: This element is always present and cannot be removed. The time defines the time range for which your pivot will return results.

- **Match**: This element enables the ability to set up matching strings such as numbers, timestamps, Booleans, and IPv4 addresses (although currently only as AND but not OR matches).

- **Limit**: This element enables you to restrict the number of results returned by your pivot.

 Note that the configuration options for the match and limit filter elements depend on the type of attribute you've chosen for the element.

Split

The Splunk configuration options that are available for split (row and column) depend on the type of attributes you choose for them.

 Some split configuration options are specific to either row or column elements, while others are available to either element type.

These configuration options, regardless of the attribute type, are as follows:

- Both split row and split column:

    ° **Max rows and max columns**: This is the maximum number of rows or columns that can appear in the results table

    ° **Totals**: This will indicate whether to include a row or column that represents the total of all others in an attribute called ALL

- Only split row elements:

    ° **Label**: This is used to override the attribute name with a different text or character string

    ° **Sort**: This is used to reorder the split rows

- Only split column:

    ° **Group others**: This indicates whether to group any results excluded by the max columns limit into a separate other column

Configuration options dependent on the attribute type are:

- String attributes:

    ° There are no configuration options specific to string attributes that are common to both split row and split column elements

- Numeric attributes:

    ° **Create ranges**: This indicates whether or not you want your numeric values represented as ranges (Yes) or listed separately (No)

- Boolean attributes:

    ° You can provide alternate labels for true and false values

- Timestamp attributes:

    ° **Period**: You can use this to bucket your timestamp results by `Year`, `Month`, `Day`, `Hour`, `Minute`, or `Second`

Column values

You will find a column value element that provides the total results returned by a selected object over all time spans. You have the option to keep this element, change its label, or remove it. In addition, you can add new column value elements such as:

- List distinct values
- First/last value
- Count / distinct count
- Sum
- Average
- Max/min
- Standard deviation
- List distinct values
- Duration
- Earliest/latest

Pivot table formatting

You can format the results of your pivot in many ways. You can set the number of results displayed per page (10, 20, or 50) using the pagination dropdown.

If you use the format dropdown, you can even control table wrapping, the display of row numbers, and determine the drilldown and data overlay behavior. The pivot table drilldown is set to cell mode by default and works in a similar way to the Splunk table drilldown (discussed earlier in this chapter).

A quick example

Earlier, we chose a sample data model named `Jims FCST` and from the **Select an Object** page, we chose **Prior Forecast**, which made us land on **New Pivot** (pivot editor):

To build a simple pivot, we need to perform the following steps:

1. Add/verify the filters:

   Remember, **All time** is the default; this will include all the results found over time. We'll click on the pencil icon and edit this filter to be based on **Date Range**:

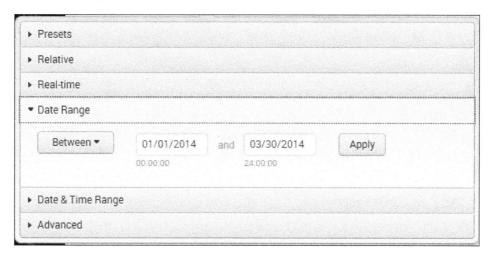

2. Configure **Split Rows**:

   For **Split Rows**, I've selected **Business Unit**:

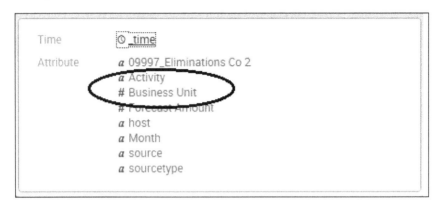

3. Configure **Split Columns**:

   For **Split Columns**, I've selected **Month**:

4. Configure **Column Values**:

   Finally, for **Column Values**, I've removed the default column (the total count) and added a sum of the value FCST and labeled it as **FCST Amount**:

5.   View the results (saved as **Jims Fcst Amount Sample**):

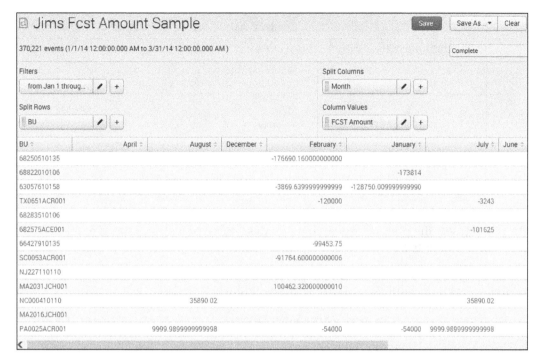

Sparklines

Growing in popularity as a data visualization option, sparklines are inline charts that represent the general shape of a variation (typically over time) in some measurement (such as miles per gallon or home value), in a simple and highly condensed way. Splunk provides you with the ability to add sparklines to statistics and chart searches, improving their usefulness and overall information density.

A prior Splunk search example is as follows:

```
sourcetype=csv "Current Forecast" "Direct"  "513500" | rename 100000
as "FCST", "FY 2012" as "Year"| eval RFCST= round(FCST) | chart
avg(RFCST) by Year
```

The preceding search creates the following results table:

	Year ⬍	avg(RFCST) ⬍
1	FY 2008	28291.947891
2	FY 2009	19064.995775
3	FY 2010	14514.582763
4	FY 2011	14017.654286
5	FY 2012	12894.081541
6	FY 2013	17644.403556
7	FY 2014	46413.303071
8	FY 2015	108945.781609

Events (6,056) | Statistics (8) | Visualization

20 Per Page ▾   Format ▾   Preview ▾

As you can see, the preceding search generates a table that shows the average forecasted amounts by fiscal year in just two columns.

If you add the keyword **sparkline** to the search pipeline, you can have Splunk include sparklines with the results, as shown here:

```
sourcetype=csv "Current Forecast" "Direct"  "513500" | rename 100000
as "FCST", "FY 2012" as "Year"| eval RFCST= round(FCST) | chart
sparkline avg(RFCST) by Year
```

 Note that you will always use the sparkline feature in conjunction with charts and stats because it is a function of these two search commands, not a command by itself.

If we run the preceding Splunk search, it generates a table similar to the earlier command, except that now, for each row, you have a sparkline chart, as shown here:

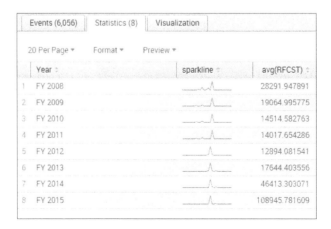

Here is an additional example of using `sparkline` to view the variations of the total forecast for a year by month:

```
sourcetype=csv 2014 "Current Forecast" "Direct"    | rename 100000 as
"FCST", "May" as "Month" | eval RFCST= round(FCST) | chart sparkline
sum(RFCST) by Month
```

The output obtained is as follows:

	Month ⟂	sparkline ⟂		sum(RFCST) ⟂
1	April			111247168
2	August			118660766
3	December			97932199
4	February			116236507
5	January			123165499
6	July			102186565
7	June			112638116
8	March			112393478
9	May			132132300

Events (54,779)   Statistics (12)   Visualization

20 Per Page ▾   Format ▾   Preview ▾

Now, you can easily see patterns in the data that might have been invisible before.

 Note that the Splunk sparkline displays information with relation to the events represented in that sparkline but not in relation to the other sparklines.

Summary

In this chapter, we reviewed Splunk tables, charts, and fields and then explored the drilldown from within both tables and charts. The pivot and the pivot editor were discussed and finally we finished with the sparkline in our results.

In the next chapter, we will introduce Splunk lookups and explain the best practices, purpose, and use of this feature within Splunk solutions.

4
Lookups

This chapter will discuss Splunk lookups and workflows. The topics that will be covered in this chapter are as follows:

- The value of a lookup
- Design lookups
- File lookups
- Script lookups

Introduction

Machines constantly generate data, usually in a raw form that is most efficient for processing by machines, but not easily understood by "human" data consumers. Splunk has the ability to identify unique identifiers and/or result or status codes within the data. This gives you the ability to enhance the readability of the data by adding descriptions or names as new search result fields. These fields contain information from an external source such as a static table (a CSV file) or the dynamic result of a Python command or a Python-based script.

 Splunk's lookups can use information within returned events or time information to determine how to add other fields from your previously defined external data sources.

To illustrate, here is an example of a Splunk static lookup that:

- Uses the Business Unit value in an event
- Matches this value with the organization's business unit name in a CSV file
- Adds the definition to the event (as the Business Unit Name field)

So, if you have an event where the Business Unit value is equal to 999999, the lookup will add the Business Unit Name value as Corporate Office to that event.

More sophisticated lookups can:

- Populate a static lookup table from the results of a report.
- Use a Python script (rather than a lookup table) to define a field. For example, a lookup can use a script to return a server name when given an IP address.
- Perform a time-based lookup if your lookup table includes a field value that represents time.

Let's take a look at an example of a search pipeline that creates a table based on IBM Cognos TM1 file extractions:

```
sourcetype=csv 2014 "Current Forecast" "Direct"  "513500" |
rename May as "Month" Actual as "Version" "FY 2012" as Year
650693NLR001 as "Business Unit" 100000 as "FCST" "09997_Eliminations
Co 2" as "Account" "451200" as "Activity" | eval RFCST= round(FCST) |
Table Month, "Business Unit", RFCST
```

The following table shows the results generated:

Month	Business Unit	RFCST
1 June	999999	3049034
2 May	999999	3049034
3 April	999999	3049034
4 March	999999	3048728
5 February	999999	3225361
6 January	999999	6567749
7 December	999999	3726281

Now, add the lookup command to our search pipeline to have Splunk convert Business Unit into Business Unit Name:

```
sourcetype=csv 2014 "Current Forecast" "Direct"  "513500" |
rename May as "Month" Actual as "Version" "FY 2012" as Year
650693NLR001 as "Business Unit" 100000 as "FCST" "09997_Eliminations
Co 2" as "Account" "451200" as "Activity" | eval RFCST= round(FCST) |
lookup BUtoBUName BU as "Business Unit" OUTPUT BUName as "Business
Unit Name" | Table Month, "Business Unit", "Business Unit Name", RFCST
```

The `lookup` command in our Splunk search pipeline will now add `Business Unit Name` in the results table:

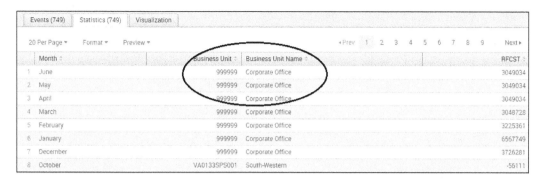

Configuring a simple field lookup

In this section, we will configure a simple Splunk lookup.

Defining lookups in Splunk Web

You can set up a lookup using the **Lookups** page (in Splunk Web) or by configuring stanzas in the `props.conf` and `transforms.conf` files. Let's take the easier approach first and use the Splunk Web interface.

Before we begin, we need to establish our lookup table that will be in the form of an industry standard comma separated file (CSV). Our example is one that converts business unit *codes* to a more user-friendly business unit *name*. For example, we have the following information:

Business unit code	Business unit name
999999	Corporate office
VA0133SPS001	South-western
VA0133NLR001	North-east
685470NLR001	Mid-west

In the events data, only business unit codes are included. In an effort to make our Splunk search results more readable, we want to add the business unit name to our results table. To do this, we've converted our information (shown in the preceding table) to a CSV file (named `BUtoBUName.csv`):

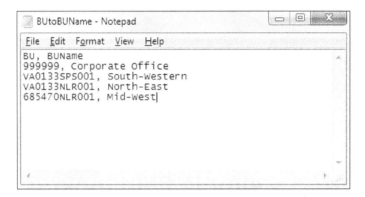

For this example, we've kept our lookup table simple, but lookup tables (files) can be as complex as you need them to be. They can have numerous fields (columns) in them.

A Splunk lookup table has a few requirements, as follows:

- A table must contain a minimum of two columns
- Each of the columns in the table can have duplicate values
- You should use (plain) ASCII text and not non-UTF-8 characters

Now, from Splunk Web, we can click on **Settings** and then select **Lookups**:

From the **Lookups** page, we can select **Lookup table files**:

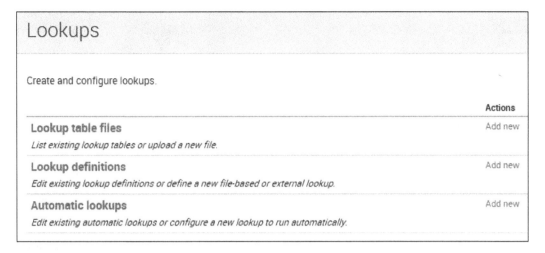

From the **Lookup table files** page, we can add our new lookup file (`BUtoBUName.csv`):

By clicking on the **New** button, we see the **Add new** page where we can set up our file by doing the following:

1. Select a **Destination app** (this is a drop-down list and you should select **Search**).

2. Enter (or browse to) our file under **Upload a lookup file**.

3. Provide a **Destination filename**.

Then, we click on **Save**:

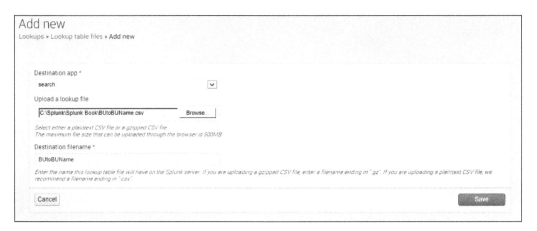

Once you click on **Save**, you should receive the **Successfully saved "BUtoBUName"** **in search**" message:

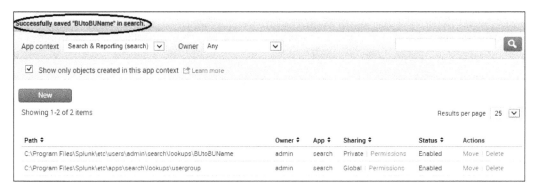

 In the previous screenshot, the lookup file is saved by default as **private**. You will need to adjust permissions to allow other Splunk users to use it.

Going back to the **Lookups** page, we can select **Lookup definitions** to see the **Lookup definitions** page:

In the **Lookup definitions** page, we can click on **New** to visit the **Add new** page (shown in the following screenshot) and set up our definition as follows:

- **Destination app**: The lookup will be part of the Splunk **search** app
- **Name**: Our file is `BUtoBUName`
- **Type**: Here, we will select **File-based**
- **Lookup file**: The filename is `ButoBUName.csv`, which we uploaded without the `.csv` suffix

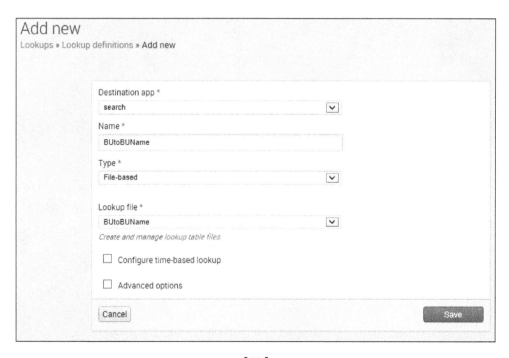

Again, we should see the **Successfully saved "BUtoBUName" in search** message:

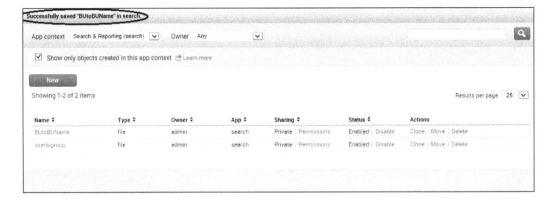

Now, our lookup is ready to be used:

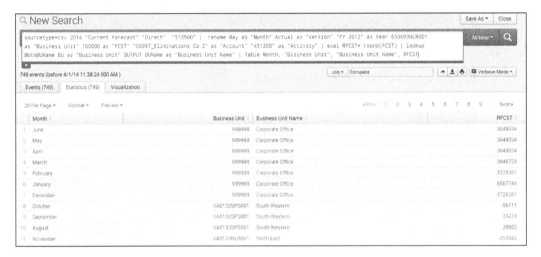

Automatic lookups

Rather than having to code for a lookup in each of your Splunk searches, you have the ability to configure automatic lookups for a particular source type. To do this from Splunk Web, we can click on **Settings** and then select **Lookups**:

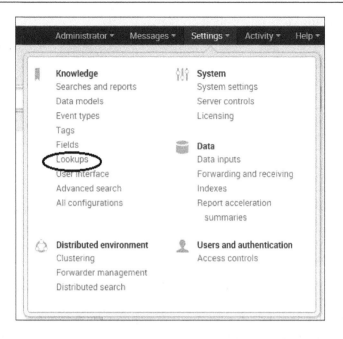

From the **Lookups** page, click on **Automatic lookups**:

In the **Automatic lookups** page, click on **New**:

In the **Add New** page, we will fill in the required information to set up our lookup:

- **Destination app**: For this field, some options are **framework**, **launcher**, **learned**, **search**, and **splunk_datapreview** (for our example, select **search**).

- **Name**: This provide a user-friendly name that describes this automatic lookup.

- **Lookup table**: This is the name of the lookup table you defined with a CSV file (discussed earlier in this chapter).

- **Apply to**: This is the type that you want this automatic lookup to apply to. The options are **sourcetype**, **source**, or **host** (I've picked **sourcetype**).

- **Named**: This is the name of the type you picked under **Apply to**. I want my automatic search to apply for all searches with the **sourcetype** of csv.

- **Lookup input fields**: This is simple in my example. In my lookup table, the field to be searched on will be BU and the = field value will be the field in the event results that I am converting; in my case, it was the field 650693NLR001.

- **Lookup output fields**: This will be the field in the lookup table that I am using to convert to, which in my example is BUName and I want to call it Business Unit Name, so this becomes the = field value.

- **Overwrite field values**: This is a checkbox where you can tell Splunk to overwrite existing values in your output fields — I checked it.

The Add new page

The Splunk **Add new** page (shown in the following screenshot) is where you enter the lookup information (detailed in the previous section):

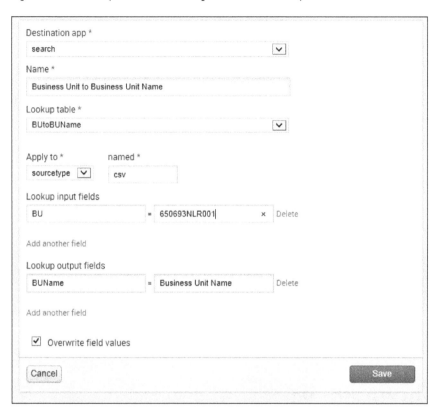

Once you have entered your automatic lookup information, you can click on **Save** and you will receive the **Successfully saved "Business Unit to Business Unit Name" in search** message:

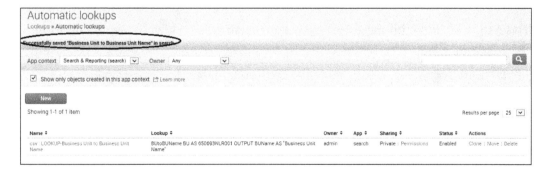

Now, we can use the lookup in a search. For example, you can run a search with `sourcetype=csv`, as follows:

```
sourcetype=csv 2014 "Current Forecast" "Direct"  "513500" |
rename May as "Month" Actual as "Version" "FY 2012" as Year
650693NLR001 as "Business Unit" 100000 as "FCST" "09997_Eliminations
Co 2" as "Account" "451200" as "Activity" | eval RFCST= round(FCST) |
Table "Business Unit", "Business Unit Name", Month, RFCST
```

Notice in the following screenshot that **Business Unit Name** is converted to the user-friendly values from our lookup table, and we didn't have to add the lookup command to our search pipeline:

	Business Unit	Business Unit Name	Month		RFCST
	Events (749)	Statistics (749)	Visualization		
	20 Per Page ▾	Format ▾	Preview ▾	◂ Prev 1 2 3 4 5 6 7 8 9 ...	Next ▸
1	999999	Corporate Office	June		3049034
2	999999	Corporate Office	May		3049034
3	999999	Corporate Office	April		3049034
4	999999	Corporate Office	March		3048728
5	999999	Corporate Office	February		3225361
6	999999	Corporate Office	January		6567749
7	999999	Corporate Office	December		3726281
8	VA0133SPS001	South-Western	October		-56111

Configuration files

In addition to using the Splunk web interface, you can define and configure lookups using the following files:

- `props.conf`
- `transforms.conf`

To set up a lookup with these files (rather than using Splunk web), we can perform the following steps:

1. Edit `transforms.conf` to define the lookup table. The first step is to edit the `transforms.conf` configuration file to add the new lookup reference. Although the file exists in the Splunk default folder (`$SPLUNK_HOME/etc/system/default`), you should edit the file in `$SPLUNK_HOME/etc/system/local/` or `$SPLUNK_HOME/etc/apps/<app_name>/local/` (if the file doesn't exist here, create it).

Whenever you edit a Splunk `.conf` file, always edit a local version, keeping the original (system directory version) intact.

In the current version of Splunk, there are two types of lookup tables: static and external. Static lookups use CSV files, and external (which are dynamic) lookups use Python scripting.

You have to decide if your lookup will be static (in a file) or dynamic (use script commands). If you are using a file, you'll use `filename`; if you are going to use a script, you use `external_cmd` (both will be set in the `transforms.conf` file). You can also limit the number of matching entries to apply to an event by setting the `max_matches` option (this tells Splunk to use the first <integer> (in file order) number of entries).

I've decided to leave the default for `max_matches`, so my `transforms.conf` file looks like the following:

```
[butobugroup]
filename = butobugroup.csv
```

2. This step is optional. Edit `props.conf` to apply your lookup table automatically. For both static and external lookups, you stipulate the fields you want to match in the configuration file and the output from the lookup table that you defined in your `transforms.conf` file.

It is okay to have multiple field lookups defined in one source lookup definition, but each lookup should have its own unique lookup name; for example, if you have multiple tables, you can name them LOOKUP-table01, LOOKUP-table02, and so on, or something perhaps more easily understood.

 If you add a lookup to your `props.conf` file, this lookup is automatically applied to *all events from searches that have matching source types* (again, as mentioned earlier; if your automatic lookup is very slow, it will also impact the speed of your searches).

3. Restart Splunk to see your changes.

Implementing a lookup using configuration files – an example

To illustrate the use of configuration files in order to implement an automatic lookup, let's use a simple example.

Once again, we want to convert a field from a unique identification code for an organization's *business unit* to a more user friendly descriptive name called *BU Group*. What we will do is match the field bu in a lookup table butobugroup.csv with a field in our events. Then, add the bugroup (description) to the returned events.

The following shows the contents of the butobugroup.csv file:

```
bu, bugroup
999999, leadership-group
VA0133SPS001, executive-group
650914FAC002, technology-group
```

You can put this file into $SPLUNK_HOME/etc/apps/<app_name>/lookups/ and carry out the following steps:

1. Put the butobugroup.csv file into $SPLUNK_HOME/etc/apps/search/lookups/, since we are using the search app.

2. As we mentioned earlier, we edit the transforms.conf file located at either $SPLUNK_HOME/etc/system/local/ or $SPLUNK_HOME/etc/apps/<app_name>/local/. We add the following two lines:

    ```
    [butobugroup]
    filename = butobugroup.csv
    ```

3. Next, as mentioned earlier in this chapter, we edit the props.conf file located at either $SPLUNK_HOME/etc/system/local/ or $SPLUNK_HOME/etc/apps/<app_name>/local/. Here, we add the following two lines:

    ```
    [csv]
    LOOKUP-check = butobugroup bu AS 650693NLR001 OUTPUT bugroup
    ```

4. Restart the Splunk server.

 You can (assuming you are logged in as an admin or have admin privileges) restart the Splunk server through the web interface by going to **Settings**, then select **System** and finally **Server controls**.

Now, you can run a search for `sourcetype=csv` (as shown here):

```
sourcetype=csv 2014 "Current Forecast" "Direct"  "513500" |
rename May as "Month" ,650693NLR001 as "Business Unit" 100000 as
"FCST"|  eval RFCST= round(FCST) |
Table "Business Unit", "Business Unit Name", bugroup, Month, RFCST
```

You will see that the field **bugroup** can be returned as part of your event results:

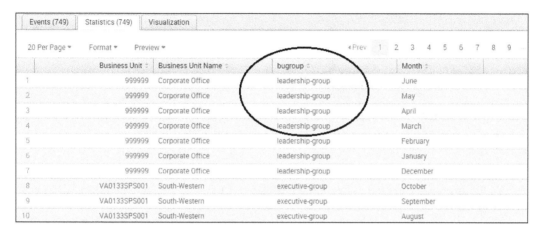

Populating lookup tables

Of course, you can create CSV files from external systems (or, perhaps even manually?), but from time to time, you might have the opportunity to create lookup CSV files (tables) from event data using Splunk. A handy command to accomplish this is `outputcsv` (which is covered in detail later in this chapter).

The following is a simple example of creating a CSV file from Splunk event data that can be used for a lookup table:

```
sourcetype=csv "Current Forecast" "Direct"  |  rename 650693NLR001
as "Business Unit"  | Table "Business Unit", "Business Unit Name",
bugroup | outputcsv splunk_master
```

The results are shown in the following screenshot:

Of course, the output table isn't quite usable, since the results have duplicates. Therefore, we can rewrite the Splunk search pipeline introducing the dedup command (as shown here):

```
sourcetype=csv   "Current Forecast" "Direct"   | rename 650693NLR001
as "Business Unit" | dedup "Business Unit" | Table "Business Unit",
"Business Unit Name", bugroup | outputcsv splunk_master
```

Then, we can examine the results (now with more desirable results):

Handling duplicates with dedup

This command allows us to set the number of duplicate events to be kept based on the values of a field (in other words, we can use this command to drop duplicates from our event results for a selected field). The event returned for the dedup field will be the first event found (if you provide a number directly after the dedup command, it will be interpreted as the number of duplicate events to keep; if you don't specify a number, dedup keeps only the first occurring event and removes all consecutive duplicates).

The dedup command also lets you sort by field or list of fields. This will remove all the duplicates and then sort the results based on the specified sort-by field. Adding a sort in conjunction with the dedup command can affect the performance as Splunk performs the dedup operation and then sorts the results as a final step. Here is a search command using dedup:

```
sourcetype=csv   "Current Forecast" "Direct"   | rename 650693NLR001
as "Business Unit"  |  dedup "Business Unit" sortby bugroup |  Table
"Business Unit", "Business Unit Name", bugroup | outputcsv splunk_
master
```

The result of the preceding command is shown in the following screenshot:

	Business Unit	Business Unit Name	bugroup
1	ADMIN	North-East	ADMIN
2	TX04267004	Accounting	Accounting-1-gorup
3	TX03287002	Accounting	Accounting-2-group
4	WA2069FF01	FPM	FPM-1-group
5	WA20697103	FPM	FPM-2-group
6	WA20697002	FPM	FPM-3-group

Events (6,885) Statistics (6,885) Visualization

20 Per Page ▾   Format ▾   Preview ▾   ‹Prev 1 2 3 4 5 6 7 8 9 … Next›

Now, we have our CSV lookup file (`outputcsv splunk_master`) generated and ready to be used:

```
splunk_master - Notepad

File   Edit   Format   View   Help
"Business Unit","Business Unit Name",bugroup
ADMIN,"North-East",ADMIN
TX04267004,Accounting,"Accounting-1-gorup"
TX03287002,Accounting,"Accounting-2-group"
WA2069FF01,FPM,"FPM-1-group"
WA20697103,FPM,"FPM-2-group"
WA20697002,FPM,"FPM-3-group"
WA20527002,FPM,"FPM-4-group"
WA20097002,FPM,"FPM-5-group"
WA0014FF01,FPM,"FPM-6-group"
OR20267002,Maintenance,"Maintenance-group"
105631,,"Unassigned-group"
VA0133SPS001,"South-Western","executive-group"
999999,"Corporate Office","leadership-group"
"MTG-COMMITTEE",Marketing,"marketing-group"
60538610110,"Mid-west","sales-group"
WA20387003,Techincal,"teachincal-1-gorup"
WA00147002,Techincal,"techinical-2-group"
TX0426FF01,Accounting,
TX04267002,Accounting,
TX02947103,Accounting,
PR9999MEMDEP,"Public Relations",
PR9999IPMM019,"Public Relations",
PR9990DMS017,"Public Relations",
PR9990DMS016,"Public Relations",
PR9990DMS010,"Public Relations",
NM2012FF01,Legal,
"MTG-VALUES CONF",Marketing,
```

 Look for your generated output file in `$SPLUNK_HOME/var/run/splunk`.

Dynamic lookups

With a Splunk static lookup, your search reads through a file (a table) that was created or updated prior to executing the search. With dynamic lookups, the file is created at the time the search executes. This is possible because Splunk has the ability to execute an external command or script as part of your Splunk search.

At the time of writing this book, Splunk only directly supports Python scripts for external lookups. If you are not familiar with Python, its implementation began in 1989 and is a widely used general-purpose, high-level programming language, which is often used as a scripting language (but is also used in a wide range of non-scripting contexts).

Keep in mind that any external resources (such as a file) or scripts that you want to use with your lookup will need to be copied to a location where Splunk can find it. These locations are:

- `$SPLUNK_HOME/etc/apps/<app_name>/bin`
- `$SPLUNK_HOME/etc/searchscripts`

The following sections describe the process of using the dynamic lookup example script that ships with Splunk (`external_lookup.py`).

Using Splunk Web

Just like with static lookups, Splunk makes it easy to define a dynamic or external lookup using the Splunk web interface. First, click on **Settings** and then select **Lookups**:

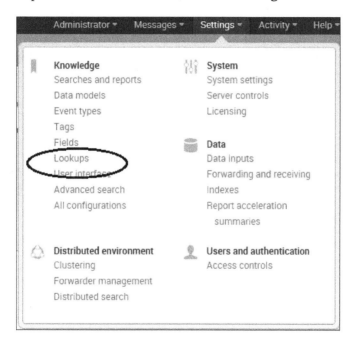

On the **Lookups** page, we can select **Lookup table files** to define a CSV file that contains the input file for our Python script. In the **Add new** page, we enter the following information:

- **Destination app**: For this field, select **Search**
- **Upload a lookup file**: Here, you can browse to the filename (my filename is `dnsLookup.csv`)
- **Destination filename**: Here, enter `dnslookup`

The **Add new** page is shown in the following screenshot:

Now, click on **Save**. The lookup file (shown in the following screenshot) is a text CSV file that needs to (at a minimum) contain the two field names that the Python (py) script accepts as arguments, in this case, host and ip. As mentioned earlier, this file needs to be copied to $SPLUNK_HOME/etc/apps/<app_name>/bin.

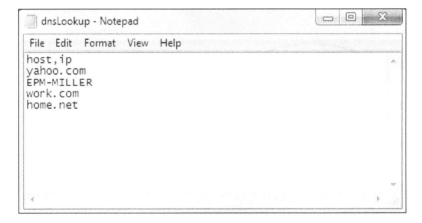

Next, from the **Lookups** page, select **Lookup definitions** and then click on **New**. This is where you define your external lookup. Enter the following information:

- **Type**: For this, select **External** (as this lookup will run an external script)
- **Command**: For this, enter external_lookup.py host ip (this is the name of the py script and its two arguments)
- **Supported fields**: For this, enter host, ip (this indicates the two script input field names)

The following screenshot describes a new lookup definition:

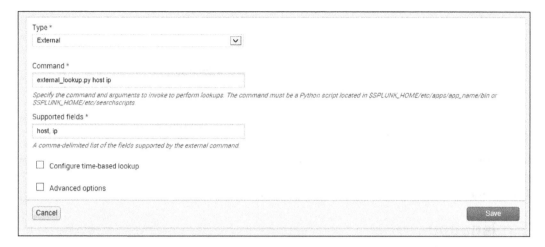

Now, click on **Save**.

Using configuration files instead of Splunk Web

Again, just like with static lookups in Splunk, dynamic lookups can also be configured in the Splunk `transforms.conf` file:

```
[myLookup]
external_cmd = external_lookup.py host ip
external_type = python
fields_list = host, ip
max_matches = 200
```

Let's learn more about the terms here:

- `[myLookup]`: This is the report stanza.

- `external_cmd`: This is the actual runtime command definition. Here, it executes the Python (py) script `external_lookup`, which requires two arguments (or parameters), `host` and `ip`.

- `external_type` (optional): This indicates that this is a Python script. Although this is an optional entry in the `transform.conf` file, it's a good habit to include this for readability and support.

- `fields_list`: This lists all the fields supported by the external command or script, delimited by a comma and space.

The next step is to modify the `props.conf` file, as follows:

```
[mylookup]
LOOKUP-rdns = dnslookup host ip OUTPUT ip
```

 After updating the Splunk configuration files, you will need to restart Splunk.

External lookups

The external lookup example given uses a Python (py) script named `external_lookup.py`, which is a DNS lookup script that can return an IP address for a given host name or a host name for a provided IP address.

Explanation

The lookup table field in this example is named `ip`, so Splunk will mine all of the IP addresses found in the indexed logs' events and add the values of `ip` from the lookup table into the `ip` field in the search events. We can notice the following:

- If you look at the py script, you will notice that the example uses an MS Windows supported `socket.gethostbyname_ex(host)` function
- The `host` field has the same name in the lookup table and the events, so you don't need to do anything else

Consider the following search command:

```
sourcetype=tm1* | lookup dnslookup host | table host, ip
```

When you run this command, Splunk uses the lookup table to pass the values for the `host` field as a CSV file (the text CSV file we looked at earlier) into the external command script. The py script then outputs the results (with both the `host` and `ip` fields populated) and returns it to Splunk, which populates the `ip` field in a result table:

Output of the py script with both the host and ip fields populated

Time-based lookups

If your lookup table has a field value that represents time, you can use the `time` field to set up a Splunk fields lookup. As mentioned earlier, the Splunk `transforms.conf` file can be modified to add a lookup stanza.

For example, the following screenshot shows a file named `MasteringDCHP.csv`:

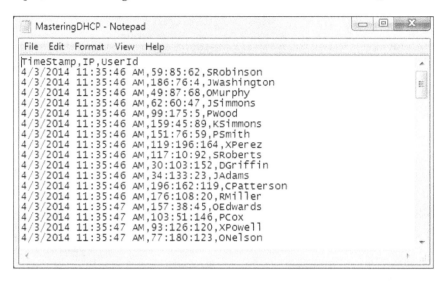

You can add the following code to the `transforms.conf` file:

```
[MasteringDCHP]
filename = MasteringDCHP.csv
time_field = TimeStamp
time_format = %d/%m/%y %H:%M:%S $p
max_offset_secs = <integer>
min_offset_secs = <integer>
```

The file parameters are defined as follows:

- `[MasteringDCHP]`: This is the report stanza
- `filename`: This is the name of the CSV file to be used as the lookup table
- `time_field`: This is the field in the file that contains the time information and is to be used as the timestamp
- `time_format`: This indicates what format the time field is in
- `max_offset_secs` and `min_offset_secs`: This indicates min/max amount of offset time for an event to occur after a lookup entry

Be careful with the preceding values; the offset relates to the timestamp in your lookup (CSV) file. Setting a tight (small) offset range might reduce the effectiveness of your lookup results!

The last step will be to restart Splunk.

An easier way to create a time-based lookup

Again, it's a lot easier to use the Splunk Web interface to set up our lookup. Here is the step-by-step process:

1. From **Settings**, select **Lookups**, and then **Lookup table files**:

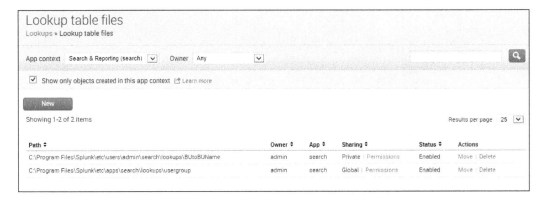

2. In the **Lookup table files** page, click on **New**, configure our lookup file, and then click on **Save**:

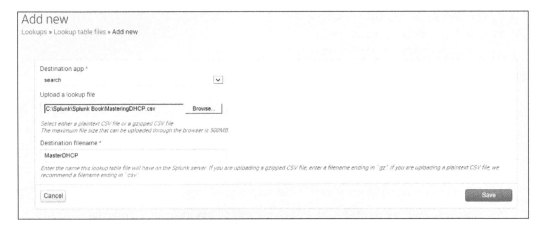

3. You should receive the **Successfully saved "MasterDHCP" in search** message:

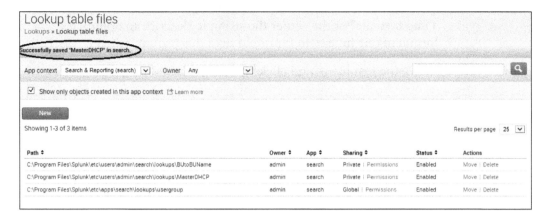

4. Next, select **Lookup definitions** and from this page, click on **New**:

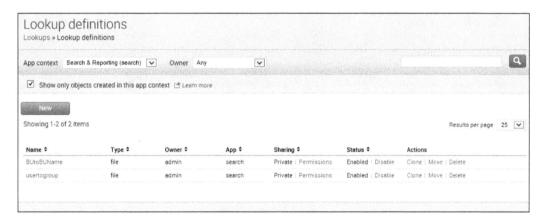

5. In the **Add new** page, we define our lookup table with the following information:
    ○ **Destination app**: For this, select **search** from the drop-down list
    ○ **Name**: For this, enter `MasterDHCP` (this is the name you'll use in your lookup)
    ○ **Type**: For this, select **File-based** (as this lookup table definition is a CSV file)
    ○ **Lookup file**: For this, select the name of the file to be used from the drop-down list (ours is **MasteringDCHP**)
    ○ **Configure time-based lookup**: Check this checkbox

- ○ **Name of time field**: For this, enter `TimeStamp` (this is the field name in our file that contains the time information)

- ○ **Time format**: For this, enter the string to describe to Splunk the format of our time field (our field uses this format: `%d%m%y %H%M%S`)

6. You can leave the rest blank and click on **Save**.

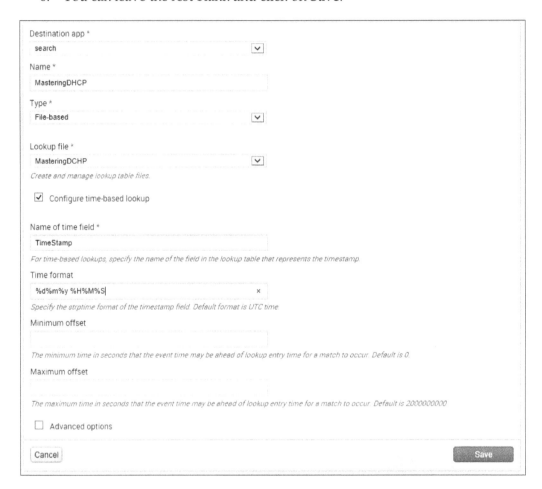

You should receive the **Successfully saved "MasterDHCP" in search** message:

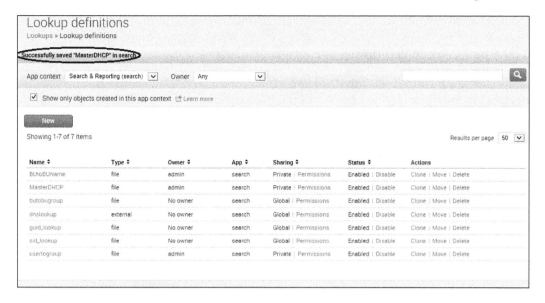

Now, we are ready to try our search:

```
sourcetype=dh* | Lookup MasterDHCP IP as "IP" | table DHCPTimeStamp,
IP, UserId | sort UserId
```

The following screenshot shows the output:

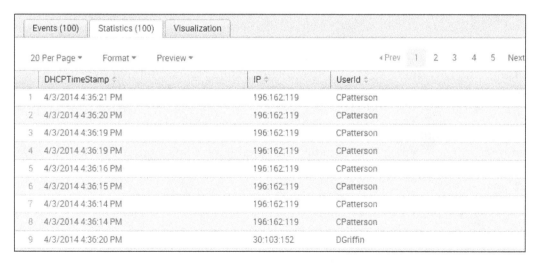

Seeing double?

Lookup table definitions are indicated with the attribute LOOKUP-<class> in the Splunk configuration file, props.conf, or in the web interface under **Settings** | **Lookups** | **Lookup definitions**.

If you use the Splunk Web interface (which we've demonstrated throughout this chapter) to set up or define your lookup table definitions, Splunk will prevent you from creating duplicate table names, as shown in the following screenshot:

However, if you define your lookups using the configuration settings, it is important to try and keep your table definition names unique. If you do give the same name to multiple lookups, the following rules apply:

If you have defined lookups with the same stanza (that is, using the same host, source, or source type), the first defined lookup in the configuration file wins and overrides all others. If lookups have different stanzas but overlapping events, the following logic is used by Splunk:

- Events that match the host get the host lookup
- Events that match the sourcetype get the sourcetype lookup
- Events that match both only get the host lookup

It is a *proven practice* recommendation to make sure that all of your lookup stanzas have unique names.

Command roundup

This section lists several important Splunk commands you will use when working with lookups.

The lookup command

The Splunk `lookup` command is used to manually invoke field lookups using a Splunk lookup table that is previously defined. You can use Splunk Web (or the `transforms.conf` file) to define your lookups.

If you do not specify OUTPUT or OUTPUTNEW, all fields in the lookup table (excluding the lookup match field) will be used by Splunk as output fields. Conversely, if OUTPUT is specified, the output lookup fields will overwrite existing fields and if OUTPUTNEW is specified, the lookup will not be performed for events in which the output fields already exist.

For example, if you have a lookup table specified as `iptousername` with (at least) two fields, `IP` and `UserId`, for each event, Splunk will look up the value of the field `IP` in the table and for any entries that match, the value of the `UserId` field in the lookup table will be written to the field `user_name` in the event. The query is as follows:

```
... Lookup iptousernameIP as "IP" output UserId as user_name
```

Always strive to perform lookups after any reporting commands in your search pipeline, so that the lookup only needs to match the results of the reporting command and not every individual event.

The inputlookup and outputlookup commands

The `inputlookup` command allows you to load search results from a specified static lookup table. It reads in a specified CSV filename (or a table name as specified by the stanza name in `transforms.conf`). If the `append=t` (that is, true) command is added, the data from the lookup file is appended to the current set of results (instead of replacing it). The `outputlookup` command then lets us write the results' events to a specified static lookup table (as long as this output lookup table is defined).

So, here is an example of reading in the `MasterDHCP` lookup table (as specified in `transforms.conf`) and writing these event results to the lookup table definition `NewMasterDHCP`:

```
| inputlookup MasterDHCP | outputlookup NewMasterDHCP
```

After running the preceding command, we can see the following output:

Note that we can add the `append=t` command to the search in the following fashion:

```
| inputlookup MasterDHCP.csv | inputlookup NewMasterDHCP.csv append=t
|
```

The inputcsv and outputcsv commands

The `inputcsv` command is similar to the `inputlookup` command; in this, it loads search results, but this command loads from a specified CSV file. The filename must refer to a relative path in `$SPLUNK_HOME/var/run/splunk` and if the specified file does not exist and the filename did not have an extension, then a filename with a `.csv` extension is assumed. The `outputcsv` command lets us write our result events to a CSV file.

Here is an example where we read in a CSV file named `splunk_master.csv`, search for the text phrase FPM, and then write any matching events to a CSV file named `FPMBU.csv`:

```
| inputcsv splunk_master.csv  | search "Business Unit Name"="FPM" |
outputcsv FPMBU.csv
```

The following screenshot shows the results from the preceding search command:

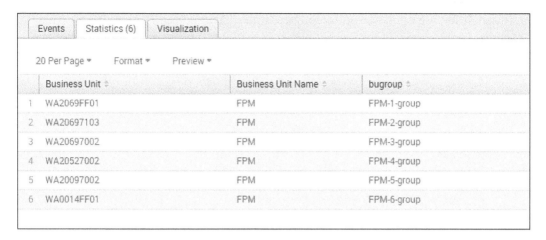

The following screenshot shows the resulting file generated as a result of the preceding command:

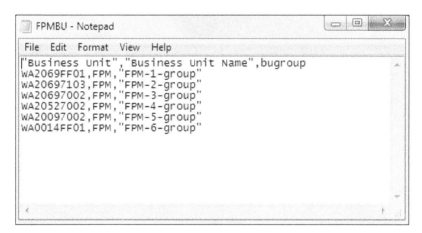

Here is another example where we read in the same CSV file (splunk_master.csv) and write out only events from 51 to 500:

```
| inputcsv splunk_master start=50 max=500
```

Events are numbered starting with zero as the first entry (rather than 1).

Summary

In this chapter, we defined Splunk lookups and discussed their value. We also went through the two types of lookups, static and dynamic, and saw detailed, working examples of each. Various Splunk commands typically used with the lookup functionality were also presented.

In the next chapter, we will dive deep into the topic of dashboarding with Splunk.

5
Progressive Dashboards

This chapter will explain the default Splunk dashboard and then expand on the advanced features offered by Splunk for making business-effective dashboards.

In this chapter, we will cover the following topics:

- Creating effective dashboards
- Using panels
- XML
- Searching
- Dynamic drilldowns
- Real-time solutions

Creating effective dashboards

Splunk makes it easy to build and edit dashboards without writing a single line of code. However, the question is what is a dashboard?

 A dashboard provides a visual interface that displays the key indicators to users in a single view. This view – called a dashboard – is designed to consolidate numerous areas of interest in order to increase the visibility of critical information.

In Splunk Web, every single (web) page is known as a **view**. Some of these views are shipped with and installed with Splunk by default (such as the Search & Reporting app). Splunk allows you to add new views to its apps and when you create your own Splunk apps, you can design and build views for them.

In Splunk, a dashboard is always associated with a specific app and is a type of view that is made up of panels. These panels can contain modules such as:

- Search boxes
- Fields
- Charts
- Tables
- Lists

So, let's take a closer look at these objects.

Views

A Splunk view is a user interface that you build using Splunk's app framework. Dashboards and forms are common examples of views. A good example is the Splunk search app that centers on a default search view, which is shipped with Splunk. Again, views are made from modules (discussed later in this chapter).

Splunk provides a **Web Framework** library that provides several prebuilt views, including visualizations (such as charts and tables), search controls (such as the search bar and timeline), form inputs (such as the checkbox, check group, dropdowns, and so on), and the Splunk headers and footers.

Panels

A Splunk panel can be thought of as a piece of Splunk view. When we talk about dashboards, we need to understand that every dashboard is made up of a number of panels. These panels are commonly set with the *saved* searches (Splunk searches that you have saved for later use) that run when the dashboard is initially loaded to provide the dashboard with up-to-date information.

The dashboard panel types determine the kind of information displayed in the dashboard. For example, tables and charts are two different panel types. In the visual dashboard editor, there are four available panel types:

- Tables
- Charts
- Event lists
- Single values

 Dashboards can (and usually do) have multiple panels.

Modules

Pretty much everything you see (and don't see) in a Splunk Web view is referred to as a module, from the search bar to the results. Splunk modules are used in dashboards, form searches, and other custom user interfaces within Splunk. The Splunk **Module System** exposes the core Splunk knowledge base for the purpose of customizing Splunk for your application domain.

All of these Splunk's standard modules are built with HTML, CSS, JavaScript, and sometimes even Python scripting. Splunk stores all of its modules at `$$SPLUNK_HOME/share/splunk/search_mrsparkle/modules/`.

Here's a hint: in order to browse the list of modules, you can use your web browser. Navigate to `http://localhost:8000/modules` on your Splunk server (replace it with your host and port); mine is shown in the following screenshot:

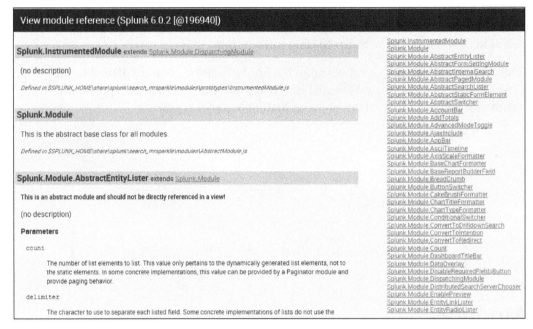

List of modules as shown in my web browser

Form searching

Some Splunk dashboards contain search forms. A search form is just another Splunk view (and is actually very similar to a Spunk dashboard) which provides an interface for users to supply values to one or more search terms.

Using textboxes, drop-down menus, or radio buttons, a search form allows users to focus only on what they are searching for (and the results, which can be displayed in the tables, event listings, or any of the visualizations available), as discussed here:

- **Textboxes**: They take specific field values or display a default value
- **Drop-down menus and lists**: They contain dynamically defined collections of search terms
- **Radio buttons**: They force to choose particular field values
- **Multiple result panels**: They generate different kinds of visualizations

An example of a search form

Take an example of the following simple Splunk search pipeline:

```
sourcetype=TM1* Error
```

Based on the preceding Splunk search pipeline, we can use the Splunk search page to run the search and receive the results, shown as follows:

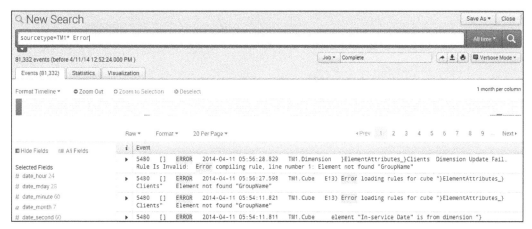

Splunk search page and the results for the search obtained

Generally speaking, the user is looking through the Cognos TM1 logs for a text string occurrence (in this case, **Error**). In this simple example, I wanted to create a Splunk search form that hides the search pipeline and allows the users to simply type into a textbox and click on search.

The easiest method of accomplishing this is to create a new dashboard and then edit it to give us what we want. On the Splunk **Dashboard** page, click on **Create New Dashboard**, fill in the blank fields, and then click on **Create Dashboard**, as shown here:

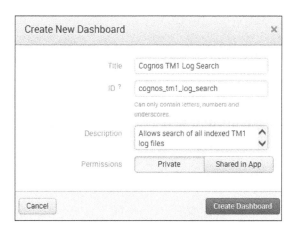

After creating the dashboard, click on **Edit Source**. Here is where you need to be comfortable with XML (more on XML later in this chapter). For now, we'll just point out the changes that were done to create the Cognos TM1 search form, as shown in the following screenshot:

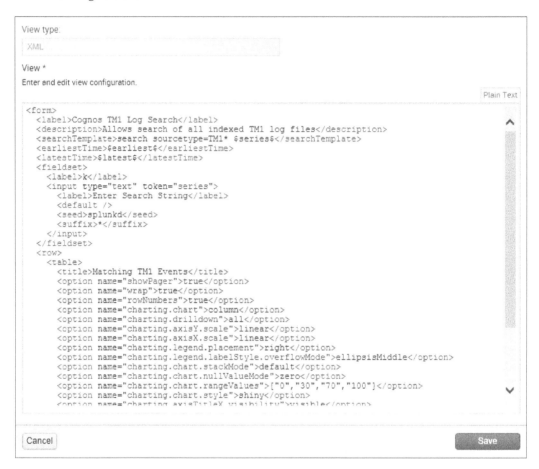

The changes that were made in the XML are as follows:

1. The outermost tags were converted from `<dashboard></dashboard>` to `<form></form>`.

2. The search was modified to `search sourcetype=TM1* $series$`.

This keeps the source as "all indexed TM1 logs" and creates an argument (or parameter) for the search, named `series`. This will be filled in at search runtime.

3.   The user input field (a textbox) was defined with the `<fieldset></fieldset>` and `<input type></input>` tags.

The following is the source XML:

```
<form>
  <label>Cognos TM1 Log Search</label>
  <description>Allows search of all indexed TM1 log files</description>
  <searchTemplate>search sourcetype=TM1* $series$</searchTemplate>
  <earliestTime>$earliest$</earliestTime>
  <latestTime>$latest$</latestTime>
  <fieldset>
    <label>k</label>
    <input type="text" token="series">
      <label>Enter Search String</label>
      <default />
      <seed>splunkd</seed>
      <suffix>*</suffix>
    </input>
  </fieldset>
  <row>
    <table>
      <title>Matching TM1 Events</title>
      <option name="showPager">true</option>
      <option name="wrap">true</option>
      <option name="rowNumbers">true</option>
      <option name="charting.chart">column</option>
      <option name="charting.drilldown">all</option>
      <option name="charting.axisY.scale">linear</option>
      <option name="charting.axisX.scale">linear</option>
      <option name="charting.legend.placement">right</option>
      <option name="charting.legend.labelStyle.
overflowMode">ellipsisMiddle</option>
      <option name="charting.chart.stackMode">default</option>
      <option name="charting.chart.nullValueMode">zero</option>
      <option name="charting.chart.
rangeValues">["0","30","70","100"]</option>
      <option name="charting.chart.style">shiny</option>
      <option name="charting.axisTitleX.visibility">visible</option>
      <option name="charting.axisTitleY.visibility">visible</option>
```

```
        <option name="charting.chart.sliceCollapsingThreshold">0.01</
option>
        <option name="charting.gaugeColors">8710400,16771072,12529712</
option>
        <option name="drilldown">row</option>
        <option name="count">10</option>
      </table>
    </row>
</form>
```

 Note that the `<table></table>` section doesn't really matter. It's just the formatting for the results to be displayed and can be created by experimenting with the web interface.

So, here's our **Cognos TM1 Log Search** form example:

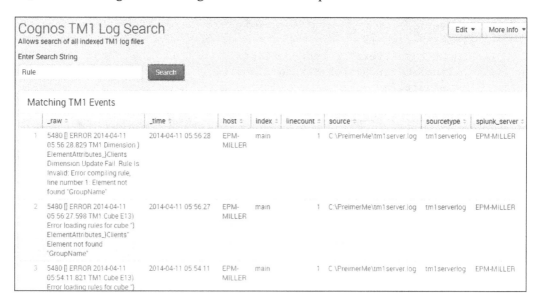

Dashboards versus forms

Splunk dashboards differ from simple XML forms in the following ways:

- The top-level (and bottom or closing) elements of both are different (`<dashboard></dashboard>` and `<form></form>`)

- Forms usually include user inputs (perhaps time range pickers, drop-down lists, radio groups, or textboxes)

- Most forms take advantage of postprocess searches, while dashboards usually do not
- The sequences of the XML elements differ slightly

Everything else—such as the layout of the rows and panels and the visualizations in the panels—will essentially be the same.

Going back to dashboards

You can use the Splunk Dashboard Editor to create your new dashboards, add/remove panels from dashboards, edit existing dashboards, and generate PDFs for a dashboard. The Dashboard Editor is really a series of dialogs that you fill out to accomplish what you want. Once you have created a dashboard, you focus on its panels and visualizations (using the appropriate editor).

The Panel Editor

Once you enable your Splunk dashboard to edit it, you can access a series of panel dialogs. Using the Panel Editor, you can modify the panel's properties and the underlying search. In addition, you have the ability to choose a different visualization and to configure it to fit your needs.

The Visualization Editor

The Visualization Editor is a series of dialogs that are provided to give you the ability to configure a selected visualization. Based on choices (the nature of the visualization), the editing dialog changes, allowing you to set each visualization property. Splunk provides similar editing for the Splunk search page and report page. From these pages, you can define visualizations that you export to your dashboard.

XML

> *Extensible Markup Language (XML) is a markup language that defines a set of rules for encoding documents in a format that is both human-readable and machine-readable.*

> *– Wikipedia 2014.*

For some features in Splunk, you can directly edit the source code. If you are fluent in XML (or HTML), you can opt to use your favorite editor (you need access to the Splunk instance on the host server for this), but Splunk provides a reasonably fine editor that you can use to edit your source in either simple XML or HTML. Editing the source code allows you to:

- Have much more control over the dashboard panel formatting properties
- Create geographic maps that display location markers
- Set up advanced and dynamic drilldown behaviors
- Create HTML panels that display static text, images, and HTML formatting
- Construct panels where you overlay charts
- Design forms that:
  ○ Include textboxes, drop-down lists, and dynamic radio buttons
  ○ Have different searches for each panel that make use of the input from the form controls (textbox, list, or radio button)
  ○ Make use of postprocess searches (searches whose results are postprocessed by child panels using reporting commands such as `timechart`, `chart`, and `stats`)
  ○ Autorun on page load with a default value. Users can rerun the page after it loads with different values if they wish.

Let's walk through the Dashboard Editor

What I love about the Splunk Dashboard Editor is that it gives you a starting framework for your dashboard. Rather than coding XML from line 1 (or copying an existing dashboard), the Dashboard Editor lets you create a dashboard with the basics to start customizing with a few simple clicks. Using the Dashboard Editor, you can:

- Create simple dashboards that can later be populated with panels
- Add a time range picker
- Reorganize panels by dragging-and-dropping
- Edit the search used by the dashboard
- Change each panel's details
- Convert a dashboard to HTML
- Use a different visualization for a panel
- Set formatting options for panel visualization
- Edit the dashboard source code

Constructing a dashboard

There are four main steps to construct a Splunk dashboard. They are:

- Constructing the framework
- Adding panels and panel content
- Specifying visualizations
- Setting permissions

Constructing the framework

Using Splunk's Dashboard Editor, you can easily create a new dashboard framework by following these steps:

1. On the **Dashboards** page of an app, click on **Create New Dashboard**.
2. Provide **Title**, **ID** (you can use the default), and **Description**. Specify **Permissions**. Then, click on **Create Dashboard**, as shown in the following screenshot:

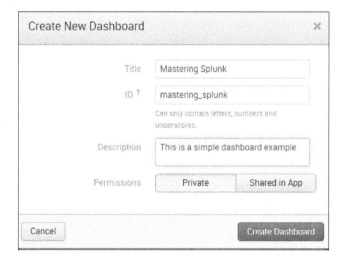

Adding panels and panel content

Once the Splunk dashboard framework has been created, you can use the Dashboard Editor to add the desired content to the dashboard by adding one or more panels (we defined panels earlier in this chapter) and a time range picker or by jumping directly into the dashboard's source code to make more specific customizations (more on this later):

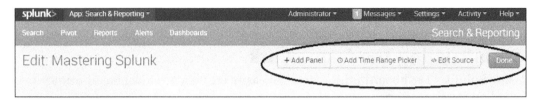

Adding a panel

To add a panel, click on **Add Panel**. Then, in the **Add Panel** dialog (shown in the following screenshot), you can add a title for your panel, select panel's **Content Type** (search, pivot, or report), and then provide the Splunk **Search String** (if you are creating an inline search panel; more on *content types* coming up soon) to be used by the panel, as shown in the following screenshot:

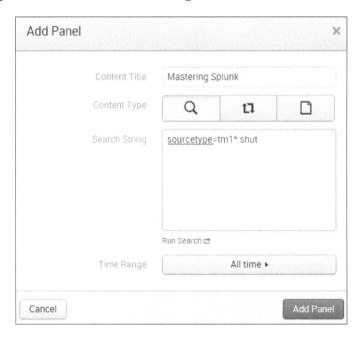

When you're done, click on **Add Panel**; we have the first panel of our sample dashboard, as shown here:

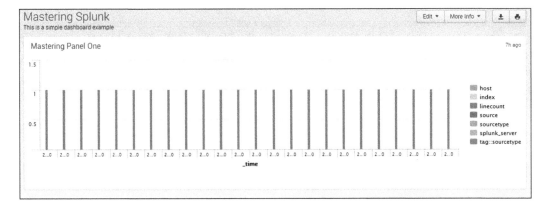

Specifying visualizations for the dashboard panel

Okay, this was a good start (although perhaps not very interesting). You might think that in this humble example, the resulting chart really doesn't add much value. However, when you add a search to your dashboard panel, you select how the panel will display the results (and you can later change your selection from the Dashboard Panel Editor).

What you can do it is you can go back into the edit mode for your dashboard and click on **Edit**, then click on **Edit Panels**, and finally go to the upper-right corner of the visualization editor icon, as shown in the following screenshot:

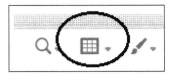

From here, Splunk allows you to select from a variety of visualizations for your event results, including **Statistics Table**, which I think makes more sense, as shown in my example:

In this chapter, we've already discussed how to edit the source code of a dashboard, so for now, let's take a look at how to add a time range picker.

The time range picker

The Splunk time range picker empowers you to set boundaries on your searches. It can restrict a search to a preset time range, custom relative time range, and custom real-time range. Moreover, you can use it to specify your own date range or a date and time range.

On the **Dashboards** page, you can edit the dashboard that you want to edit and then select **Edit Panels**, shown as follows:

Now that you are in the edit mode (for the selected dashboard), you can click on **Add time Range Picker**. Splunk automatically adds a drop-down selector to your panel that defaults to **All time**, shown as follows:

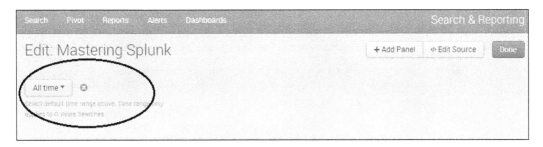

Now, your dashboard panel offers the ability to research with different time boundaries.

Adding panels to your dashboard

To add more panels to your dashboard, you can re-enter the edit mode of your dashboard, click on **Edit**, and then select **Edit Panels**. This time, since your dashboard already contains a panel, you have the option to click on **Add Panels** in order to add an additional panel using the **Add Panel** dialog (as shown in the preceding screenshot). Another (perhaps easier) way to do this would be to use an existing (saved) search (or report or pivot) and to add it to your dashboard (rather than recreate it using **Add Panel**).

Splunk gives you the ability to add a panel directly from the **Search**, **Reports**, or **Pivot** pages:

1. From the **Search** page or from the **Pivot** page, you can go to **Save As | Dashboard Panel**.
2. On the **Report** page, you can click on **Add to Dashboard**.

Depending on the source (search, reports, or pivot), the way you save a dashboard panel will vary. This also depends on whether you are creating a new dashboard or adding a panel to an existing dashboard.

Controlling access to your dashboard

Once you have constructed your dashboard, Splunk gives you some control over it, that is, where (in Splunk) it will be visible (known as the Display from) and who you want to allow to be able to edit it (read-only or write access also). To set these controls, on the **Dashboards** page, select **Edit** and then click on **Edit Permissions**, as shown in the following screenshot:

The **Edit Permissions** dialog is displayed where you can select **Display For** (**Owner**, **App**, or **All Apps**) that best suits your dashboard, as shown here:

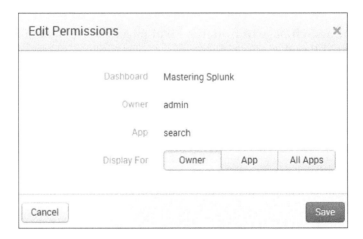

Your individual (user) role (and capabilities defined for this role) might limit the type of access that you can define for a dashboard.

Cloning and deleting

You can clone (create a copy of) any existing dashboard as the starting point for a new dashboard (rather than creating one from scratch), and you can also delete (remove) a dashboard that is no longer needed. Once you are in the dashboard's edit mode, you can perform the cloning and deleting operations as follows:

- **To clone a dashboard**: Go to **Edit | Clone** and then (give your new dashboard a title, ID, and description) click on **Clone Dashboard**. After Splunk clones your dashboard, you can view (and reset, if necessary) permissions for the dashboard.

- **To delete a dashboard**: Go to **Edit | Delete** (you'll be asked to confirm whether you want to delete the dashboard).

Keeping in context

Splunk dashboards are associated with (or are in context with) a particular Splunk app. The dashboards are:

- Framework
- Home page
- Learned
- Data preview
- Admin

You can set the permissions of a dashboard to global (to make it available to all Splunk apps), or you can change (move) the app context for the dashboard from one app to another, as follows:

1. In Splunk Web, navigate to **Settings | User interface | Views**.
2. Locate the dashboard that you want to move and from **Actions**, select **Move**.
3. Select your app's context and then click on **Move**.

Some further customization

You can use the Splunk Dashboard Editor for the basics (such as creating a basic dashboard); however, to customize your dashboard with additional features that are not available in the Dashboard Editor, you can do the following:

- Edit the XML directly to implement advanced features (we discussed a simple example of using this method earlier in this chapter when we created a Splunk search form from a dashboard).

- Edit the dashboard style sheets or add custom CSS style sheets. A dashboard can import CSS and JavaScript files as well as image files and static HTML files, allowing you to further customize your dashboard (more on this later).

- Convert or export the dashboard to HTML. After converting the dashboard to HTML, edit the HTML code, JavaScript, and style sheets to specify custom behavior (more on this later).

Using panels

Earlier in this chapter, we defined what a panel is and how it is related to a dashboard. Let's review the facts:

- A dashboard contains at least one (usually more) panel

- Typically, multiple panels are organized in rows

- A search delivers the content of each panel (displayed as a table or visualization)

- A panel's search can be of the following types:
    - An inline search
    - An inline pivot
    - A reference to a search report
    - A reference to a search pivot

 Note that you can also apply a global search to all dashboard panels and then modify (postprocess) the (global) search to display the results in a different way within each panel of the dashboard.

Adding and editing dashboard panels

The procedure to add a panel to a dashboard (go to **Edit | Edit Panels, | Add Panel**) is straightforward (and we've covered the topic earlier in this chapter). Once you are done with adding panels to your dashboard, you might want to:

- Rearrange the panels within the dashboard:

  If you are in the edit mode (if not, go to **Edit | Edit Panels**), just grab a panel and drag it to its new position.

- Edit the panel searches:

  How you edit a panel search hinges on the content type of the panel containing the search. The panel editor displays an icon for each type (inline search, inline pivot, report search, and report pivot). When you are in the edit mode of the dashboard (go to **Edit | Edit Panels**) and select the panel properties icon (the options available will depend on the type of base search), as shown in the following screenshot:

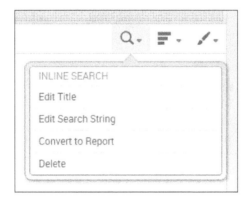

For all panel content types, you can modify (edit) the panel title or you can delete the panel. For report panels (panels that contain a reference to a report), you can perform the following steps:

1. View the report.
2. Open the panel search in search or pivot.
3. Make a clone of an inline search or pivot.
4. Change the report for the panel.
5. Select the visualization specified in the report for this panel.

For panel content types that are inline searches or inline pivots (panels that contain a reference to a search pivot), you can:

- Edit the search, specifying the inline search or inline pivot
- Convert the inline search or pivot to a report

Visualize this!

Along with the typical event listing, Splunk provides a number of options for search result visualization, as shown in the following screenshot. You can configure results (assuming that you have write permissions to the dashboard) to be displayed in the form of tables and charts, and for certain searches, you can visualize your results with a variety of gauge and single-value displays. Also, you can configure the visualization properties.

(Panel Properties, Visualization Type, Visualization Format)

The visualization type

This is the table or chart that you want to use to visualize your event results. Again, from the dashboard's edit mode (go to **Edit** | **Edit Panels**), you can click on the visualization icon (to the right-hand side of the panel properties icon) and select your desired visualization. The graphic for the visualization icon reflects the type of visualization currently selected, and Splunk lists the visualization options available, and is nice enough to note which ones are recommended for the base search.

The visualization format

In addition, farther on the right-hand side (of the visualization icon) is the visualization format icon, which lets you set the properties for the selected visualization. Every Splunk visualization contains a set of configuration properties that you can change. Many charts share the same properties, but some properties only apply to specific types of charts. General properties include the sacked mode (how to represent data in a chart), multiseries mode (enabled/disabled), drilldown mode (enabled/disabled), null value (specify how to represent missing values), style (of the visualization), x/y axis properties, title, scale, and legend.

Dashboards and XML

Splunk dashboards (and forms actually) can be created (and maintained) with simple XML. The `views` directory of an app will contain the source XML files for dashboards coded in simple XML. The location depends on the permissions for the dashboard, shared in-app or private, which is given as follows:

- The source XML files for shared permission can be found at `$SPLUNK_HOME/etc/apps/<app>/local/data/ui/views/<dashboard_file_name>`

- The source XML files for private permissions can be found at `$SPLUNK_HOME/etc/users/<user>/<app>/local/data/ui/views/<dashboard_file_name>`

The following simple XML elements are required for a Splunk dashboard (you can refer to the product documentation for the optional elements):

- The top-level element:

  ```
  <dashboard></dashboard>
  ```

- Rows (each row contains one or more panels):

  ```
  <row> </row>
  ```

- Panels (each panel contains a visualization of the search results):

  ```
  <chart></chart>
  <event></event>
  <list></list>
  <map></map>
  <single></single>
  <table></table>
  ```

- Searches defined for panels:

  ```
  <searchName></searchname>
  <searchString></string>
  <searchPostProcess></searchPostProcess>
  ```

Editing the dashboard XML code

By default, dashboards in Splunk are based on simple XML code. As we saw earlier in this chapter, you can use Splunk's interactive editor to create and edit dashboards without having to edit the simple XML, but you also have the option to edit the XML source directly (from the dashboard, go to **Edit | Edit Source**) to add features that are not available in the Dashboard Editor. We'll go over some real-world examples of editing the dashboard's XML code later in this chapter, but for now, let's take a look at using XML to expand the usability of a dashboard.

Dashboards and the navigation bar

You can add your dashboard to the Splunk navigation bar for an (any) Splunk app by directly editing the navigation menu's XML from the Splunk **Settings** menu, as described in the following steps:

1. In the dashboard, select **Settings** and then click on **User interface**, as shown in the following screenshot:

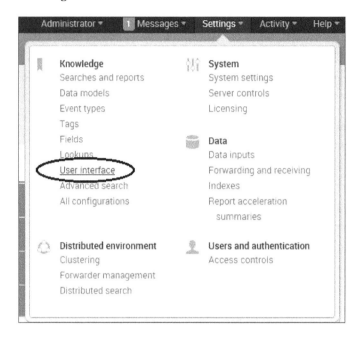

2. Next, select **Navigation menus**, as shown here:

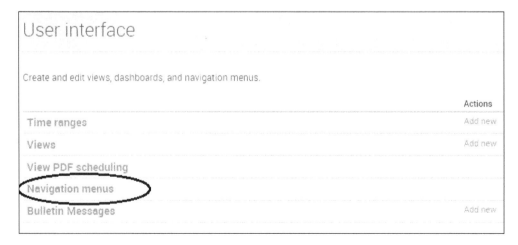

3. Select the app from **App context**, as shown in the following screenshot:

4. Under **Nav name**, select **default** to open the navigation menu's XML in the Splunk source editor:

Now, you can begin editing the XML directly! You can add dashboards to the Splunk navigation bar using the XML `<view>` element (as a child of the `<nav>` element to specify the IDs of the dashboards that you want to add) and the `<collection>` element (to create a drop-down list of dashboards in the navigation bar).

You can also set the default view for your Splunk app using the default attributes to the `<view>` element. (By default, the search view is the home view of an app, and in my example, I have designated dashboards as the default view.) The XML code is as follows:

```
<nav search_view="search" color="#993300">
  <view name="search" default='true' />
  <view name="data_models" />
  <view name="reports" />
  <view name="alerts" />
  <view name="dashboards" default="true"/>
  <collection label="Mastering Dashboards">
   <view name="Mastering_Splunk"/>
    <view name="jims_awesome_dashboard"/>
  </collection>
</nav>
```

Here's the result:

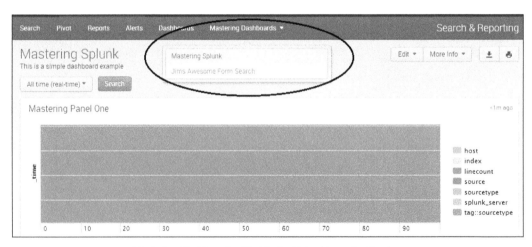

Mastering Dashboard added to the Splunk's navigation bar

Color my world

If you haven't noticed, I have used the `color` attribute of the `<nav>` element to change the color of my navigation bar:

```
<nav search_view="search" color="#993300">
```

More on searching

Earlier (in this chapter), we said that a search delivers the content of each dashboard panel. A dashboard panel can be one of the several content types. Here, we will take a look at examples of each.

When you add a (new) panel to an existing dashboard, you get to select the panel's content type simply by clicking on the appropriate icon, as shown in the following screenshot:

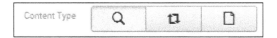

Inline searches

Dashboard panels can use live, inline searches as the source for the content displayed in the panel. Once you have added a panel to your dashboard, you can click on the panel edit icon and then select **Edit Search String**. In the **Edit Search** dialog, edit the Splunk search pipeline, select **Time Range**, and then click on **Save**, as shown here:

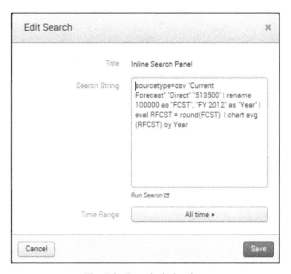

The Edit Search dialog box

A saved search report

In addition to panels that execute inline searches for content, you can add panels that use a saved Splunk report. Once you add a panel (to a dashboard), you can click on the panel edit icon and select **New Report**.

An easy way to do this is to convert an existing inline search panel by clicking on the inline search panel edit icon and then selecting **Convert to Report**, as shown in the next screenshot:

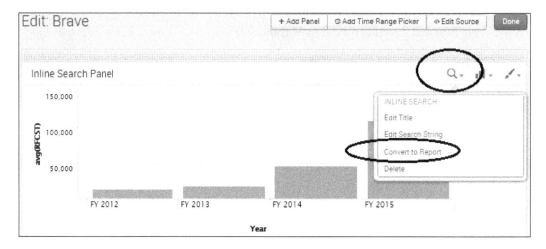

In the **Convert to Report** prompt, you can name your saved report panel and click on **Save** to view the results, as shown in the following screenshot:

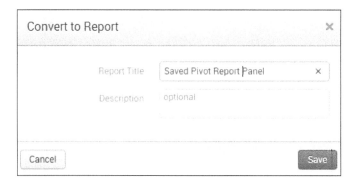

Another way to do this would be to construct (or edit) an inline search and then click on **Save As**. Then, click on **Dashboard Panel**, as shown here:

In the **Save As Dashboard Panel** dialog, you can select **Existing** and the name of the dashboard you want to add the report to, and then make sure that you select **Report** for **Panel Powered By** (you have the option to create a new dashboard panel as an inline search or as a saved report), as shown in the following screenshot:

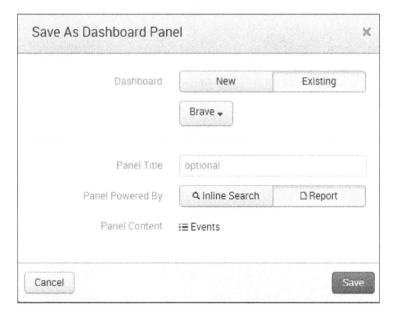

The inline pivot

To add an inline pivot panel to an existing dashboard, use the Splunk pivot tool (explained earlier in this book) to construct a new (or edit an existing) pivot. Then, click on **Save As** and then select **Dashboard Panel**, as shown here:

The **Save As Dashboard Panel** dialog allows you to select **Existing** (to add this pivot to an existing dashboard) and then select the dashboard name you want to add the pivot panel to (in my example, the dashboard is named **Brave**). You can add **Panel Title** and then click on **Save**, as shown in the following screenshot:

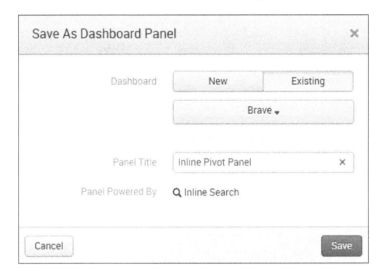

Splunk will add your pivot panel and then display the "has been created" prompt. From here, you can click on **View Dashboard** to see the results, as shown here:

The saved pivot report

Once you have a pivot panel, you might want to convert it to a pivot report panel. To do this, you can click on the pivot report panel's edit icon and select **Convert to Report**, as shown here:

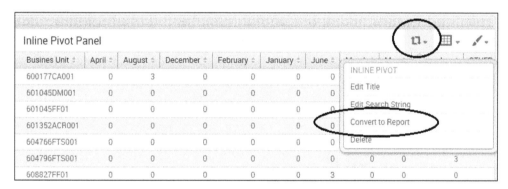

From here, you can simply name your new pivot report and click on **Save** to see the results, as shown in the following screenshot:

The following dashboard shows the final result of our example that uses four panels—each with a different content type. Starting from the top—left to right—you can see the inline search, saved search report, inline pivot, and saved pivot report, as shown here:

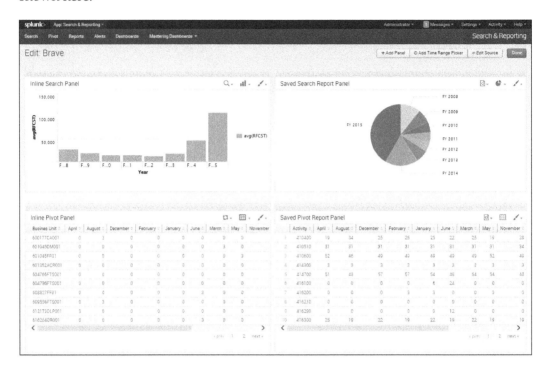

Dynamic drilldowns

You can include the dynamic drilldown functionality in dashboards by defining destinations to link to when a user clicks on fields in your dashboard. The value captured by the mouse-click can be sent to the defined destination. This destination can be another dashboard, form, view (within your Splunk installation), or an external web page.

The essentials

The key to implementing drilldowns within a Splunk dashboard is to use the XML tags:

```
<drilldown></drilldown>
<link></link>
```

Within the `<drilldown>` tag, you can optionally specify a `target=` attribute if you wish to direct the drilldown destination (which defaults to `target="_self"` and the link will open in the current window).

Between the `<drilldown>` tags, you can add one or more `<link>` tags and use the `<link>` tags to specify a destination for the drilldown.

There are many ways to use the `<link>` tag, as follows:

1. Use a relative path to connect to the dashboard:

   ```
   <link> path/viewname </link>
   ```

2. Use a relative path to connect to a form, passing in a token to populate the form:

   ```
   <link> path/viewname?form.token=$dest_value$ </link>
   ```

3. Pass in the earliest and latest time ranges from the original search (requires the use of CDATA, as indicated in the following sections):

   ```
   <link> path/viewname?form.token=$dest_value$&earliest=$earliest$&latest=$latest$ </link>
   ```

    Note that CDATA is used to make sure that characters such as & are interpreted correctly.

4. Use a URL and query argument to pass a value to the destination page:

   ```
   <link> URL?q=$dest_value$ </link>
   ```

Examples

The token $row.<fieldname>$ specifies the field from the selected row or column from which the value for drilldown is captured.

The following example shows a Splunk dashboard, drilling down to a Splunk search form, passing a value of the field series (of the row that the user clicks on) as the source type for the search form to search on, as shown in the following screenshot:

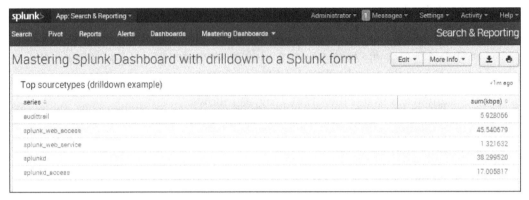

Splunk dashboard drilling down to a Splunk search form

Here's the source XML code for the dashboard (with the drilldown code in bold):

```
<dashboard>
 <label>Mastering Splunk Dashboard with drilldown to a Splunk form</label>
   <row>
     <table>
       <searchString>
          index="_internal" group="per_sourcetype_thruput" |
          chart sum(kbps) over series
       </searchString>
       <title>Top sourcetypes (drilldown example)</title>
       <earliestTime>-60m</earliestTime>
       <latestTime>now</latestTime>
       <option name="count">15</option>
       <option name="displayRowNumbers">false</option>
       <option name="showPager">true</option>
     <drilldown target="My New Window">
       <link>
        /app/search/search_form_from_dashboard?
          form.sourcetype=$row.series$
       </link>
     </drilldown>
     </table>
   </row>
</dashboard>
```

The following screenshot shows the Splunk search form with the search field filled in (from the preceding drilldown of the dashboard):

Here's the XML source code of the Splunk search form (shown in the preceding screenshot):

```
<form>
  <label>Basic form search</label>
  <fieldset>
    <html>
      <p>
        Enter a sourcetype in the field below.
      </p>
    </html>
      <!-- the default input type is a text box -->
      <input token="sourcetype" />
  </fieldset>
  <!-- search with replacement token delimited with $ -->
  <searchTemplate>
   index=_internal source=*metrics.log
      group=per_sourcetype_thruput sourcetype="$sourcetype$"
      | head 1000
  </searchTemplate>
  <row>
    <!-- output the results as a 50 row events table -->
    <table>
    <title>Matching events</title>
    <option name="count">50</option>
    </table>
  </row>
</form>
```

Another example is a dashboard that uses drilldown on a website page, passing the value that is clicked on to the web page search form, as shown here:

Here's the dashboard's XML source code:

```
<dashboard>
  <label>Drilldown to Splunk-base</label>
  <row>
    <table>
      <title>Sourcetypes by source (Dynamic drilldown to a
        form)</title>
      <searchString>
        index="_internal" | stats dc(sourcetype) by sourcetype,
          source
      </searchString>
      <earliestTime>-60m</earliestTime>
      <latestTime>now</latestTime>
      <option name="count">15</option>
      <option name="displayRowNumbers">false</option>
      <option name="showPager">true</option>
      <drilldown target="My New Window">
       <link>
          http://splunk-base.splunk.com/integrated_search/
           ?q=$click.value$
       </link>
      </drilldown>
    </table>
  </row>
</dashboard>
```

The following screenshot shows the resulting drilldown to Splunk answers (after searching for `splunkd_access`):

No drilldowns

You can also use the drilldown option to disable drilldown for a panel:

```
<option name="drilldown">none</option>
```

Real-world, real-time solutions

Today, Splunk and Splunk dashboards are making creative inroads by providing real-world, real-time solutions in new and interesting ways. The following is an example of such creativeness.

An international organization utilizes IBM Cognos TM1 for its budgeting, forecasting, and planning. They want the ability to leverage visualizations with their (TM1) data, providing dashboarding with the ability to drill into the underlying detail data if desired. However, they did not want to rollout TM1 across the organization (TM1 was only used by their planners) and native TM1 didn't really provide the rich visualizations that they desired. A variety of software solutions were considered and were plausible, but the organization happened to own Splunk. With Splunk's dashboard and visualization capabilities, it was an easy solution to implement!

The IBM Cognos TM1 model is where the budgeting, planning, and forecasting takes place. Source systems feed actuals and metadata into the model, and TM1 rules are implemented to drive automated forecasting based on the organization's business logic. Planners review and make adjustments, and the TM1 engine consolidates the data in real time. By scheduled TM1 chores, up-to-date views of the data are sliced and written (as text files) to a designated network location where they are automatically indexed by the Splunk server. Individuals who have access to Splunk view dashboards that contain (near) real-time visualizations of the TM1 data and also have the ability to drilldown to any area of the raw underlying detail data. Splunk also delivers scheduled PDFs of the dashboard data as e-mail attachments to those without Splunk access (more experienced Splunk users created their own Splunk searches on the data).

The information displayed on the Splunk dashboards allows the organization's analysts to visualize versions or views of the data, such as current versus prior forecasts, forecasts versus actuals, and track budgets, in multiple currencies. In addition, statistics such as (who) and when and where adjustments being made are available. All this information is visualized graphically on a dashboard (complete with drilldowns and printability), without programming or report creation. Take a look at the following screenshot, which shows the budget versus forecast data:

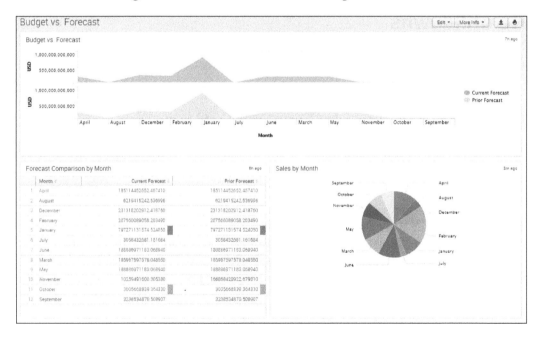

Summary

In this chapter, we covered all the aspects of Splunk dashboards, including construction, editing, drilldowns, and setting permissions. We also looked at the editing dashboard's source XML code to take advantage of the more complex features of a Splunk dashboard, which are not supported by the dashboard editor.

In the next chapter, we will cover the topic of indexes and indexing within Splunk.

6
Indexes and Indexing

This chapter will explain the idea of indexing, how it works, and why it is important. This chapter will take you through the basic and advanced concepts of indexing, step by step.

In the chapter, we'll cover the following topics:

- The importance of indexing
- Indexes, indexers, and clusters
- Managing your indexes

The importance of indexing

To understand the importance of indexing, you need to understand what an index is and its purpose.

In a typical database, an index is an internal structure that is used to *increase the speed of data retrieval*. An index is a copy of selected data that can be searched very efficiently, which might also include a file-level disk block number or even a direct connection to the entire set of data it was copied from.

Although Splunk indexes are structured a bit differently than typical database indexes, the objective is basically the same. Splunk uses its indexes to facilitate flexibility in searching and to improve data retrieval speeds.

What is a Splunk index?

As mentioned on `http://www.splunk.com`, a Splunk index can be defined as follows:

> *"A Splunk index is a repository for Splunk data."*

Data that has not been previously added to Splunk is referred to as raw data. When the data is added to Splunk, it indexes the data (uses the data to update its indexes), creating event data. Individual units of this data are called events. In addition to events, Splunk also stores information related to Splunk's structure and processing (all this stuff is not event data), transforming the data into its **searchable events**.

Splunk stores the data it indexed and its indexes within flat files (actually, files in a structured directory), meaning that it doesn't require any database software running in the background. These files are called **indexers**. Splunk can index any type of time series data (data with timestamps). During data indexing, Splunk breaks data into events based on the timestamps it identifies.

Event processing

Splunk event processing refers to the *processing of raw data* (which is a series of events) and *writing the processed data to an index file* (we'll talk about which index file later in this chapter).

Event processing is part of the **Splunk data pipeline**. The data pipeline consists of four parts:

* Input (data)
* Parsing
* Indexing
* Searching

Event processing refers to the parsing and indexing that occurs as part of the Splunk data pipeline.

Parsing

During parsing, data is separated into events and processed. The processing of data includes the following actions:

* Identifying the default fields (for each event)
* Configuring character set encoding

- Line termination using line break rules; events can be short (such as a single line) or long (many lines)

- Time stamping—identification or creation

- Applying custom logic in some cases—for example, masking certain event data

Indexing

During indexing, additional processing occurs, including the following:

- Segmentation of events

- Building the index data structure(s)

- Writing the raw data and index files to the disk

Indexing begins when you specify the data that you want Splunk to input. As more input is (data is) added, Splunk will automatically begin indexing them.

Index composition

As mentioned earlier, all data input to Splunk is written to indexes and stored in them (or index files). Index files are subdirectories that are located in `$SPLUNK_HOME/ var/lib/splunk` by default.

Two file types make up the composition of a Splunk index. They are as follows:

- Raw files

- Index files (some might refer to these files as **tsidx files**)

Raw files are compressed events data with additional information that the indexing process has added, which can be used by Splunk for efficiency. Index files contain information known as metadata that is used to access and search the raw files. Raw files and index files together make up a Splunk **bucket** (this will be discussed later in this chapter). Index file directories are organized by age.

Default indexes

When you install Splunk, there are three indexes that are configured automatically:

- **Main (main)**: This is Splunk's default index where all the processed data is stored (unless indicated otherwise)

- **Internal (_internal)**: This index is where Splunk's internal logs and processing metrics are stockpiled

- **Audit (_audit)**: This index contains events related to the file system change monitor, auditing, and all user history

 A Splunk administrator has the ability to construct indexes, edit and remove properties, and delete and move indexes.

Indexes, indexers, and clusters

Remember that Splunk indexes are a repository for all the Splunk data. Indexing (part of the Splunk data pipeline) is performed by an **indexer**.

Indexers create and use indexes. An indexer is simply a Splunk instance configured to only index data. A Splunk instance can perform indexing as well as everything else, but typically in a larger, distributed environment, the functions of data input and search management are allocated to different Splunk instances. In a larger, scaled environment, you will include forwarders and search heads.

Forwarders consume the data, indexers search and index the data, and search heads coordinate searches across the set of indexers.

A cluster is a group of indexers (sometimes referred to as nodes) that copy each other's data (you will find more on this later in this chapter).

There are three types of nodes in a cluster:

- **Master node**: The master node is a specialized type of indexer to manage the cluster
- **Peer nodes** (multiple): These nodes handle the indexing function for a cluster, indexing and maintaining multiple copies of the data and running searches across the data
- **Search heads** (multiple): These search heads will coordinate searches across all the peer nodes

Note that clusters require additional configuration beyond what's needed for a standalone indexer.

Managing Splunk indexes

When you add data to Splunk, the indexer processes it and stores it in a designated index (either, by default, in the main index or in the one that you identify). You can (if you are an administrator) manage Splunk indexes to suit your environmental needs or meet specific business requirements.

Getting started

Splunk index management starts with gaining an understanding of which indexes currently exist. To see a list of the indexes (using Splunk Web) you can go to **Settings** and then click on **Indexes**:

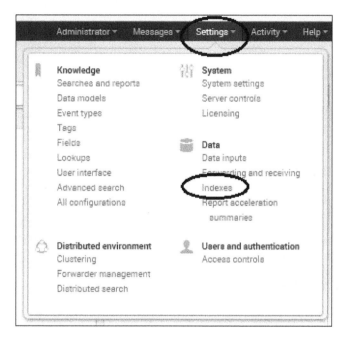

The **Indexes** page lists every index that is currently defined, including Splunk's preconfigured indexes: **_audit**, **main**, and **_internal**:

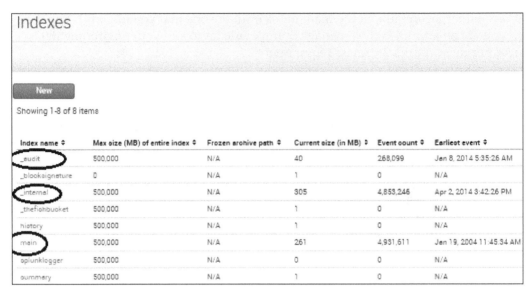

Index name ‡	Max size (MB) of entire index ‡	Frozen archive path ‡	Current size (in MB) ‡	Event count ‡	Earliest event ‡
_audit	500,000	N/A	40	268,099	Jan 8, 2014 5:35:25 AM
_blocksignature	0	N/A	1	0	N/A
_internal	500,000	N/A	305	4,853,246	Apr 2, 2014 3:42:26 PM
_thefishbucket	500,000	N/A	1	0	N/A
history	500,000	N/A	1	0	N/A
main	500,000	N/A	261	4,931,611	Jan 19, 2004 11:45:34 AM
splunklogger	500,000	N/A	0	0	N/A
summary	500,000	N/A	1	0	N/A

Index page listing the _audit, main, and _internal indexes

 In a distributed environment, where the indexer(s) and search head are potentially not part of the same Splunk instance, you should repeat this exercise for each instance.

Managing Splunk indexes can be kept simple or it can become very intricate. Index management tasks can include the following:

- Dealing with multiple indexes
- Removing or deactivating indexes
- Configuring index storage properties
- Relocating the index database
- Partitioning indexes
- Limiting index sizes
- Limiting the index disk usage
- Backing up indexed data
- Developing an index-archiving strategy

Dealing with multiple indexes

If you do not set a specific index for a search, Splunk will use its main or default index (this might vary depending on the role(s) assigned to you and the default indexes currently configured). As a Splunk administrator, you can use Splunk Web, the CLI, or edit the `indexes.conf` file to create an unlimited number of additional indexes.

Reasons for multiple indexes

There are three main reasons why you might want (or need) to consider setting up more indexes in your Splunk environment. These are as follows:

- **Security**: You can secure information using indexes by limiting which users can gain access to the data that is in particular indexes. When you assign users to **roles**, you can limit a user's searches to certain indexes based on the their role.

- **Retention**: The data that Splunk indexes might have to be preserved for an explicit amount of time and then be discarded based on certain business requirements. If all the data uses the same index, it is difficult to parse and manage it; by using more than one index, you can write data to different indexes, setting different archive or retention policies for each index.

- **Performance**: As data volumes are always increasing, performance considerations are serious. You can usually improve the search performance with a good indexing strategy. A simple example is to write higher volume search data to particularly named indexes while keeping smaller volume search data in others. In particular, it is good practice to construct devoted indexes for each Splunk data source and then send the data from this source to its dedicated index. This way you can specify which index to search (which is covered later in this chapter).

Creating and editing Splunk indexes

You can create an index with Splunk Web, the command-line interface (CLI), or by editing the indexes.conf file. Of course, the easiest method might be to use Splunk Web.

Here is the process of creating a Splunk index:

1. Go to **Settings** and then go to **Indexes**.

2. On the **Indexes** page (shown in the following screenshot), click on **New**:

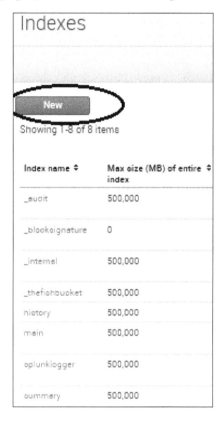

3. On the **Add new** page, enter the following information:

  ○ The index name

  ○ Path/location for the storage of the index

  ○ Maximum size for the index (the default is 500,000 MB)

  ○ Maximum size of the currently written-to portion of the index

  ○ The frozen archive path

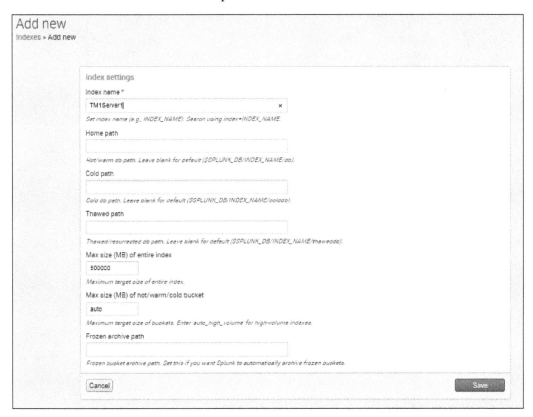

The Add new page

4. Click on **Save** and the following screenshot is displayed:

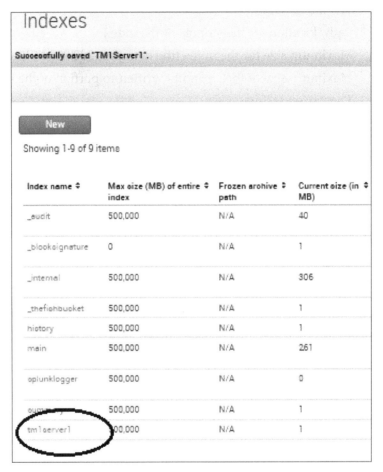

Screen displaying the saved Splunk index

Important details about indexes

Let's see some of the features of Splunk indexes:

- **Index names**: A Splunk index's name can contain only digits, lowercase letters, underscores, and hyphens and cannot start with an underscore or a hyphen.

- **Path locations**: These can be home, cold, or thawed/resurrected and can be left blank (if you want Splunk to use the following):

```
$SPLUNK_DB/<index_name>/db
$SPLUNK_DB/<index_name>/colddb
$SPLUNK_DB/<index_name>/thaweddb
```

- **Max sizes**: The maximum size of indexes defaults to 500,000 MB. There are various schools of thought on how to size your index. The maximum size of the index will depend on how much data you expect to index.

- **Frozen archive path**: This is an optional parameter—you can set this field if you want to archive frozen buckets.

 Splunk uses the terminologies home/hot, cold, and thawed/resurrected to describe the state of the index, with *home/hot* meaning *newly written or currently writing*, cold meaning *rolled off from hot, not current*, and *thawed/resurrected* meaning *unzipped or archived for reuse*.

Other indexing methods

As with most Splunk administrative tasks, there are two other methods (other than using Splunk Web) to create and edit indexes; they are the command-line interface (CLI) and editing the Splunk index configuration (indexes.conf) files. Indexes defined using these methods must adhere to the same requirements as those indexes managed through the web interface. When using the CLI, you do not need to restart Splunk to create or edit an index, but (as always) when editing the indexes.conf file, you must stop and restart Splunk. (If your environment is a distributed environment, all the instances of Splunk that are involved must be restarted.)

 If you are working in a simple, single-installation Splunk environment, I recommend that you stay with Splunk Web. For our discussion, we'll stick to Splunk Web and the index configuration (indexes.conf) files methods.

Editing the indexes.conf file

As usual, when it comes to configuration files, Splunk provides samples. Seek out the following .spec and .example files before you proceed with modifying your indexes.conf file:

- indexes.conf.example
- indexes.conf.spec

The indexes.conf.spec file (usually found at $SPLUNK_HOME/etc/system/default/) contains all the possible options for a indexes.conf file. You can refer to this file (in addition to Splunk's online documentation) for examples to configure your actual indexes.conf file in order to easily add indexes or update specific index properties.

To add a new Splunk index, you can use the following syntax example:

```
[newindex]
homePath=<path for hot and warm buckets>
coldPath=<path for cold buckets>
thawedPath=<path for thawed buckets>
```

Once you've made the changes to your version of the file, it should be saved at `$SPLUNK_HOME/etc/system/local/`.

You will then need to restart Splunk to enable the configurations. Here is a simple example; I've added the following lines to my local `indexes.conf` file:

```
# new index example for the future splunk masters
[masteringsplunk]
homepath     = $SPLUNK_DB/masteringsplunk/db
coldpath     = $SPLUNK_DB/masteringsplunk/colddb
thawedPath   = $SPLUNK_DB/masteringsplunk/thaweddb
```

On the **Indexes** page in Splunk Web, we can see our new index (**masteringsplunk**):

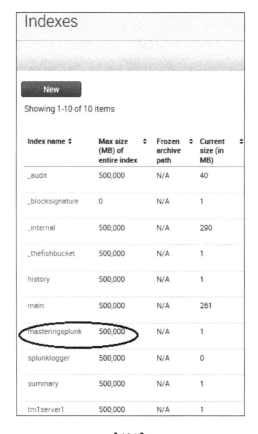

Using your new indexes

When you input data, Splunk just takes care of indexing it. If you haven't *remanaged* your indexes, all of the data (all of the events) will be written to Splunk's main index.

If you've gone to the trouble of creating additional indexes, then you'll most likely want to use them by directing data (events) to a specific index.

Splunk gives you the ability to route *all the data from an input* to a specified index as well as send certain event data to a particular index.

Sending all events to be indexed

Each and every event from an (data) input can be sent to a specified index; you can leverage Splunk Web or go back to editing the configuration files.

In Splunk Web, you can go to the **Data inputs** page (under **Settings**) and select **Files & directories**:

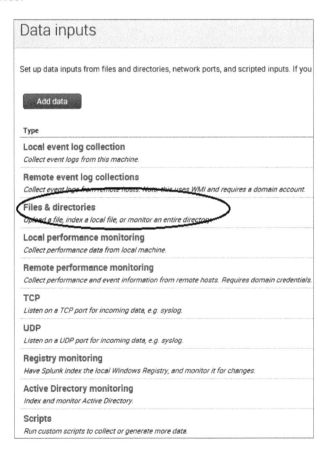

On the **Files & directories** page, you can set the destination index for each defined input source:

When you click on the desired (input) source, you can review and change various settings, including the destination (or target) index, as shown in the following screenshot:

If you want to use the configuration file approach to assign indexes, you need to review and modify the `inputs.conf` file (similar to the `indexes.conf` file). Splunk has supplied you with the `inputs.conf.spec` and `input.conf.example` files, which contain documentation and examples.

To direct *all events* from an input source, you will use the `monitor:` and `index=` commands in the `inputs.conf` file.

The following is the default syntax for Splunk's internal index (used to send all the Splunk logs to Splunk's `_internal` index):

```
[monitor://$SPLUNK_HOME\var\log\splunk]
index = _internal
```

The following example sends *all the data* from `/tm1data/logs` to an index named `tm1servers`:

```
[monitor:///tm1data/logs]
disabled = false
index = tm1servers
```

Sending specific events

If you have the ability to identify certain events within your data with a specific attribute(s), then you can use that attribute to send those specific events to a selected index. To route specific events to a specific index, you can again use Splunk Web or edit the configuration files (the `props.conf` and `transforms.conf` files).

As detailed earlier, using Splunk Web, you can go to the **Data inputs** page (under **Settings**), select **Files & directories,** and then click on the desired source to once again review and change the settings. Under the **Index** settings (where you selected the destination index), there are two more fields that you can set: **Whitelist** and **Blacklist**. These are the regex (regular expressions) that Splunk will use when you specify an entire directory. It can also be a regex for the `monitor://` setting, but you might want to include (whitelist) or exclude (blacklist) certain files. These options are shown in the following screenshot:

Some examples of sending specific events might include specifying events where the `_raw` field includes a particular computer IP address or the event includes a particular web address:

```
_raw="(?<!\d)11.\d{1,3}\.\d{1,3}\.\d{1,3}(?!d)"
(?m)packtlib.packtpub.com
```

Again, rather than using Splunk Web, you can edit Splunk's configuration files. Once you have identified a common event attribute, you can edit the `props.conf` file (where you specify a source, source type, or host) and the `transforms.conf` file (where you set your regular expressions).

Using these files, you can do the following:

1. Define a props stanza in the `$SPLUNK_HOME/etc/system/local/props.conf` file. The stanza is where you define the relationship:

```
[<spec>]
TRANSFORMS-<class_name> = <transforms_name>
```

Your `<spec>` value can be a source type of your events, the host of your events, or a particular source itself. The `<class_name>` value is any unique identifier. The `<transforms_name>` value is the unique identifier you want to give to your transformation rule in the `transforms.conf` file.

2. Set up a transformation rule in the `$SPLUNK_HOME/etc/system/local/transforms.conf` file:

```
[<transforms_name>]
REGEX = <your_custom_regex>
DEST_KEY = _MetaData:Index
FORMAT = <alternate_index_name>
```

The `<transforms_name>` value must match the `<transforms_name>` value you specified in the `props.conf` file. The `<your_custom_regex>` value is the regular expression you provide to match for your event attribute. The `DEST_KEY` value must be set to the `_MetaData:Index` index attribute. The `<alternate_index_name>` value specifies the specific index that the events will be written to.

A transformation example

Consider the following `props.conf` example:

```
[tm1serverlog]
TRANSFORMS-index = TM1LogsRedirect
```

This directs events of the `tm1serverlog` source type to the `TM1LogsRedirect` stanza in the `transforms.conf` file. The `transforms.conf` file will be as follows:

```
[TM1LogsRedirect]
REGEX = \s+Shutdown
DEST_KEY = _MetaData:Index
FORMAT = masteringsplunk
```

This processes the events directed here by the `props.conf` file. Events that match the regex (because they contain the `Shutdown` string in the specified location) get routed to the desired index, `masteringsplunk`, while any other event will be sent to the default index.

Searching for a specified index

When Splunk performs the search, it always reads the Splunk main index (or an index based on the user's assigned role) unless the search explicitly specifies a different index. The following search command, for example, will search in the `tm1server` index:

```
index=tm1server userid=jim.miller
```

Deleting your indexes and indexed data

While Splunk continues to write data (events) to its indexes, you can remove specified indexed data or even an entire index from your Splunk environment. So, let's have a look at how to do this.

Deleting Splunk events

Splunk affords the `delete` special operator to delete events from your Splunk searches. The Splunk `delete` operator flags all the events returned so that future searches don't return them. This data will not be visible to any user (even *admin* permission users) when searching. However, just flagging this data using `delete` does not free up the disk space, as data is not removed from the index; it is just invisible to searches.

In *Chapter 2, Advanced Searching*, we discussed the Splunk search pipeline and various operators. The `delete` operator is an extraordinary operator that can only be run by a user granted the **delete_by_keyword** capability. Even the Splunk admin user does not have this capability granted; you must explicitly grant it to users who you think should have it.

To provide this ability, you can (in Splunk Web) go to **Settings** and then go to **Access controls**:

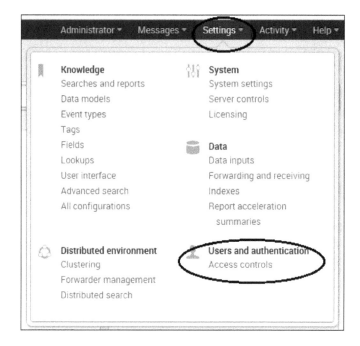

The next step is to select **Roles** from the **Access controls** page:

On the **Roles** page, click on the specific user role that you want to edit:

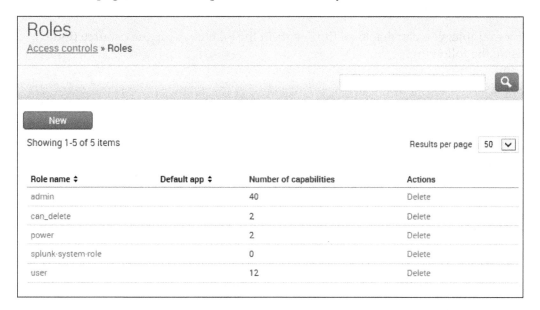

When Splunk displays the selected role's current properties, you can locate (under the **Capabilities** section) and click on the **delete_by_keyword** capability to add it to the **Selected capabilities** list and then click on the **Save** button:

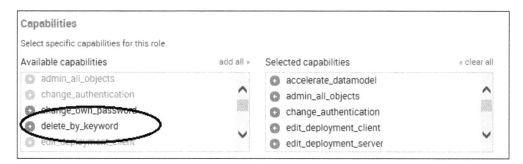

Once you have granted this capability to your user role, you can use the `delete` operator in a Splunk Web search pipeline.

For example, you can delete all the events in the `masteringsplunk` source (index), using the following:

```
source=mastersplunk | delete
```

Not all events!

In the following Splunk search, I am searching a particular input source for a very specific set of events:

```
source="c:\\logging\\sales.cma" May 2015 421500 "current Forecast"
"83100"
```

This search results in one event being returned, as shown in the following screenshot:

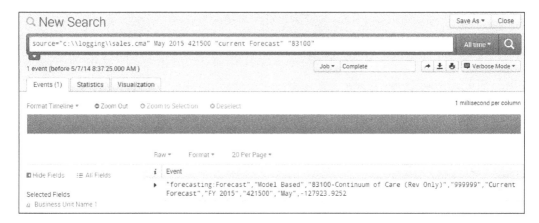

Next, I *pipe my search* to the `delete` operator:

```
source="c:\\logging\\sales.cma" May 2015 421500 "current Forecast"
"83100" | delete
```

After executing this search, when I rerun the original search, I have a different result: no events are returned! This is shown in the following screenshot:

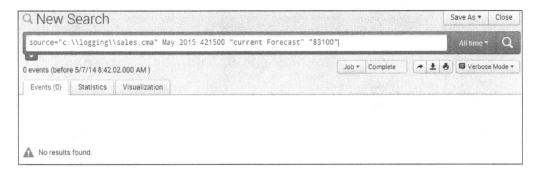

Deleting data

Again, using the `delete` operator does not permanently remove data from Splunk. You need to use the Splunk command-line interface (CLI) to actually erase indexed data permanently from your environment.

Splunk's `clean` command will completely remove the data from one or all the indexes, depending on whether you provide an `<index_name>` argument. In most cases, you will use the `clean` command before reindexing all your data.

Administrative CLI commands

Splunk administrative CLI commands are the commands used to manage or configure your Splunk server and its environment. Your Splunk role's configuration dictates which actions (commands) you can execute, and most actions require you to be a Splunk admin.

The general syntax for a CLI command is as follows:

```
<command> [<object>] [[-<parameter>] <value>]...
```

It is always advisable to run a `help` command before executing a Splunk CLI command. For example, to see the help information on the `clean` command, you can run the following:

```
splunk help clean
```

You should get something similar to what is shown in the following screenshot:

The clean command

To run the `clean` command, you need to stop Splunk first. The following example removes the event data from the index named `masteringsplunk`, and the `-f` append forces Splunk to skip the confirmation prompt:

```
splunk stop
splunk clean eventdata -index masteringsplunk -f
```

You should get something similar to what is shown in the following screenshot:

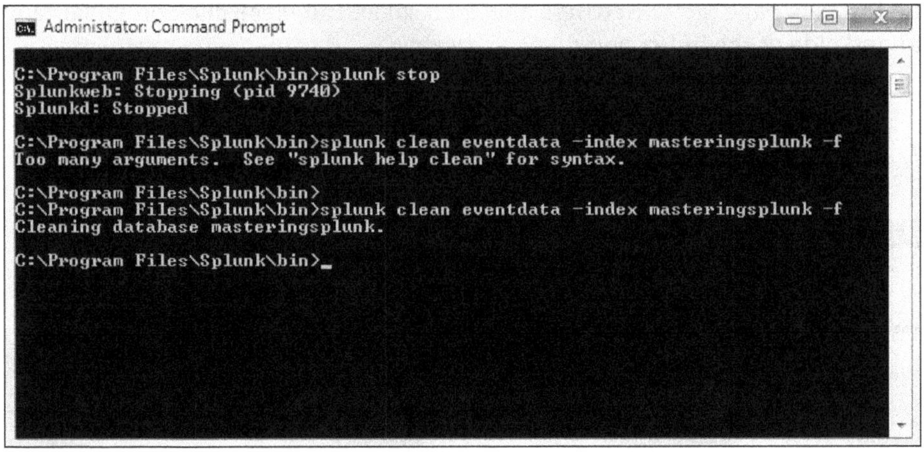

Deleting an index

If you want to delete a Splunk index entirely (not just the data in it but all of it), you can use the `remove index` CLI command. This command will delete the index's data directories and permanently remove the index from the Splunk configuration file, `indexes.conf`. The syntax is as follows:

```
splunk remove index <index_name>
```

Although the `remove` command cleans up the `indexes.conf` file, it is *up to you as the administrator* to make quite sure that all the `inputs.conf` files are reviewed for references to the index you are going to delete. If you delete the index and a reference to it still exists in the `inputs.conf` file, any data being sent to the (deleted) index will be discarded by Splunk and lost.

Disabling an index

To disable a Splunk index (and not delete it or delete data from it), you can use the `disable index` CLI command. Keep in mind that unlike the `remove index` command, the `disable index` command does not delete the index data and can be undone using the `enable index` CLI command. The syntax is as follows:

```
splunk disable index <index_name>
splunk enable index <index_name>
```

You can also disable a particular index using Splunk Web.

On the **Indexes** page (go to **Settings** and then select **Indexes**), click on **Disable** to the right-hand side of the index you want to disable:

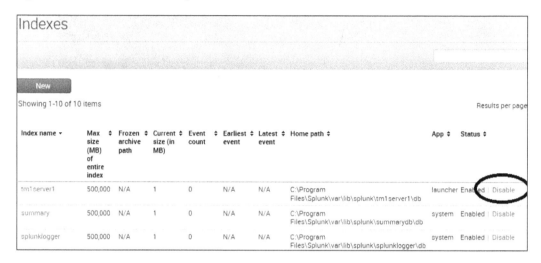

Retirements

Splunk retires data based on time or volume. These are limit settings that you, as the Splunk administrator, can set as part of your retirement policy.

For processing, Splunk retires its data by freezing it (moving it to a frozen state), which means it gets deleted from the index. You do have the ability to archive the data before deleting it. Typically, a retirement policy will manage index buckets from *hot to warm, warm to cold*, and *cold to frozen* (we'll talk more about this later in this chapter).

Configuring indexes

Splunk will allow you to set the location (path) to your nonclustered indexes using Splunk Web, but the majority of the configurations must be done by editing the indexes.conf file (for this discussion, we will stick to nonclustered indexes).

The indexes.conf file should be saved at $SPLUNK_HOME/etc/system/local/ or in a custom app directory, in $SPLUNK_HOME/etc/apps/.

The following are the most interesting index configuration attributes (you can use the product documentation to review the full list):

- `homePath`, `coldPath`, and `thawedPath`: These attributes are all required settings. These indicate where Splunk will place the index buckets (hot/warm are stored in home, cold in cold, and thawed in thawed). The `ColdToFrozenDir` attribute is optional and indicates where Splunk will archive data before deleting it from an index.

- `maxHotBuckets`: This attribute is the limit of hot or live index buckets, and `maxDataSize` is the attribute to limit how big a hot or live bucket can grow.

- `maxWarmDBCount`: This is the attribute that sets the maximum number of warm buckets allowed before Splunk moves warm buckets to cold.

- `maxTotalDataSizeMB`: This is the attribute that sets the maximum size of an index before Splunk begins moving cold buckets to frozen.

- `frozenTimePeriodInSecs`: This attribute sets the maximum time before Splunk begins moving cold buckets to frozen.

- `coldToFrozenScript`: This is the attribute where, as its name implies, you indicate a script for Splunk to run just before a cold bucket moves to frozen.

Moving your index database

If you need to, you can actually transport your Splunk index database or individual indexes (or parts of an index) to entirely new locations.

This process simply involves the following steps:

1. Stop Splunk.
2. Copy the files required for the index.
3. Unset the `Splunk_DB` variable.
4. Reset the `Splunk_DB` variable (by editing the `%SPLUNK_HOME%\etc\splunk-launch.conf` file).
5. Restart Splunk.
6. Delete the old index folder/files.

You can change the path to your indexes with Splunk Web; however, this method only affects the data written to the index after the path change is made. Splunk Web should really only be used for setting paths to new indexes, which we discussed earlier in this chapter.

Spreading out your Splunk index

You can spread out your Splunk index data across multiple disks and partitions. It is recommended that the manner in which you approach this should be based on a well thought out strategy and not merely on *availability of storage*.

In Splunk, paths (the locations) are set on an index-by-index basis, using the previously mentioned path attributes (`homePath`, `coldPath`, and `thawedPath`) in the `indexes.conf` file. Your fastest storage should be used for home data and progressively slower (and cheaper) storage for cold data.

Size matters

When it comes to the sizing of indexes, it is important to allow appropriate extra or buffer space as Splunk, during normal processing, can sporadically exceed indexes' set maximum size. Again, configuring the sizes of indexes is done by editing the `indexes.conf` file.

Index-by-index attributes

You can set index sizes (using the `maxTotalDataSizeMB` attribute) in the `indexes.conf` file based on your knowledge of the data.

Bucket types

Index sizing can also be done using bucket types. A bucket is a location or folder on a disk that contains all or parts of a Splunk index. You can set a maximum size for all hot and warm buckets using the following syntax:

```
homePath.maxDataSizeMB = 10000
```

To set the maximum size for all cold bucket storage, you can use the following syntax:

```
coldPath.maxDataSizeMB = 5000
```

Volumes

Finally, a popular method used to organize and direct index sizes is through the use of **volumes**. A volume is basically the disk space that is set aside for a particular use and in this case, where your Splunk index data will reside. Volumes can hold data from one or multiple indexes. By setting data size limits on a volume, you can control the disk usage for the indexes.

Creating and using volumes

To create a volume (and optionally specify the maximum size for the volume), you can use the following syntax:

```
[volume:<volume_name>]
path = <pathname_for_volume>
maxVolumeDataSizeMB = <max size>
```

To use the volumes you've created, you can set an index's `homePath` and/or `coldPath` attributes to those volumes, as follows:

```
[masteringsplunk]
homePath = volume:volumenameidefined/masteringsplunk
coldPath = volume:othervolumenameidefined/masteringsplunk
```

Hitting the limits

We've discussed many topics concerning the management of the space that Splunk indexes consume. Of the space that Splunk uses, its indexes consume most of the space. Once you've implemented a strategy for index space management, you will still need to keep monitoring it (and perhaps amending it) as once the available disk space drops below the minimum allowed limit, Splunk indexing and searching will stop (don't worry though, Splunk will resume once space is freed up).

We'll talk some more about how to determine potential space needs a little later, but for now, consider the following factoids:

- Splunk routinely looks for free disk space on all the partitions that contain indexes. If the free disk space limit has been reached, *Splunk stops.*

- Before executing a Splunk search, the amount of free space available is checked. If the free disk space limit has been reached, *Splunk does not execute the search.*

- By default, the minimum free disk space required is 5,000 MB.

- Splunk *does not clear* any disk space on its own.

- Data coming into Splunk *will be lost* while Splunk waits for space.

- You can set space minimums through Splunk Web, the CLI, or the `server.conf` file.

Setting your own minimum free disk space

Using Splunk Web, you can set your own minimum free disk space; simply click on **Settings** and then select **System settings**:

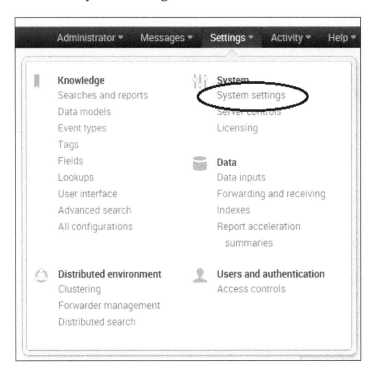

On the **System settings** page, click on **General settings**:

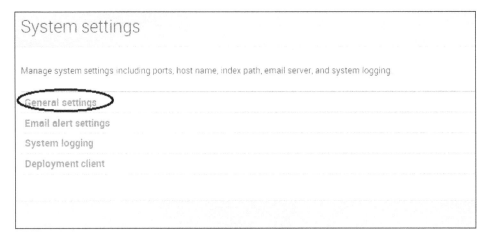

On the **General settings** page, locate the section named **Index settings** and the field named **Pause indexing if free disk space (in MB) falls below**:

Here, you can enter the minimum free disk space that you want and then click on **Save**. After you've made the change, you will need to restart Splunk for your changes to take effect.

You can also use the CLI to set the free disk limits using the following commands:

```
splunk set minfreemb 20000
splunk restart
```

Finally, you can set the minimum free disk space by editing the `server.conf` file using the following syntax:

```
[diskUsage]
minFreeSpace = <num>
```

Summary

In this chapter, we introduced indexes in general, talked about the objectives behind Splunk indexing, identified the existing indexes within your Splunk environments, defined indexes and indexers, and went through the basic operations of managing your indexes, such as setting attributes (index by index) and even moving or removing an index.

In the next chapter, we will go over the forward-thinking topics for Splunk applications and add-ons, such as navigation, searching, and sharing.

7
Evolving your Apps

This chapter starts with some Splunk app basics and then covers more advanced topics for Splunk applications and add-ons, such as navigation, searching, and sharing. Sources to find additional application examples are also provided.

In this chapter, we will cover the following topics:

- Basic applications
- Navigation and searching
- Resources
- More applications

Basic applications

So, what are Splunk apps? The product documentation at `http://www.splunk.com` defines Splunk apps as follows:

> *"A self-service out-of-the box extension that has its own UI context and which can be selected from the App list that appears at the upper right-hand corner of the Splunk UI."*

> *Splunk.com, 2014*

The app list

To access Splunk's app list, select **Apps** from Splunk Web, as shown in the following screenshot:

Search & Reporting is Splunk's search interface and can be accessed by clicking on the **Search & Reporting** link. If you click on **Find More Apps**, Splunk takes you to the **Browse more apps** page, where you can go through page after page of existing downloadable apps (or you can use the search field to search for apps that are relevant to your interests or needs).

When you click on **Manage Apps**, Splunk displays the **Apps** page, listing all the apps currently configured in your environment, as shown in the following screenshot:

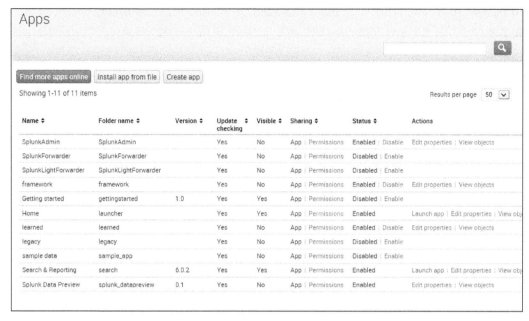

The Apps page

On this page, you can view and modify each app's properties (more details on this later in this chapter).

More about apps

Splunk apps are most often referred to as knowledge objects. You can think of a knowledge object as an arrangement of objects within Splunk, based on some business logic or agreed upon by consideration or need (you can call this user requirement).

Knowledge objects can be (saved) searches, event types, transactions, tags, field extractions and transforms, lookups, dashboards, add-ons, workflow actions, or views. Basically, apps are knowledge objects designed and implemented for the specific needs of a team or user or to solve a specific problem. Apps themselves can utilize or leverage other apps or add-ons. Splunk can run any number of apps simultaneously.

Using Splunk apps and add-ons, you can transform a Splunk instance into distinct interfaces for different user communities. Using this approach, all the users can use the same Splunk instance, but they can access only the data and functionalities that you decide to grant them.

Out of the box apps

When you log in to Splunk, you land on an app (typically, this is the Splunk *Search* app, but this might depend on the user's role). In addition, the Splunk *Getting Started* app is also available for use. As mentioned earlier in this chapter, you can find and install additional apps or even create your own. When you're logged in (or are using Splunk), you're almost always using an app (even if it's just the default Splunk *Search*). The intent is for most apps to work straight out of the box, without additional configurations or customizations.

Add-ons

Also related to apps are add-ons. Add-ons provide you with the ability to input or collect specific data types for use in your configured (default or custom) Splunk apps. Add-ons can be data feeds, input forms, scripts, or other logic collected for the purpose of data input.

An example of a Splunk add-on is *Splunk_TA_Windows*, which includes predefined inputs to collect data from Windows systems and to normalize the data for use in **Common Information Model** (**CIM**) compliant Splunk apps. There are three types of Splunk add-ons: domain (for example, views for domains within an app), supporting (provides support tools and more, used by a domain add-on), and other (typically used to get and map data from specific sources within apps).

Earlier (in *The app list* section) in this chapter, we walked through the steps of how to view your installed Splunk apps. Keeping in mind that Splunk apps as well as add-ons are made up of typically more than one Splunk knowledge object, there is a way to view and manage these objects.

Splunk Web

To view all the knowledge objects in your Splunk instance using Splunk Web, you can go to **Settings** and then click on the link you are interested in, such as the following:

- **All configurations**: Using this option, you can see everything
- **Searches and reports**: Using this option, you can see all the saved searches and report objects
- **Event types**: Using this option, you can see all the event types
- **Fields**: Using this option, you can see all the field extractions

These options can be viewed in the following screenshot:

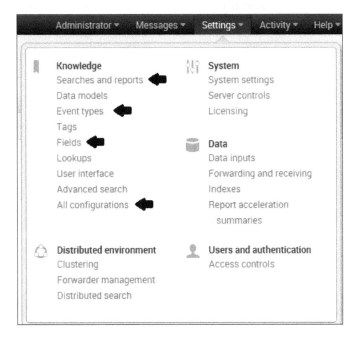

Once you've made a selection, you can view and update the knowledge objects you are interested in.

 You can sort, filter, and search each of the object lists by clicking on the field arrows or utilizing the search field on the app's context bar.

Installing an app

As mentioned earlier in this chapter, you can use Splunk Web to find the Splunk apps that are available for download and use (under **Apps**, click on **Find More Apps**). The steps for installation are as follows:

1. Once you've identified an app you are interested in, you can click on **Install free**, as shown in the following screenshot:

2. From there, you will be asked to log in to Splunk with your username and password (we discussed how to establish your username earlier in this book).

3. Once you have successfully logged in, the app will be downloaded and ready for installation. Splunk will advise you to restart it, as shown in the following screenshot:

4. You can click on **Restart Splunk**. Restarting Splunk will make your app available for use.

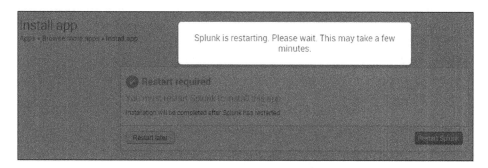

5. Once Splunk has restarted, you will receive the following message:

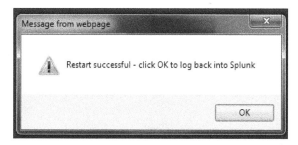

6. After Splunk has restarted, your app will be listed on the **Apps** page, as shown here:

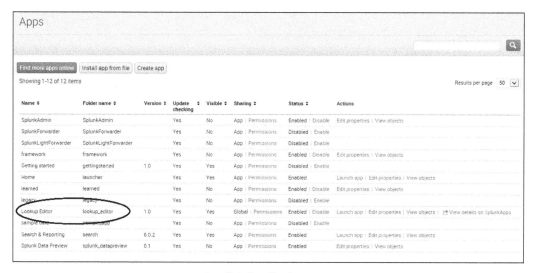

App listed on the Apps page

At this point, it is a good idea to review the app's properties and, specifically, set the value for the **Update checking** option to **Yes**, as shown in the following screenshot. This will tell Splunk to automatically check whether there are any updates available for your app, so you don't have to remember; however, take care to check whether this is appropriate for your environment. In some cases, due to proxy settings, this automatic checking might cause performance issues.

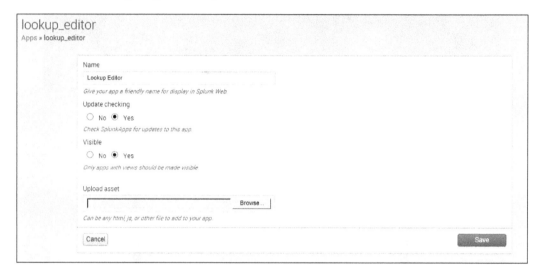

Additionally, if you'd rather install your downloaded apps directly (without using the Splunk web interface), you can do the following:

1. Copy your downloaded file into the `$SPLUNK_HOME/etc/apps` directory.

2. Untar and unzip your app.

3. Restart Splunk.

If you don't want to use the automatic updating option for your installed Splunk apps, you can also use the Splunk command-line interface to update a specific app (based on the app's installation package information):

```
./splunk install app <app_package_filename> -update 1 -auth
<username>:<password>
```

Disabling and removing a Splunk app

In addition to updating your app, you can use the command line to disable or remove an installed app. To disable a specific Splunk App, you can use the following command:

```
./splunk disable app [app_name] -auth <username>:<password>
```

To use the CLI to remove a specific installed Splunk app, you can use the following command:

```
./splunk remove app [appname] -auth <username>:<password>
```

 Using the CLI to remove a Splunk app does not delete any data indexed by the app. To remove specific data indexed by a disabled app, you need to use the `clean` command (discussed in *Chapter 6, Indexes and Indexing*). In addition, take the time to review the app you want to remove; user-specific directories used by the app might need to be manually cleaned up. Finally, after disabling or removing an app, always restart Splunk.

BYO or build your own apps

As mentioned earlier, organizations will develop familiarities specific to their needs as they use Splunk to gain information from data. In time, as the organization matures, most of them will create Splunk knowledge objects (also explained earlier in this book).

These familiarities and knowledge objects can be used to enhance or extend Splunk in various ways, including the development of custom apps and add-ons. An app contains a **user interface** (**UI**) that you can customize. Add-ons are smaller, reusable components that do not contain a navigable UI. The apps that you develop can be installed and used throughout your internal environment or can be shared globally by uploading them to `http://apps.splunk.com/`.

In addition to extending the capabilities of basic Splunk, apps can be used to create separate Splunk instances into functional environments. As Splunk can be configured with any number of apps, multiple organizational groups can use Splunk without an overlap or conflict with each other. As a Splunk developer, you can build apps that provide distinct user interfaces and functionalities tailored for each user group. Groups can have access restricted to one or numerous apps.

App FAQs

The following are some fundamental characteristics of Splunk apps:

- Apps are often referred to as a workbench or workspace
- Apps are navigable
- Apps can be opened from Splunk's home page, the **Apps** menu, or indirectly from **Settings**
- Apps tend to focus on the characteristics of data

- Apps are based on specific uses

- Apps can support varied groups

- Apps can be run at the same time as other apps

- Apps can include one or more configurations and/or knowledge objects

- Apps can be set up to be completely customized

- Apps can include HTML, CSS, and JavaScript code

Also, a Splunk add-on is reusable and similar to a Splunk app, but an add-on does not contain a navigable view. You cannot open an add-on from the Splunk Enterprise home page or the **Apps** menu.

The end-to-end customization of Splunk

Splunk app development usually starts with the UI. Based on your needs, the Splunk user interface can be modified in the simplest (changing a menu layout) to the most complex (utilizing custom HTML and JavaScript code to completely change the look and feel) way. In this book, we've already covered several interesting UI customizations:

- **Dashboards**: These visually present search results

- **Form search**: This simplifies searches by presenting a search box, which runs filters or more complex logic behind the scenes

- **Advanced views**: This allows view customization beyond what is available in simple XML syntax

Beyond the UI, a Splunk app can be further customized for handling specific types of data. Through Splunk Web, you can further develop your app's functionality with the following actions:

- Create specific indexes used only by your app

- Add specific searches, reports, and fields

- Restrict access to the app's object(s)

- Add views and navigation menus to the app

- Set up specific user roles for the app

Preparation for app development

Before you begin Splunk app development, the Splunk community recommends that you consider the following questions:

- **Which editor will you use?**: Splunk apps can be built using only Splunk Web, but the more advanced your app needs to be, the more you will find yourself creating and editing XML, CSS, and HTML code. Splunk Web includes an XML editor, but this editor is simplistic and is best used only for things such as syntax highlighting and indenting. You can pick one of your choice, but a good recommendation is Komodo Edit, which is free and available at `http://komodoide.com/komodo-edit/`.

- **Do you have a good sampling of data?**: Realistically, you cannot develop an app without real, relevant data to test with. The time that is spent to index real data to test with is time that is well spent.

- **Which are the existing knowledge objects?**: Any objects that you plan to integrate into your app, such as visualizations, searches, reports, views, or dashboards, should be identified before development begins.

- **Have you assembled your web tools?**: Common web tools (these will be different depending on your browser) help you to troubleshoot your JavaScript, CSS, and HTML code.

Beginning Splunk app development

Assuming, of course, that you have identified a use case to solve, what data is to be worked with, and how it will be imported into Splunk as well as you have a good grasp (gained perhaps though a storyboard session) of who will use your app and how they will use it, then the following diagram shows the app development life cycle:

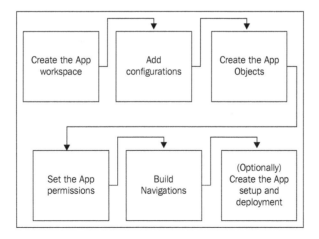

Creating the app's workspace

All Splunk apps are dependent on a specific directory structure, which can be created and modified by hand (not recommended) or by using the app builder (highly recommended). Splunk's app builder creates the directories and the required configuration files for you and even registers your app within your Splunk server. The following are the steps to create the workspace:

1. To get started, you can go to **Apps** and then click on **Manage Apps**.

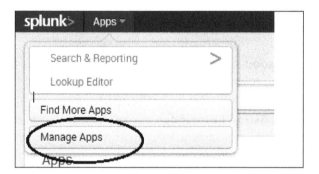

2. On the **Apps** page, click on **Create app**.

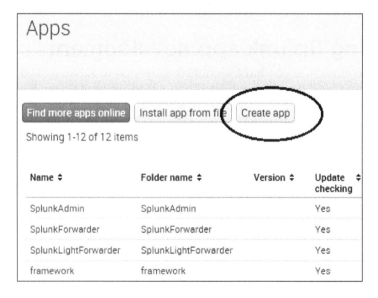

3. On the **Add new** page, you can begin building your new Splunk app by filling in the blank fields.

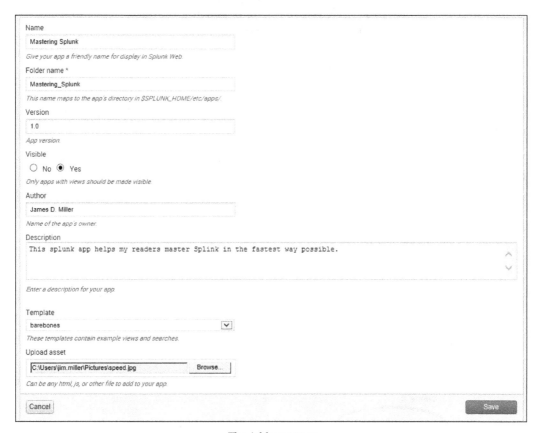

The Add new page

The fields are defined as follows:

- **Name**: You need to give a name to your app. Keep in mind that this name will be used as the label setting in the app.conf file and is visible in the **Apps** drop-down menu.

- **Folder name**: This is the name of the app's folder in the apps directory in $SPLUNK_HOME.

- **Version**: This denotes the current version of your app (as you are creating a new app, we'll assume its 1.0).

- **Visible**: You should almost always mark your app as visible.

- **Author**: This should be the original developer's name.

- **Description**: This is the description that will appear on the Splunk **Home** page.

- **Template**: Splunk provides you with two app templates (the `sample_app` and `barebones` apps). These are excellent starting points for your first few apps. Later, as a Splunk master, you can add your own additional customized templates.

- **Upload asset**: Here you can add graphics or some HTML, JavaScript, or CSS code, as well as other files to your app.

Once you've entered the information, you can click on **Save** (you don't have to restart Splunk).

Your new Splunk app should now be listed on the **Apps** page, as shown in the following screenshot:

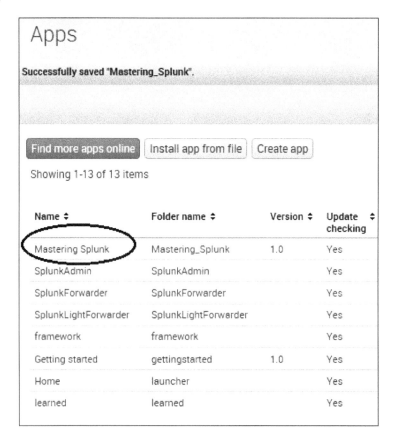

Adding configurations

Several areas of this book discuss Splunk configurations and configuration files. Splunk uses configuration files to define and control a variety of Splunk behaviors. Here, configurations are used to state how an app will interact with the splunkd server. You will find that most Splunk apps include at least some configuration.

Compared to an app's frontend (or user interface), configurations are used to define an app's backend, setting up what is referred to as the apps *data layer* and defining the following:

- The type of data that will be the input for the app
- The kind of access controls that might be needed for the app

You should know that all Splunk configuration files are, by default, global and are available to all Splunk apps currently installed. To exclude configurations that you set for your specific Splunk app, you can place those specific configurations in your app's directory.

The app.conf file

Earlier in this chapter, we mentioned the Splunk app builder. When you use the app builder, it creates the most important Splunk app configuration file: `app.conf`. Once this file is created, you will most likely want to customize it to further modify your app. As an example, in this chapter, we used the app builder to create a new app named *Mastering Splunk*. The app builder created an `app.conf` file and placed it at `$SPLUNK_HOME/etc/apps/Mastering_Splunk/default/`.

If we open this file, it looks like the following:

```
#
# Splunk app configuration file
#

[install]
is_configured = 0

[ui]
is_visible = 1
label = Mastering Splunk

[launcher]
author = James D. Miller
description = This splunk app helps my readers master Splink in the fastest way possible.
version = 1.0
```

The app.conf file

Notice that the contents of the file are based on the information I entered on the **Add new** page while working with the Splunk app builder.

Let's take a look at the file sections:

- To indicate whether the app is enabled or disabled, use the following lines of code:

```
[install]
state = enabled | disabled
```

- To make your app visible in Splunk Web, use the following lines of code:

```
[ui]
is_visible = true
label = <name>
```

- To add the app into the app launcher, use the following lines of code:

```
[launcher]
author=<author of app>
description=<textual description of app>
version=<version of app>
```

Giving your app an icon

It is good practice to include an identifying icon when developing a Splunk app. Icons can be displayed next to the name of your app in the Splunk **Home** page.

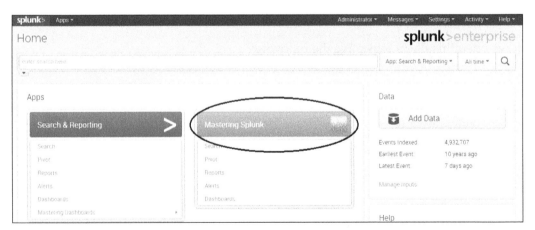

To add an icon image to your app, you don't have to modify any configuration settings. There is no setting in app.conf for such images. To include an icon, properly formatted images should be placed in the /static directory of your app, where they will be automatically detected by Splunk and displayed to the user. For example, the location of the image can be the following:

```
<app_directory>/static/appIcon.png
```

 For Splunk to identify the icon that you are using, it must be named appIcon and the capital I is required!

Your icon image must be a 36 by 36 pixel PNG-formatted file (or it will be ignored by Splunk). In addition, to ensure that your browser locates your icon, you should always clear your browser cache. To do this, you can go to Splunk's main URL and type /info after 8000. At the bottom of the page, there will be a cache control option that forces your browser to update.

Of course, you can always restart Splunk after adding an icon image to ensure that Splunk uses the image.

Until this point, the Splunk app server caches all static assets in its apps, such as images, CSS, and JavaScript code. When you release a newer version of an app, you should edit the app.conf file to make sure that all of your updated assets are available by adding a build number.

Under install, you can specify a build number, as follows:

```
[install]
build = 2
```

Other configurations

Other configurations that you can include in your Splunk app are:

- Specific data inputs
- Custom or specific indexing
- Logic and rules— segmentation, character set, or other custom data processing rules
- Custom users or roles

Creating the app objects

At this point of time, you have your app's workspace defined and have made any configuration changes you need. Now it is time to add the applicable knowledge objects. These knowledge objects are scoped to the app and made permissible. When building an app, you typically have a number of previously created (or to be created) objects in mind that will add features or functionalities to your app.

These functionalities include the following:

- Searches and/or reports
- Event types
- Dashboards, form searches, and views
- Fields and field extractions
- Tags
- Lookups

Each type of object has the ability to extend your app in a variety of ways. Most apps highly leverage searches and reports to capture unique parts of certain data, display them on a dashboard, or even use them to modify Splunk menus and more. The use of objects within your app is only limited by your imagination. Some of the objects are explained as follows:

- **Event types**: Use event types to capture and share unique knowledge specifics to your app
- **Fields**: Add your own custom fields to be used by your app
- **Tags**: Tags can also be added to your app
- **Views**: You can include dashboards and search views and present the knowledge objects you've built in your app

Once knowledge objects are created, you can add them to your app by scoping them to the app. What this means is to set the ownership for the object based on your needs. For example, a knowledge object can:

- Be available globally to all users and all apps
- Be available to all the users of a specific app
- Be available to only certain users or user roles

Setting the ownership

The simplest method to set the ownership (scoping) of an object is using Splunk Web. First, go to **Settings** and then select the type of knowledge object you are interested in, for example, **Searches and Reports**. From the list of objects (in this example, defined searches and reports), you can locate the object you want to scope.

In my example, I'm interested in the object named **Current Forecast Report**, so I click on **Move** against it, as shown in the following screenshot:

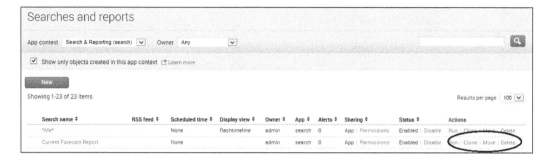

Splunk will prompt you with the **Move Object** dialog.

You can select the app you want to move (or scope) this object to and then click on **Move**.

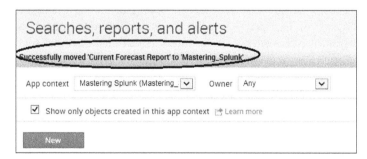

Splunk tells you that the object was moved. Now, if you click on **Permissions**, you can see that this object is available to all the users of your Splunk app, named *Mastering_Splunk*, as shown here:

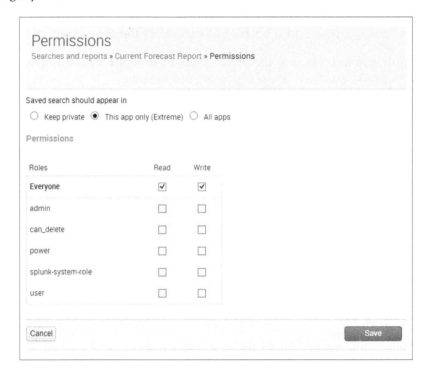

Setting the app's permissions

In Splunk, everything is either an app or an object, and each app or object can be controlled using permissions. The way Splunk permissions work is based on the *nix filesystem permissions model.

Each app or object can be set to read or read and write for each role defined within Splunk. In this way, you can manage what users can see and interact with. Users of a certain role might be allowed to only see a set of identified reporting views, or you can set certain apps to be accessed only by a particular team within the organization.

For example, you might have a forecasting app that is the only thing visible to your organization's planning team (when they log in to Splunk Enterprise).

Splunk permissions can be applied by setting up explicit users with the ability to create and/or edit objects within a Splunk app, or more characteristically, you can limit a user/users to only be able to create and/or edit within their user directory (remember that every user has their own user directory, so all the objects they create are placed in that particular directory).

Users can only promote their objects to the app level if you give them write permissions on the app or apps that they wish to promote. When a user promotes a Splunk object, Splunk moves it from the user directory to the app directory.

Using Splunk Web, you can set up permissions *per object* or *per app* using the following steps:

1. Click on **Settings**.
2. Go to **KNOWLEDGE**, click on the category that contains the object you want to edit permissions for, or click on **All configurations** to access all the configurations in a given app.
3. Next to the object you want, click on the **Permissions** link.
4. Set the permissions to read and/or write for all the roles listed.
5. Lastly, click on **Save**.

Another approach to permissions

In addition to using Splunk Web, you can also manage object permissions with the `default.meta` file. In most cases, the recommended approach is to stick to Splunk Web, but for completeness, this section describes the `default.meta` file approach.

To use the `default.meta` file approach, you need to edit the `default.meta` file in your app's default directory, as follows:

```
$SPLUNK_HOME/etc/apps/<app_name>/metadata/default.meta
```

Using this approach, you can set permissions for any object in a Splunk app by creating an entry for the object you want to set permissions for (you can also set permissions for all the objects of a certain type):

```
[<object_type>/<object_name>] access = read : [ <comma-separated list
of roles>], write : [ comma-separated list of roles>]
```

Let's discover the fields step by step:

- **Object type**: The object type entry indicates the type of object for which permissions have to be set
- **Object name**: The object name is the name of the saved search, view, event type, or any other object you want to set permissions for

 If you don't specify an object name, the permissions apply to all the objects of that type!

As with most Splunk configuration files, Splunk provides plenty of online documentation on how to edit the `default.meta` file and gives you the `default.meta.conf.spec` and `default.meta.conf.example` files as templates for various examples.

A default.meta example

As an example, earlier in this book, we created a Splunk view named `mastering_splunk`, using the `default.meta` file to set permissions; you can see this in the following code:

```
[views/mastering_splunk]
access = read : [ * ]
export = system
owner = admin
version = 6.0.2
modtime = 1397565243.759972200
```

Within this file, we have a section heading that names the object type (`views`) and the object name (`mastering_splunk`). Below this section, we set the access permissions (`read` for all user roles), export the view to make it available to all the apps, define the object owner as `admin`, define the version that the object was created in (`6.0.2`), and specify the last time when the object was modified (`modtime`).

Building navigations

Now that you've scoped in all of the knowledge objects you want to use in your app, you can build a custom navigation for it. This navigation can help users navigate to dashboards, reports, saved searches, and other views more easily. Essentially, what you can do is specify a default view (the first view users see upon launching your app) and then rearrange objects within the navigation bar in Splunk Web into an order that is more intuitive for your application.

Splunk stores the navigation menu information as an XML file named `default.xml` in your app's `nav` directory. Note that if you have created your app using the app builder, the `default.xml` file exists at `$SPLUNK_HOME/etc/apps/<app_name>/>/default/data/ui/nav/default.xml`.

You can edit this file directly with an XML editor of your choice, but I recommend that you use Splunk Web.

Let's adjust the navigation

The sample app, `mastering_splunk`, was built with Splunk Web, so we can launch the app by clicking on **Apps** and selecting **Mastering Splunk**. Then, after the app is launched, click on **Settings** and then select **User interface**, as shown in the following screenshot:

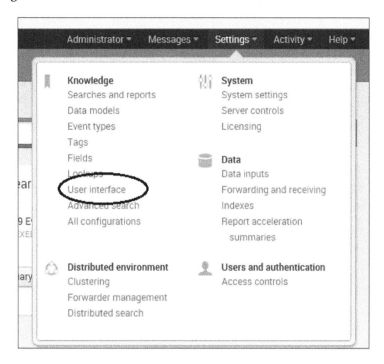

On the **User interface** page, select **Navigation menus**.

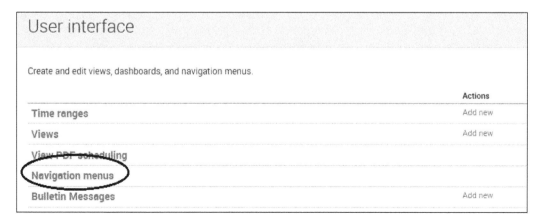

To open the XML editor, click on **default**, as shown here:

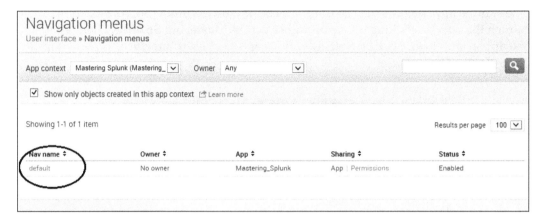

Now, modify the XML file to rearrange your apps menu. I've changed my default menu to simply say `Master` and make it a drop-down selection list starting with dashboards.

default
User interface » Navigation menus » default

Navigation menu XML *
Enter and edit navigation menu XML configuration.

Plain Text

```
<nav>
  <collection label="Master">
  <view name="dashboards" />
  <view name="search" default='true' />
  <view name="data_models" />
  <view name="reports" />
  <view name="alerts" />
  </collection>
</nav>
```

Cancel   Save

My apps menu example lists a number of Splunk views to be included as menu selections. These views are listed by their view name, but the menu will list the view's label (rather than the particular view name). For example, the view named data_models has a label **Pivot**, so this is what appears in the menu list.

It is not necessary to restart Splunk to see your changes. Simply click on **Save**, go back to the Splunk **Home** page, and select the app again. Now you can see the changes, as shown in the following screenshot:

Using the default.xml file rather than Splunk Web

I recommend that you use Splunk Web to create your apps, but if you choose not to, you can create your own default.xml file, move it to your app's nav folder, and make changes to it (outside Splunk) to reflect the navigation changes you want.

Creating an app setup and deployment

On running a Splunk app for the first time, a user might have to modify the app's default configurations. Rather than having the user edit the Splunk configuration files directly, you can have a setup screen display automatically when the app first runs. This setup screen allows the user to accept or modify the app's particular configurations.

Taking the time to create an app setup screen can make it easier for app deployment and can simplify its customization. As an example, you can use a setup screen to set the frequency of alerts for a saved search within your app.

You can click on **Apps** and then **Manage Apps**. On the Splunk **Apps** page, locate the heading **Actions**. You will notice a link labeled **Set up** (there will be other links such as **Launch app**, **Edit properties**, and **View objects**) for each app you have installed that has a setup screen associated with it, as shown in the following screenshot:

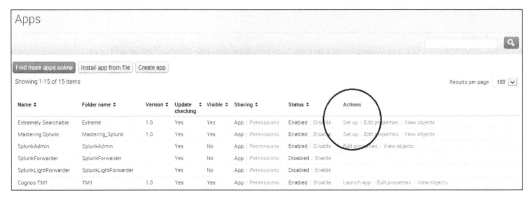

The Set up link

Clicking on the **Set up** link, will let you access the app's setup screen.

 App setup screens save app configuration changes to the `$SPLUNK_HOME/etc/apps/<app>/local` file. This local directory file will override any settings in the app's `default` directory.

Creating a setup screen

Creating a setup screen for your Splunk app is very simple (just two steps!), as follows:

1. Create a `setup.xml` file and place it in your app's default directory at `$SPLUNK_HOME/etc/apps/<AppName>/default/setup.xml`.

2. Modify the file providing values for the fields in your app's configuration files.

An example of creating a Splunk app setup screen is shown below. Earlier, we created a modest Splunk app and called it *Mastering_Splunk*. To create a setup screen for this app, we can, using any text editor such as MS Windows notepad, create a `setup.xml` file, similar to the one shown in the following screenshot:

```
<setup>
  <block title="Mastering Splunk" endpoint="saved/searches/" entity="foobar">
    <text> Jims Mastering Splunk Splunk App Setup </text>
  </block>
    <block title="Enable or Disable Automatic Update Checking" endpoint="storage/passwords" entity="_new">
        <input field="check_for_updates">
      <label>Enable Update Checking</label>
      <type>bool</type>
    </input>
  </block> |
    <block title="Add an Splunk Master Account" endpoint="storage/passwords" entity="_new">
    <input field="name">
      <label>Username</label>
      <type>text</type>
    </input>
    <input field="password">
      <label>Password</label>
      <type>password</type>
    </input>
  </block>
```

The setup.xml file

After creating your XML file, place the file at `$Splunk_Home/etc/apps/mastering_ splunkdefaul/setup.xml`.

Here is an explanation of the preceding XML file.

There are three `<block>` sections in our file, as follows:

- Title and description
- An on/off checkbox for setting the `check_for_updates` field of our app
- Two input textboxes for adding a new Splunk master username and password

Once your file is saved, Splunk will update the configuration file for your app (restarting Splunk is not required).

To view your setup screen, you can go to **Apps**, then go to **Manage Apps**, and click on the **Set up** link. The screen will look like the following screenshot:

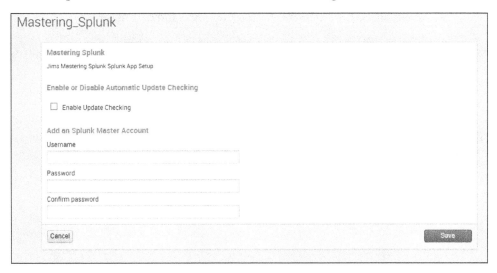

The XML syntax used

Using basic XML code, you can easily create a Splunk app `setup.xml` file as Splunk adheres to XML conventions. The following are the XML tags you need to know:

- `<setup>`: This is called the base element and contains a number of additional block elements nested inside other block elements

- `<block>`: This defines the user interface for the app's setup screen

- `<text>`: This is optional and provides text for the app's setup screen

- `<input>`: This is used to take inputs from the user and associates this input with a field

- `<label>`: This is a required child element for the `<input>` element that provides a description of the input field

- `<type>`: This is a required element within an `<input>` element, specifying the type of user interface control for capturing user input

 More XML details are provided in the Splunk documentation.

Packaging apps for deployment

If you like, you can make your apps available to the Splunk community (or the general public) by sharing them on Splunk Apps, but keep in mind that there are some very specific requirements you need to meet before your app qualifies for uploading and sharing. For example, some of the requirements are as follows:

- All Splunk apps uploaded must have the `.spl` file extension

- The name of your app and all of its references and related materials (even its documentation) must meet the requirements specified in *Naming conventions for content on Splunk Apps* (available for download from `http://www.splunk.com`)

The main point is that these specific instructions (within the product documentation) need to be reviewed before you consider packaging an app for sharing with the Splunk community.

Summary

In this chapter, we talked about some advanced topics for Splunk applications and add-ons such as adding icons and setup screens, navigation, searching, and sharing. Sources were given for finding additional application examples as well.

In the next chapter, we will explain and apply the monitoring and alerting capabilities of the Splunk technology from a desktop to enterprise level and compare Splunk with other monitoring tools.

8
Monitoring and Alerting

This chapter will explain the monitoring and alerting capabilities of the Splunk technology at a desktop level and will compare Splunk with other monitoring tools.

The following topics will be covered in this chapter:

- What to monitor
- Advanced monitoring
- Splunk Deployment Monitor
- All about alerts
- Expanded functionalities

What to monitor

Let's start by describing what we are referring to when we talk about monitoring in Splunk. So, Splunk tells us that monitoring in Splunk can be defined as follows:

> *"The act of watching a file, directory, script, or network port for new data. Also used to refer to a configured Splunk data input of the aforementioned types. When you configure a data input for an ongoing incoming data source, you are telling Splunk to monitor the input."*

> *– Splunk.com, 2014*

Earlier in this book, we covered the concept of getting data into Splunk (or indexing data). Let's refresh.

To get started with Splunk, you need to feed it with some sort of data. Once Splunk becomes aware of the new data, it instantly indexes it so that it's available for your search needs (we discussed indexes in *Chapter 6, Indexes and Indexing*). At this point, the data is transformed into Splunk events, each with its own searchable fields. There are many things that can be done to the data and with it.

So, what kind of data (actually, data source) can we ask Splunk to monitor? The answer is almost any kind of data, in fact, probably almost any kind of data created in the conceivable future. Keep in mind that Splunk is particularly efficient with all kinds of IT streaming, machine, and historical data, such as MS Windows event logs, web server logs, live application logs, network feeds, system metrics, change monitoring, message queues, archive files, or anything else of interest.

It's really this simple to start Splunk monitoring. Refer to the following steps:

1. Point Splunk to a data stream or a source of data.
2. Provide some details about the data stream or data source (which then becomes a data input).
3. Splunk begins to index the data / data source, transforming the information so that events are visible.
4. You can access the data's events right away. The results aren't exactly what you wanted them to be? So, you can tweak the indexing process until they are.

In addition, the data (for Splunk to monitor) can be on the same machine as Splunk (which we would refer to as local data) or it can exist (or will be delivered to) on a completely different machine (which, of course, we will call as remote data). Keep in mind that remote data is not a problem, as the data can be accessed by Splunk if the following conditions are met:

*   You set up a network feed
*   Install a Splunk forwarder(s) where the data originates

 Forwarders are lightweight versions of Splunk that read data and then forward it to the main Splunk instance for indexing and searching.

Of course (we spent an entire chapter on them), Splunk also uses apps and add-ons that can be preconfigured for specific data input monitoring. You can find free apps and add-ons on Splunk Apps or you can build your own.

Recipes

The Splunk product documentation refers to Splunk input recipes (or preconfigured configurations) for data and data sources. You can access them from the **Add data** section on Splunk Web. Recipes define the basic data or data sources that you will most often deal with, but if the recipes and apps don't cover your needs, then you can use the general input configuration capabilities of Splunk to specify your particular data / data source for Splunk to monitor.

Pointing Splunk to data

Pointing Splunk to data and specifying it for Splunk to monitor mean the same thing. There are several ways to accomplish this (arranged by ease of use), which are explained in the following sections.

Splunk Web

In my opinion, the easiest method you can use to configure inputs is Splunk Web and its data input pages:

1. From **Splunk Home**, select **Add data**. This takes you to the **Add data** page.
2. Select **Settings** and then click on **Data inputs**. This takes you to a page where you can view and manage your existing inputs as well as add new ones.

Splunk CLI

You can always use the Splunk CLI (command-line interface) to configure your inputs, although this method is much more like programming.

Go to the `$SPLUNK_HOME/bin/` directory and use the following command, in the command prompt, to add the new input:

```
./splunk add monitor  <fully qualified path>
```

Splunk configuration files

When using the first two methods (Splunk Web and Splunk CLI), the configurations are saved in a configuration file called `inputs.conf`. You can also directly edit this file. You can add a section (a stanza) and then configure the data input by adding attribute/value pairs to this section. You can set multiple attributes in a single input section. If you do not specify a value for the attribute, Splunk uses the default value that's preset in `$SPLUNK_HOME/etc/system/default/inputs.conf`.

Apps

As discussed in *Chapter 7, Evolving your Apps*, Splunk uses apps and add-ons that simplify and/or extend Splunk in a variety of ways, including providing preconfigured data inputs. There are an increasing number of Splunk apps available for free, and if you are up for it, you can create your own app.

 If you use forwarders to send data from outlying machines to a central Splunk instance, you can specify some inputs during the forwarder installation (according to the product documentation available at http://www.splunk.com).

Monitoring categories

Splunk monitoring categories are generally identified as follows:

- Data from files and directories
- Data and events from network ports
- Windows sources, such as:
  - Windows event log data
  - Windows registry data
  - WMI data
  - Active directory data
- Performance monitoring data
- Other sources such as:
  - FIFO queues
  - Scripted inputs to get data from APIs and other remote data interfaces and message queues

Simply put, Splunk is a very capable and flexible tool for monitoring all kinds of data (those listed are the most common).

Advanced monitoring

When planning and strategizing about what to monitor with Splunk, it is important to understand the full picture. For example, the following issues need to be taken care of:

- Where will the data reside?
- Can I leverage Splunk forwarders?

- Can I use an app for this?
- What is the best way to get Splunk to start monitoring?
- What are the proven practices to configure inputs?
- What are the specifics around MS Windows data relating to Splunk?
- What does Splunk do with the data it monitors?

Location, location, location

You might think that the question whether your data is local or remote is straightforward, but with Splunk, there are a few principles that will determine the answer. These include the following:

- The operating system on which Splunk is installed
- The kind of data that is directly connected to Splunk
- Whether any authentication or other intermediate steps are needed to access the data that you want Splunk to index
- The distance and size of the data being monitored

This is represented in the following diagram:

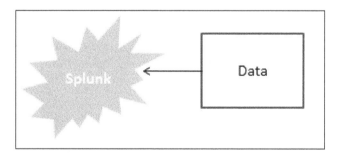

Generally speaking, if there are no intermediate steps between the data and Splunk, it's considered *local*. Examples of intermediate steps might be:

- Attaching or connecting (for example, to a specific network disk or server)
- Authentications (for example, communicating through an established firewall)
- Mapping a network drive or folder

This is represented in the following diagram:

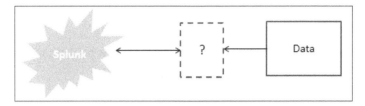

Simply put, data is considered to be remote when something needs to occur before Splunk can access the data.

> **Exceptions**
>
> Of course, there are always exceptions, where data that would normally be considered remote is not. You should check the product documentation for specific examples.

Leveraging your forwarders

Let's be forward here—what is a Splunk forwarder? A forwarder is an instance of Splunk that has a specific purpose, to input data and forward it to other instances of Splunk. In other words, forwarders have limited capabilities by design. Most forwarders don't include Splunk Web and don't have users logging in and running search pipelines; therefore, they require minimal resources and have little impact on performance. So, they can usually reside on the machines where the data originates. The following diagram gives you an idea of how you can configure Splunk using forwarders local to multiple data sources:

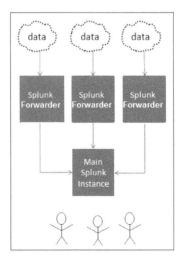

As an example, Splunk can be installed and configured as a forwarder on a number of individual servers that are all perhaps generating similar log data which you want to search centrally. You can then install Splunk on its own server where a user (or a user community) can perform searches. The forwarders on the data-generating servers can then be set up to take the data and send it to the main Splunk server, which then consolidates and indexes it and makes it available for searching. Because of their light footprint, the forwarders won't affect the performance of the source servers.

Splunk forwarders can handle exactly the same types of data and can consume this data in the same way as any Splunk instance, with one main difference: they do not index the data themselves. Instead, they input the data and refer it to a central Splunk instance, which will do the indexing and searching.

In a typical Splunk deployment, forwarders (which could number in hundreds or even thousands) will serve as the primary consumers of data. It's only in a single-machine deployment that the same Splunk instance will be the data consumer and indexer and will support user searches.

Forwarders are typically configured by editing Splunk's `inputs.conf` configuration file, either directly or using the CLI (which we discussed in a previous chapter of this book) or using Splunk Web on a test instance to configure the inputs, and then distributing the updated `inputs.conf` file to the forwarder instance.

Another method to do this is by deploying a Splunk app that contains the desired inputs.

Can I use apps?

Again, Splunk is *infinitely extendable* through its use of apps and add-ons. In particular, apps can simplify the process of data input. To this point, instead of having to configure inputs yourself, you might be able to locate an app (as mentioned in *Chapter 7, Evolving your Apps*, you can download apps from Splunk Apps) that is preconfigured for a particular environment or application and leverage it. Apps provide an opportunity to obtain specific input configurations as well as other functionalities, such as optimal views of the configured data.

The examples of Splunk apps include the following:

- *Splunk App for Windows Infrastructure*
- *Splunk App for Unix and Linux*
- *Splunk for Blue Coat ProxySG*
- *Splunk for F5*
- *Splunk for Cisco Security app*
- *Splunk App for WebSphere Application Server*

Again, in *Chapter 7, Evolving your Apps* (in the *Installing an app* section), we covered how to find and install apps, by clicking on **Apps** and then clicking on **Find More Apps** in Splunk Web. When it comes to data input, you should know that the **Add data** page actually allows access to links to a number of the most popular apps, as shown in the following screenshot:

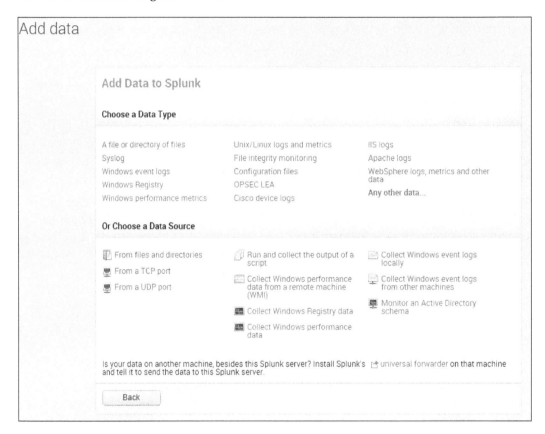

Windows inputs in Splunk

On the **Add data** page, you'll notice the mention of Windows several times. Splunk's Windows installations make the following specialized inputs available to you:

- **Windows event logs**: Splunk can monitor logs generated by the Windows event log service on any event log channel (local or remote)

- **Performance monitoring**: All performance counters that are available in the performance monitor are also available in Splunk

- **Remote monitoring over WMI**: Splunk can use WMI to access log and performance data on remote machines

- **Registry monitoring**: You can monitor changes to the local Windows registry

- **Active Directory**: Splunk can audit any modifications to Active Directory, including changes to user, group, machine, and group policy objects

Getting started with monitoring

You install Splunk and add data (configure your inputs), and Splunk is already monitoring! Obviously, after your initial exposure to Splunk and as you pursue your Splunk mastership, you'll want to approach monitoring with proven practices in mind.

A proven startup methodology is outlined here:

- **Requirements**: Gather and understand what the requirements truly are. Your needs (the requirements) will determine how you add data to Splunk: can you use an app? What about forwarders? Is there an opportunity for knowledge creation?

- **Test indexing**: Create a test index and add just a few inputs.

- **Preview the data**: Use the Splunk data preview feature to actually view the data. Then, based on what you see, you might want to modify how Splunk indexes the data.

- **Search**: Run some searches on the test data and evaluate the results. Are the results what you need?

- **Tweak events**: If necessary, tweak the Splunk input and event processing configurations until events look the way you want them to.

- **Start again**: Sometimes, it is necessary to just start over. This means that you delete the data from your test index, re-read the requirements, and get started with the process again.

- **Implement**: If you are satisfied with the results, you can drop your test index and point your inputs to the default main index (or depending on other factors, you might consider using a specific index for your data rather than using the default one); you are ready for general availability!

Custom data

Splunk can index any data, usually without needing time for additional configurations. In some cases, custom applications might yield data that will require special needs. Typical issues might be data that includes multiline events, uncommon characters, or abnormal timestamps. The approach here should be to test Splunk's default configuration first and then to tweak it as needed.

Input typing

When you specify input data, Splunk will assign an input source type to the data. This categorizes the format of the data. Splunk uses this input type when it performs indexing. Splunk installs with a large number of predefined input types, and although Splunk can assign an input type automatically, you can override what Splunk assigns or add to the set of source types to support custom data types.

It's extremely important that you assign the right source type to your data in order to ensure that the data looks the way you expect it to, has appropriate timestamps and event breaks, and the performance is at acceptable levels.

Any common data input format can be a source type (most source types are log formats). At the time of writing this book, Splunk automatically recognizes over 50 input source types.

In a lot of cases, Splunk assignment will suffice, but if you choose to assign an input source type, you can basically do one of the following:

- Assign an input source type explicitly to your data
- Create a new input source type (either from scratch or by modifying an existing input source type)

You can use the data preview feature to assign the input source type, edit the input source type settings, and create a new source type entirely.

What does Splunk do with the data it monitors?

By now, you know that you input raw data into Splunk, but do you know what Splunk Enterprise does with your data and how to make it do this in a better way?

What Splunk does is it indexes your data, making it searchable knowledge (in the form of events). Moving from data inputs to searchable knowledge is known as the Splunk data pipeline process.

The Splunk data pipeline

So, let's take a quick look at the Splunk data pipeline.

Once new data inputs are configured, Splunk picks up the new data that is generated and drops it into its parsing queue, where it waits for parsing to be done. This parsing includes the following:

- Source and event typing
- Character set normalization
- Line termination identification
- Timestamp identification and normalization
- Event boundary identification
- Regex transformation and parse-time field creation

After being sent through the Splunk parser, the data goes to an indexing queue where it waits for the Splunk indexer. The indexer completes the segmentation and index building, and what's left are indexed files, ready for searching.

Throughout this process, Splunk makes *best guesses* for the data, so that the resulting events are immediately useful and searchable. However, depending on your data and what sort of knowledge you need to extract from it, you might want to tweak one or more steps of event processing.

As mentioned, the Splunk data pipeline processing consists of two phases: parsing and indexing. Basically, all the data gets parsed into events — each of which gets passed to the indexer for final processing. During this processing, Splunk acts on the data, transforming it in various ways.

Most of the processing is configurable, so you have the ability to adjust it according to your needs. For example, you can do the following:

- You can override the extracted default fields
- You can manually select a character set
- You can modify line termination settings
- You can create timestamps or modify timestamp settings
- You can mask certain event data
- You can set the level of segmentation

The split between parsing and indexing (occurring within the Splunk data pipeline) is most relevant when your Splunk environment includes forwarders. At a very high level, forwarders can fully parse data locally and then forward it; on the other hand, data can get forwarded after very minimal parsing, with most of the parsing occurring on the receiving indexer.

Splunk

An option to monitor Splunk itself (even in the most complicated environments) is the *Splunk Deployment Monitor* app. This app is designed to help manage and troubleshoot medium- to large-scale deployments. It also keeps track of all your Splunk instances and delivers early warning signals of the potential failures.

The *Splunk Deployment Monitor* app provides you with out-of-the-box dashboards and drilldowns—giving you information that will help you monitor your Splunk environment's health, such as the following:

- Index throughput (based on time)
- Forwarder connections to the indexer over time
- Indexer and forwarder abnormalities
- Status and forwarding volume over time
- Source types being indexed by the system
- License usage

Where is this app?

Prior to Version 5.0, this app was part of the core distribution. Not anymore! You now need to download it from Splunk Apps, so do the following:

1. Go to the Splunk apps' home page to download and install the *Splunk Deployment Monitor* app with Splunk Web or using the CLI (you can search for Deployment Monitor):

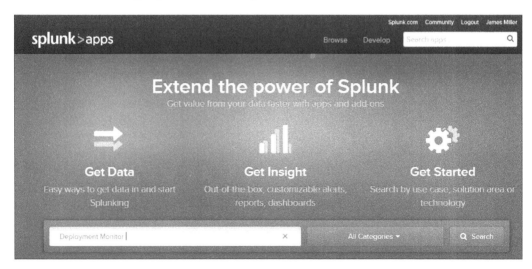

2. Click on the version of the app you are interested in:

3. Then, click on **Download**:

4. On the **Download** page, you'll need to accept the terms and conditions:

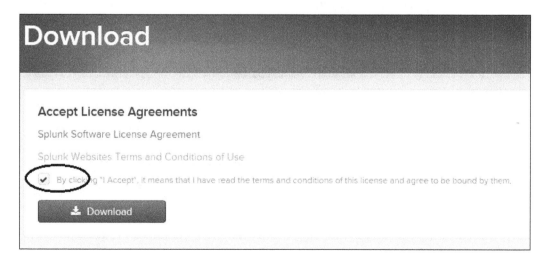

5. Once the app is downloaded, you are ready to install the app.

Let's Install!

The *Splunk Deployment Monitor* app (like most Splunk apps) can be installed using Splunk Web or the CLI. I recommend that you use Splunk Web (if you are intent on using the command line, you can check the product documentation for the sequence and the syntax of the commands you'll need).

Once you are logged in to the Splunk Web instance where you want to install and run the app, you can carry out the following steps:

1. Click on **Apps** and then click on **Manage Apps**.

2. From the **Apps** page, you can click on the **Install app from file** button.

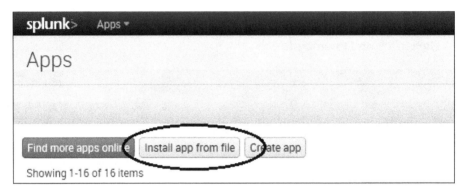

3. On the **Upload app** page, click on the **Browse** button, locate the downloaded package file (`splunk_app_deploymentmonitor-<version>-<build>.tgz`), and then click on **Open**. Finally, click on **Upload**.

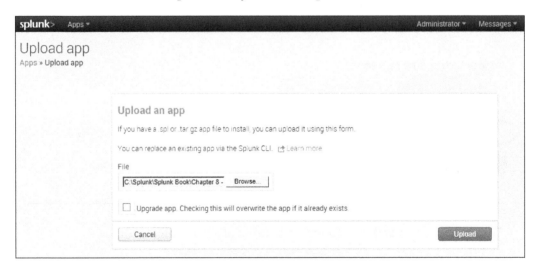

4. After Splunk installs the app, you should receive the message shown in the following screenshot:

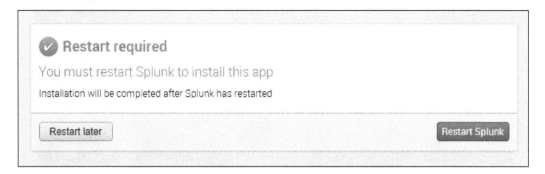

5. Click on the **Restart Splunk** button and then click on **OK**.

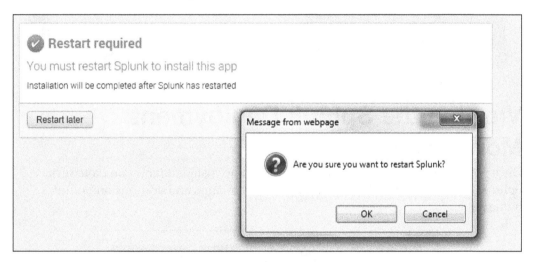

6. Success! The installation is complete.

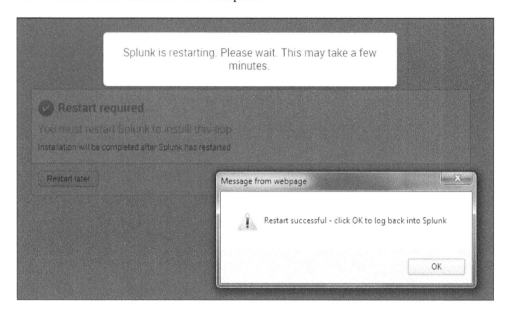

Viewing the Splunk Deployment Monitor app

Once you have the *Splunk Deployment Monitor* app installed (and you have restarted Splunk), you should see the app among the list of apps and add-ons on Splunk's home page.

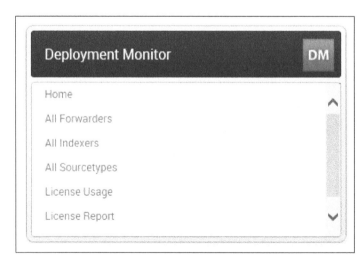

It should also appear in the **Apps** list, in the upper left-hand corner of the screen, as **Deployment Monitor**, as shown in the following screenshot:

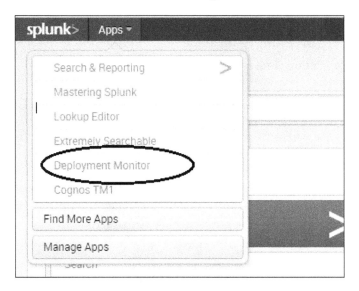

The app's documentation will tell you that the deployment monitor utilizes scheduled searches, so if you install the app and launch it immediately, the performance you experience will be less than optimal (depending on your individual Splunk environment). If you wait (the documentation recommends that you wait for several hours) and then launch the app, the performance will be typical.

At this point, I recommend that you have fun taking some time to investigate the information provided by this app—what you find most interesting will again depend upon your environment. Some of the more interesting features I found were license usage and license reports.

All about alerts

Managing an environment (machines and/or generated data) requires a continuous check of the established acceptable conditions or for the occurrence of certain events. It is one thing to leverage the power and flexibility of Splunk for searching and visualization, but once you've created searches and reports, it is unrealistic (and boring!) to expect anyone to run and rerun your searches over and over again, all the time.

As we covered earlier in this book, Splunk searches can be real time or historical. Both can be configured to *send alerts* based on an extensive set of threshold and trend-based scenarios (many real-life examples are listed on the Splunk website).

Generally speaking, Splunk enables you to design three broad types of alerts, as follows:

- Continuous every time result alerts
- Continuous over time result alerts
- Historical rolling time result alerts

> It is also possible to create scheduled reports that can initiate actions (typically, the action is to e-mail the results of the report) on each execution of the report (each time it runs). We'll visit this topic later in this chapter.

- **Real-time, "every time result" alerts**: These are typically *threshold event* alerts. For example, any time a resource reaches 100 percent utilization, an alert is sent.

- **Real-time, "over time result" alerts**: These alerts look for events in or over a given time period. For example, a single occurrence of an event (in a time period) is not interesting, but multiple occurrences of that event (within a given time period) are interesting.

- **Historical, "rolling time result" alerts**: These alerts report on the occurrence of an event that occurs in a historical period (for example, last month).

Alerting a quick startup

The absolute easiest way to create an alert is to leverage what you've got. This means that most of the searches that you can create in Splunk Web can pretty much have an alert based on them—with just a few extra clicks. For example, we can use a *very* simple search that we've seen before in this book:

```
sourcetype=TM1* Error
```

Now, run your search as follows:

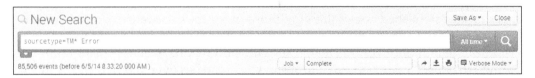

Click on **Save As** and then click on **Alert**.

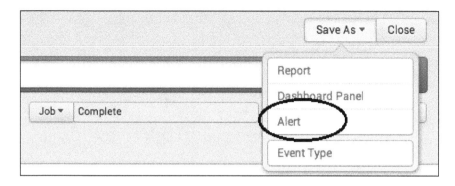

When the **Save As Alert** dialog opens, perform the following steps:

1. Give your alert a title and a description.

2. Select the alert type of the alert you want to configure (**Real Time** or **Scheduled**).

 If you select **Scheduled**, you can select the appropriate parameters (discussed later in this chapter) to schedule your search/alert.

3. Set **Trigger condition** to one of the following values:

   ° **Number of Results**: This is a trigger based on the number of search results during a rolling window of time

   ° **Number of Hosts**: This is a trigger based on the number of hosts during a rolling window of time

   ° **Number of Sources**: This is a trigger based on the number of sources during a rolling window of time

   ° **Custom**: This is a trigger based on the custom condition during a rolling window of time

The **Save As Alert** dialog is shown in the following screenshot:

Once you click on **Next**, you can enable additional actions for your alert (discussed later in this section), as shown in the following screenshot:

Finally, after you click on **Save**, the following page is displayed:

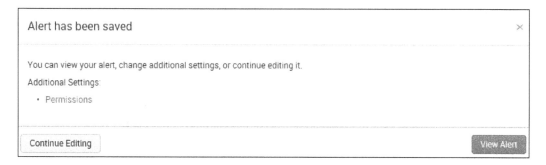

If you go ahead and click on **View Alert** at this point, Splunk will show you all the details of the alert you just set up and (if you need to) allows you to edit any of them:

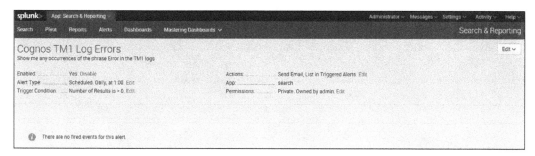

You can't do that

To schedule a search that an alert is based on, you need to have the permissions that allow you to create scheduled searches. Splunk provides the following capabilities that you need to provide to any individuals who need to create alerts based on scheduled searches. These are:

- **schedule_rtsearch**: This is for real-time searches
- **schedule_search**: This is for all other searches

Setting enabling actions

So, now let's go over the Splunk alert actions that you can enable. There are three alert actions that can be executed whenever your alert triggers.

Listing triggered alerts

Check this option to have all the triggered alerts displayed in the Splunk alert manager with a severity level that you define. You can access the Splunk alert manager by clicking on **Activity** and then selecting **Triggered Alerts**:

The Splunk alert manager is displayed in the following screenshot:

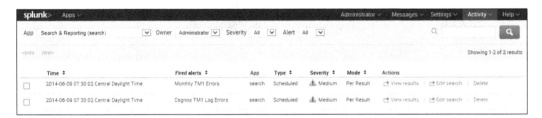

> The Splunk alert manager will show you records for the triggered alerts that are based on existing reports. They will continue to appear even if you disable the alerting aspect of those searches after the alerts were triggered. All the triggered alert records will expire and be automatically deleted from the alert manager after a set period of time. You can define triggered alert record expiration periods at the individual alert level.

Sending e-mails

You can configure Splunk to send an e-mail to a list of recipients that you define. You must configure the e-mail notification settings in **Settings** before this alert action can work.

Once you check the **Send Email** checkbox in the **Save As Alert** dialog, Splunk lets you do the following:

- Provide one or more e-mail addresses to CC and/or BCC
- Set the e-mail priority
- Specify a subject for the e-mail (which will, by default, include the name of the alert as $name$)

- Type in the message body text
- Select various **Include fields** for the e-mail message, as follows:
    ◦ Link to the alert
    ◦ Search the string
    ◦ The trigger condition
    ◦ The trigger time
    ◦ Link to the results
    ◦ The inline listing of results as a table, raw events, or CSV file
    ◦ Results as a PDF attachment
    ◦ Results as a CSV attachment

The **Send Email** checkbox is shown in the following screenshot:

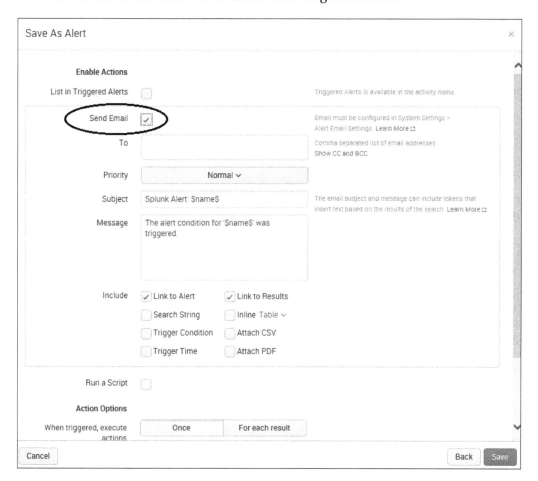

Running a script

You can have Splunk run a script that you have specified to perform some other action. The **Run a Script** checkbox is shown in the following screenshot:

All the alert scripts must be placed in `$SPLUNK_HOME/bin/scripts` or `$SPLUNK_HOME/etc/<AppName>/bin/scripts`. Splunk looks in these two directories for any script triggered by an alert.

Action options – when triggered, execute actions

An important Splunk alert action option is the **When triggered, execute actions** option. This allows you to tell Splunk to execute the action options (the ones you set):

*   Once for each time the alert is triggered
*   One time for each result (or event returned) when the alert is triggered

These options are shown in the following screenshot:

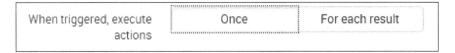

If the **Once** option is selected, it will also affect how throttling can be configured (discussed in the next section).

Throttling

Throttling, also known as **alert suppression**, defines the rules that govern the frequency with which an alert is triggered. For example, alerts might be triggered numerous times within a certain period of time. Using throttling, you can define rules to reduce the frequency of events triggering your alert. In other words, you can tell Splunk to ignore some of the events.

If you have selected **Once** as the option for the **When triggered, execute actions** option, then you can check the **Throttle** checkbox and enter a **Suppress triggering for** numeric value as the total time for which Splunk will ignore similar events (in other words, once an event triggers an alert, subsequent events of this type will be ignored for the given period of time). In addition, you can specify the time parameter (seconds, minutes, or hours).

The following screenshot shows the trigger rule defined to suppress or ignore events for 60 seconds:

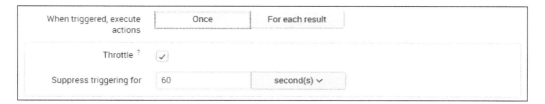

If you have selected **For each result** as the option for the **When triggered, execute actions** option, then you can check the **Throttle** checkbox and enter a **Suppress triggering for** numeric value as the total time for which Splunk will ignore similar events (in other words, once an event triggers an alert, subsequent events of this type will be ignored for the given period of time). In addition, you can specify the time parameter (seconds, minutes, or hours).

In addition, Splunk also allows you to enter a **Suppress results containing field value** option. This means that, for example, you can ignore similar events that occur within a period of time and have a particular field value within them. As a simple example, suppose that you have an alert set up that triggers when Cognos TM1 errors occur within a certain period of time. Suppose that in your environment, TM1 TurboIntegrator scripts connect to external systems through ODBC datasources. When ODBC errors occur, such as an inability to connect to the ODBC datasource, TM1 retries the process multiple times, resulting in multiple error events triggering multiple Splunk alerts. To avoid the multiple alerts trigger, you can do the following:

1. Check the **Throttle** checkbox.
2. Enter the phrase ODBC in the **Suppress results containing field value** field.

3. Enter `120` in the **Suppress triggering for value** field and select **second(s)**, as shown in the following screenshot:

As a best practice, when you set up throttling for a real-time search, it's best to start with a throttling period that is equal to the length of the base search's window and then expand the throttling period from there (this prevents you from getting duplicate notifications for a given event).

Editing alerts

There are several ways to edit alerts when using Splunk Web. For example, within an app, you can click on **Alerts** and then from the **Alerts** page, you can click on **Edit**.

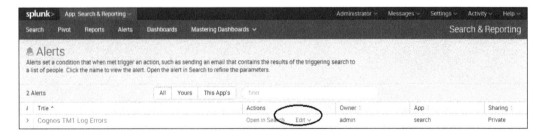

From the drop-down menu, you can select **Edit Actions**, as shown in the following screenshot:

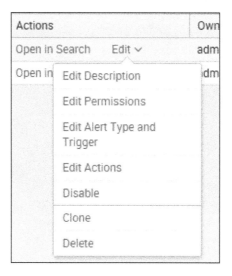

Editing the description

Clicking on **Edit Description** shows you the alert name (title) and allows you to edit the description of the alert:

Editing permissions

Clicking on **Edit Permissions** shows you the alert name (title), the owner, the app (context), and its display permissions:

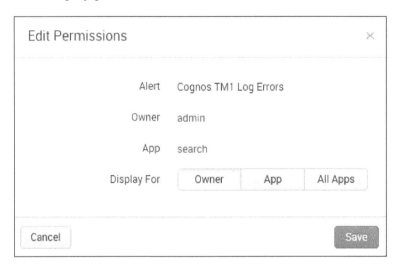

You can set your alert permissions to the following:

- **Display for Owner**: With this, only the current owner of the alert can access the alert and its results
- **Display for App**: Using this, the alert is only accessible for the app it is currently in context of, for example, **Search & Reporting**
- **Display for All Apps**: Using this, the alert is accessible within all Splunk apps

Editing the alert type and trigger

When you go to the **Edit Alert** page, Splunk does the following:

- Shows you the alert title
- Allows you to edit the description
- Allows you to set the type: **Scheduled** or **Real Time** (more on this later in this chapter)
- Allows you to set the schedule (if **Scheduled** is selected)
- Allows you to set **Trigger condition**

The **Edit Alert** page is shown in the following screenshot:

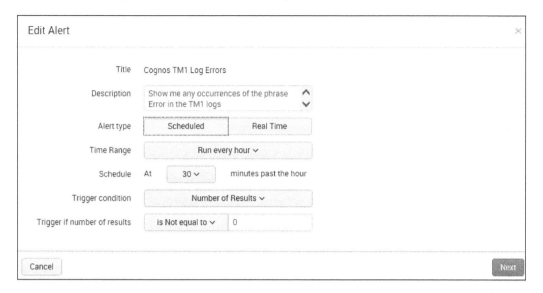

Editing actions

After you click on **Edit Actions**, Splunk does the following:

- Shows you the alert title
- Allows you to check/uncheck the **List in Trigger Alerts** option and set the severity level, if it is checked
- Allows you to tell Splunk to send an e-mail if the alert is triggered and to set e-mail options, which we discussed earlier in this chapter, if the **Send Email** checkbox is checked
- Allows you to tell Splunk to run a script if the alert is triggered
- Allows you to set the **When triggered, execute actions** option (**Once** or **For Each Result** — discussed earlier in this chapter)
- Allows you to set Splunk's **Throttle** options (discussed earlier in this chapter)

The preceding options are shown in the following screenshot:

Disabling alerts

Clicking on **Disable** allows you to temporarily turn off the alert, as shown in the following screenshot:

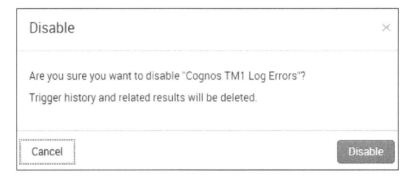

Cloning alerts

Clicking on **Clone** allows you to make an editable copy of the alert, as shown in the following screenshot:

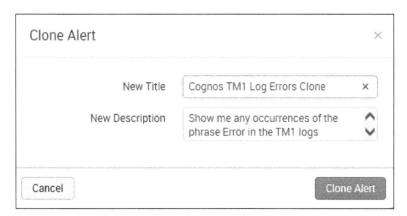

Deleting alerts

Clicking on **Delete** allows you to remove (delete) the alert from Splunk:

Scheduled or real time

We've looked at scheduled alerts in detail in this chapter, so now, let's take a look at Splunk's ability to provide real-time alerts.

With real-time searching, you can search for events before they are indexed and preview the results as the events stream in. Based on real-time searches, you can create alerts that run continuously in the background to deliver timelier notifications than alerts that are based on scheduled searches.

In a similar fashion, in order to create a scheduled alert, we need to do the following to create a real-time alert:

1. On the **Search** page, click on **Save As**.

2. When the **Save As Alert** dialog opens, give your alert a name and a description.

3. Select **Alert type** of the alert you want to configure (**Real Time**):

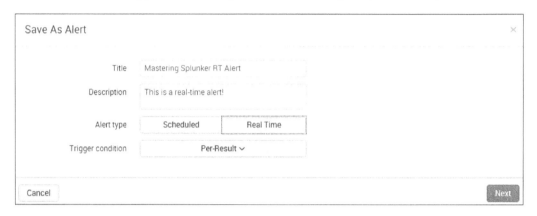

When you select **Real Time** (no scheduling information is required), you can select a **Trigger condition** option as follows:

- **Per-Result**: This is triggered whenever a search returns a result
- **Number of Results**: This is triggered based on the number of search results during a rolling window of time
- **Number of Hosts**: This is triggered based on the number of hosts during a rolling window of time
- **Number of Sources**: This is triggered based on the number of sources during a rolling window of time
- **Custom**: This is triggered based on a custom condition during a rolling window of time

Similar to creating a scheduled alert, once you click on **Next**, you can enable additional actions (detailed earlier in this chapter).

Extended functionalities

When using Splunk Web (again, I recommend this), you can edit all the alert properties in a single place.

Navigate to **Settings | Searches, reports, and alerts**; you can locate the search/alert and click on the name. From here, Splunk shows you and allows you to edit all the information for this alert. In addition, there are a few extended functionalities, as follows:

- Acceleration
- An expiration for the alert
- Summary indexing

Splunk acceleration

Splunk acceleration is a technique that Splunk uses to speed up searches which take a long time to complete, because they have to cover a large amount of data. You can enable acceleration for the search that your alert is based on by checking the **Accelerate this search** checkbox and selecting a **Summary range** value, as shown in the following screenshot:

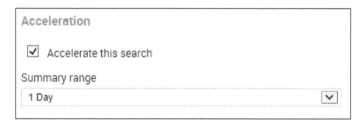

Expiration

You can determine the length of time for which Splunk keeps a record of your triggered alerts. On the **Details** page for an alerting report, you can use the **Expiration** field to define the amount of time for which an alert's triggered alert records (and their associated search artifacts) are retained by Splunk.

You can choose a preset expiration point for the alert records associated with a search, such as **After 24 hours**, or you can define a custom expiration time.

Summary indexing

You can also enable summary indexing for any report or alert. Summary indexing allows you to write the results of a search to a specific *specialized* index and allows faster searches overall by limiting the amount of results to what the report generates. To enable this feature, click on the **Enable** checkbox under the **Summary indexing** section.

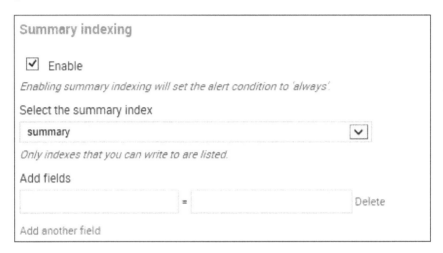

Summary

In this chapter, we talked about how Splunk monitors data inputs and how to take advantage of Splunk's alerting ability. We also detailed various topics such as Splunk monitoring, pointing to data, forwarders, Windows inputs in Splunk, input typing, and the data pipeline. We dived deeper into the *Splunk Deployment Monitor* app's download and installation, alerts, and other actions. Disabling, deleting, and cloning alerts and adjusting other permissions were shown subsequently.

In the next chapter, we will define and describe Splunk transactions from an enterprise's perspective.

9
Transactional Splunk

This chapter will define and describe Splunk transactions from an enterprise (or global to the organization) perspective.

The following topics will be covered in this chapter:

- Transactions and their types
- Advanced use of transactions such as:
    - ° Configuring transaction types
    - ° Grouping events
    - ° Concurrent events
    - ° What to avoid?

In *Chapter 2*, *Advanced Searching*, we talked briefly about Splunk transactional searching. In this chapter, we will take a much closer look at this important topic.

Transactions and transaction types

We'll start by defining two important Splunk terms: transactions and transaction types.

> "*A transaction is any group of conceptually-related events that spans time.*"
>
> *Splunk documentation*

To illustrate, an out of disk space condition might trigger several server events to be recorded (possibly even from multiple hosts or applications), and they can all be grouped together into a single transaction.

It is important to understand that events don't have to be physically linked to be thought of as a transaction. Experience with an organization's environment or knowledge of an application, for example, might provide information that *logically relates* events.

Reiterating a transaction is defined as a collection of conceptually-related events that occur over a period of time. A transaction type is a transaction that has been saved or defined in Splunk. Note that what we mean by *saved in Splunk* is that the transaction has been configured (that is, set up in the `transactiontypes.conf` file) so that Splunk understands it.

Splunk masters will usually look for opportunities to leverage searches on the basis of creating transaction types. For example, you can create a Splunk search that groups together all transactions of a particular Cognos TM1 user over a time range and save it as a transaction type.

Before we proceed, let's refresh our familiarity with several other essential terms:

- **Fields and default fields**: These fields are searchable labels in Splunk event data that provide accuracy in your searches. When Splunk indexes data, it will identify certain fields in each event that will become part of the index's event data. The fields that Splunk adds automatically are known as default fields. Default fields are of three types: internal, basic, and datetime.

- **Tags and aliases**: These tags are simply a way of providing a *friendlier* name or label to a specific group of event data to make your searching easier.

- **Configuration files**: These configuration (or `.conf`) files are text files used to hold a variety of Splunk settings. Splunk updates these files and certain Splunk administrators can also manually modify them.

- **Event data**: This data is given as input to Splunk and added to Splunk's indexes. The individual atomic units of data are called events.

Let's get back to transactions

Earlier, we mentioned that Splunk transactions might comprise of:

- Different events coming from the same source

- Different events coming from different sources

- Comparable events coming from different sources

Examples of event data that can qualify and be configured as Splunk transaction types are only limited to your imagination (and perhaps the availability of the data). Transaction types are events grouped together and referred to with a specific identifier or name.

Transaction search

To help identify events that occur over a period of time and can be configured as a transaction, you can use a Splunk transaction search. The transaction search command, which works with both Splunk Web and the command-line interface, produces groups of indexed events as its output. This output can of course be used in reports or configured as a transaction type for later reuse (we'll explain this later in this chapter).

To use a transaction search, you can perform one of the following tasks:

- Call a transaction type that you configured in the `transactiontypes.conf` file

- Define transaction constraints in your search by setting the search options of the `Transaction` command

There are many options that allow the Splunk transaction search to recognize and group events into a Splunk transaction that meet your particular needs. For example, you can perform the following actions:

- You can identify (as a transaction) where the first and last events are separated by a time span that does not exceed a maximum time with `maxspan`

- You can identify (as a transaction) events where the time between identified events does not exceed a specific value with `maxpause`

- You can identify (as a transaction) where the total number of identified events does not exceed a certain number with `maxevent`

- You can identify (as a transaction) a final identified event that contains a certain string of characters with `endswith`

 You can also use the `Transaction` command to override transaction options that you have configured in the `transactiontypes.conf` file. Again, we'll talk about this later in this chapter.

An example of a Splunk transaction

A simple example of a Splunk transaction search is as follows:

```
sourcetype=tm* TM1.Process error | transaction maxpause=1m maxspan=5m
```

In the preceding example, I'm looking for all Cognos TM1 process errors that occurred within the indexed source data type and met the following criteria:

- The time between the errors that occurred did not exceed one minute

- The time span between the error's first and last events did not exceed five minutes

The events that meet the search criteria are grouped together and returned, as shown in the following screenshot:

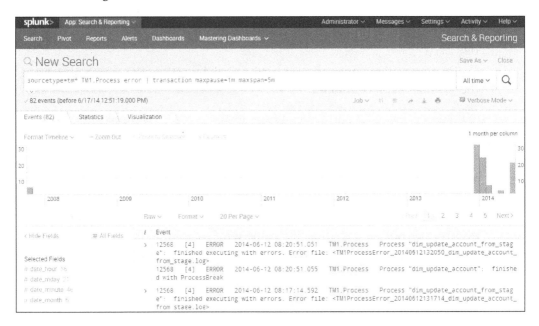

This search takes events from the Cognos TM1 logs and creates groups of events (or transactions) from events that meet the criteria specified.

After reviewing the results of the search, you can save it for reuse by configuring it within Splunk (adding it to `transactiontypes.conf` as a transaction type). We'll cover this later in this chapter.

It's possible to add a transaction to any of your Splunk searches. Pipe (|) simply searches for the `Transaction` command (as illustrated in the preceding example).

The Transaction command

Transactions returned at search time (for example, the grouped events returned in the preceding example) will consist of the following:

- Raw text of each event matching the search criteria
- Any shared event types
- Certain field values

The Splunk `Transaction` command supports the `field-list`, `match`, `maxspan`, `maxpause`, `startswith`, and `endswith` options.

In addition to the preceding list, transactions will also have additional data stored in the fields named `duration` and `transactiontypes`:

- `duration`: The `duration` field will contain the duration of the transaction. This is the difference between the timestamps of the first and last event of each group of events (each transaction).

- `transactiontype`: The `transactiontype` field is the name of the transaction (as defined in the `transactiontypes.conf` file).

- `field-list`: A comma-separated list of fields, which, if set, requires each event to have the same field(s) to be grouped into the same transaction (events with the same field names, but different values will not be included).

- `match`: The `match` option is designed to allow you to search based on the match type; currently, the only value supported is *closest* (as of Splunk version 6.1.1).

- `maxspan`: As mentioned earlier in this chapter, the `maxspan` (or maximum span) option is the time between the first and last event in the transaction group. This can be set in seconds, minutes, hours, or days (the default is -1, for an all time time span).

- `maxpause`: As mentioned earlier in this chapter, the `maxpause` (or maximum pause) option sets the maximum time allowed between the transaction events. Unlike `maxspan`, the default for `maxpause` is -1, which means `maxpause` is disabled.

- `startswith`: The `startswith` option allows you to use an expression to mark the beginning of a new transaction. The expression can be a string literal or *eval-filtering* expression. The syntax will depend on the choice for the option. The `startswith` option defaults to " ".

- `endswith`: The `endswith` option allows you to use an expression to mark the end of a transaction. Similar to the `startswith` option, the expression can be a string literal or *eval-filtering* expression. The syntax will depend on the choice for the option. The `endswith` option defaults to " ".

The Splunk product documentation (`http://docs.splunk.com/Documentation`) provides numerous examples and describes the specific syntax of using `startswith` and `endswith`.

For `startswith` and `endswith`, the `<transam-filter-string>` value is defined with the following syntax:

```
"<search-expression>" | (<quoted-search-expression>) | eval(<eval-
expression>
```

In the preceding expression, the following values can be defined:

- `<search-expression>`: This will be a search expression that cannot have quotes

- `<quoted-search-expression>`: This will be a search expression that can contain quotes

- `<eval-expression>`: This will be an eval expression evaluating to a Boolean value

Some examples are as follows:

- **Search expression**: `name="splunkmaster"`
- **Search expression**: `user=millerj`
- **Search expression**: any search phrase
- **Eval bool expression**: `eval(rotations/time < max_speed)`

Transactions and macro searches

In *Chapter 2*, *Advanced Searching*, we introduced Splunk macros.

A Splunk macro can be thought of as a (hopefully, previously tested and otherwise validated) reusable assembly of Splunk (or business) logic, basically, any part or even all of a Splunk search you don't want to type in again. Saved macros can even be defined to receive arguments when reused. Splunk macros are an integral part of knowledge management.

Macros are very powerful, and when used with transactions, can extend the power and value of your Splunk transactions. Macros in transactions support substitution through the use of `$field$`.

Let's have a quick review of Splunk macros.

A refresher on search macros

Remember, a search macro can be reused in multiple searches (both saved and ad hoc searches) and in multiple places within a particular search. In addition, search macros aren't required to be complete commands. Macros can also take arguments.

As always, Splunk Web is the easiest way to create your macros. The process is as follows:

1. Go to **Settings** and then **Advanced search**, as shown in the following screenshot:

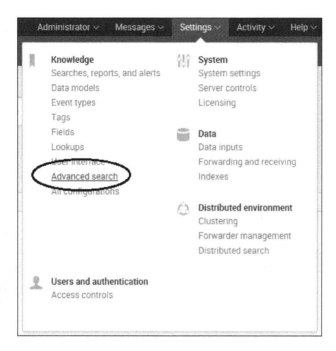

2. Then, from the **Advanced search** page, select **Search macros**:

3. In the **Search macros** page, click on **New** to create a new macro:

Defining your arguments

In the **Add new** page, you can fill in the following appropriate macro arguments:

- **Destination app**: This defaults to the Splunk search app, but you can select (from the convenient drop-down list) any existing Splunk app to restrict your macro to that app.

- **Name**: This is just a name for your macro; however, if you are planning on passing values (arguments) to your macro, you'll need to indicate in the name field the number of arguments you will pass (just the number, not the name or names of the arguments). An example is `supermacro(3)` (if you are passing three arguments to the macro named `supermacro`). Interestingly enough, Splunk does allow you to create different macros using the same name as long as each has a different argument count. This means that `supermacro` and `supermacro(3)` are unique and separate macros. This is not recommended; however, you should assign different names to different macros. In addition, if you plan to use the pipe character, it can cause you problems, and you should review the product documentation for the specific allowances for its use.

- **Definition**: This is the string that the macro evaluates to when referenced in another Splunk search.

For a user to input arguments into a (search) macro, you must wrap each argument with dollar signs (an example would be $arg1$). The actual values of each argument are specified when the macro is invoked.

- **Use eval-based definition?**: This is a checkbox that indicates whether the macro definition is an eval expression (that is, it returns a string that represents the expansion of a macro).

- **Arguments**: This is simply a comma-delimited string of your argument names (if your macro has any). The names can only contain the characters a-z, A-Z, 0-9, underscore _, and dash -. They cannot contain any duplicate names. Quotes will need to be escaped if you use them in your arguments (I recommend you try and avoid quotes).

- **Validation Expression** and **Validation Error Message**: You can enter a string that is an eval expression and evaluates to a Boolean value or a string to validate your arguments. The result of the valuation expression will be displayed in the **Validation Error Message** textbox.

Applying a macro

So, picking up from where we left off earlier in this chapter, we can take the following transaction example:

```
sourcetype=tm* TM1.Process error | transaction maxpause=1m maxspan=5m
```

We can turn this search into a macro. From the **Advanced search** page, select **Search macros**. Then, in the **Search macros** page, click on **New**. We can create a transaction search macro to return groups of events that meet the search criteria. Remember, our example uses all data indexed as tm* (all TM1 message log data sources) that contain the phrases TM1.Process and error. The idea is to see all events generated from TurboIntegrator process errors. In addition, I want to group errors that occur within a certain time span (maxspan) and with a maximum pause (maxpause) between the events.

So, to create my macro, I use the following information:

- **Destination app**: We'll let this field default to **search** (we can always change this later).

- **Name**: TM1ProcessTransactions(2) seems like a good name, and I am going to pass it to two arguments.

- **Definition**: This will be `sourcetype=tm1* TM1.Process error | transaction maxpause=$argme$ maxspan=$argmeagain$`. Notice that I've turned the values for `maxspan` and `maxpause` into arguments using the $ character.
- **Use eval-based definition?**: We can leave this field unchecked.
- **Arguments**: We'll just call the arguments `argme` and `argmeagain`.
- **Validation Expression** and **Validation Error Message**: We'll leave these blank as well.

The preceding information is shown in the following screenshot:

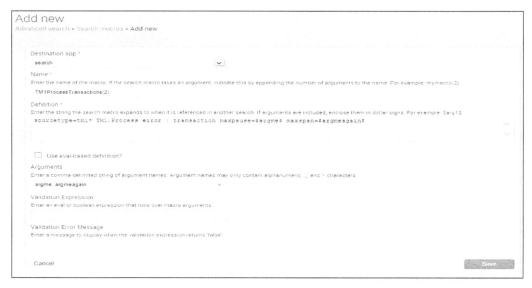

The Add new page to create a macro

Now, if we want to run our macro transaction search, we type the following code:

```
`TM1ProcessTransactions(1d, 5m)`
```

Notice that to use my macro as a search, I need to use the left quote (also known as a grave accent) character; on most English-language keyboards, this character is located on the same key as the tilde (~).

Also, notice that the arguments `maxspan` and `maxpause` can be entered at runtime as any values that you want to return to your desired report. This is shown in the following screenshot:

The macro transaction search screen

To use Splunk transactions, you can define your transaction constraints in your searches by setting search options (as we just demonstrated), or by calling a transaction type that has been configured in the `transactiontypes.conf` file.

Advanced use of transactions

Let's consider some more advanced uses of Splunk transactions.

Configuring transaction types

As we stated earlier in this chapter, a transaction is defined as a collection of conceptually-related events that occur over a period of time, and a transaction type is a transaction that has been saved or defined in Splunk. To this point, any series of events (transactions) can be turned into a transaction type. To create transaction types, you use the `transactiontypes.conf` file.

The transactiontypes.conf file

As with most features of Splunk, configuration (or .conf) files are used. To create (configure) transaction types in Splunk, you use the transactiontypes.conf file.

If you perform a search of your Splunk installation files, you should find two versions of this file named as follows:

- transactiontypes.conf.example
- transactiontypes.conf.spec

These files can be used for reference.

You should create your version of the transactiontypes.conf file and place it at $SPLUNK_HOME/etc/system/local/.

You can also create this in your own custom app directory at $SPLUNK_HOME/etc/apps/.

Transaction types are defined by creating a section header in the file and listing specifications for each transaction within the section (Splunk refers to these section headers as *stanzas*).

You can create as many transaction types as you want or need (each represented by a section header, and with any number of defining specifications). You can then utilize the Splunk Transaction command (in Splunk Web) to call the transactions you have defined, using their transaction type name. If you want, you can also override defined transactions within your search command.

Use the following syntax to create a transaction type:

```
[<transactiontype>]
maxspan =   [<integer> s|m|h|d|-1]
maxpause = [<integer> s|m|h|d|-1]
fields = <comma-separated list of fields>
startswith = <transam-filter-string>
endswith=<transam-filter-string>
```

Let's take a closer look at each of the lines in the preceding code (and some related options):

- [<transactiontype>]: The section header (or stanza) is the name of the transaction type to search for in Splunk Web. You could, in fact, only have the section header; if you do not specify entries or specifications for the transaction type, Splunk will just use the default values.

- maxspan = [<integer> s|m|h|d|-1]: This sets the maximum allowable time span for a transaction. You can set this parameter, using seconds, minutes, hours, or days (or unlimited if you set it to -1).

- `maxpause = [<integer> s|m|h|d|-1]`: This sets the maximum time between events in a transaction. This can be in seconds, minutes, hours, or days (or unlimited if you set it to `-1`).

- `maxevents = <integer>`: This sets the limit of the number (must be positive) of events in a transaction (defaults to 1000).

- `fields = <comma-separated list of fields>`: This indicates that each event in the transaction must contain the same field or fields.

- `connected= [true|false]`: This is related to `fields` and used only if `fields` is not empty. It controls if an event opens a new transaction or just becomes part of the current transaction. The default is `connected = true`.

- `startswith = <transam-filter-string>`: This is a (search or eval) filtering expression that indicates the start of a new transaction (defaults to " ").

- `endswith=<transam-filter-string>`: A search or eval filtering expression (similar to `startswith`), which if satisfied by an event marks the end of a transaction (defaults to " ").

The following string applies to both the `startswith` and `endswith` specifications:

```
<transam-filter-string>
```

This specification is made up of the following keywords:

```
"<search-expression>" | (<quoted-search-expression> | eval(<eval-
expression>)
```

The keywords shown in the preceding line of code (making up the `<transam-filter-string>` value) are defined as follows:

- `<search-expression>`: This is a search expression that does not allow quotes

- `<quoted-search-expression>`: This is a search expression that allows quotes

- `<eval-expression>`: This is an eval expression that evaluates to a Boolean

You'll also want to consider the following optional parameters:

- `delim=<string>`: This sets the delimiter for the original event values in the transaction event fields (defaults to `delim= )`

- `nullstr=<string>`: This sets the value to be used by Splunk for missing field values as part of multivalue fields in a transaction (defaults to `nullstr=NULL`)

An example of transaction types

So, here is a simple example to illustrate the power of defining transaction types in the `transactiontypes.conf` file.

Using the Splunk `Transaction` command (explained earlier in this chapter), we can construct the following transaction search:

```
sourcetype=TM* | Transaction fields=host startswith="TM1.Process"
```

This search produces a report of grouped events (transactions) that are related by two criteria:

* Similar hosts
* The event begins with the phrase `TM1.Process`

If we run the search, the following report is generated:

The search result

Using the ability to define transaction types, we can create our local version of the `transactiontypes.conf` file, as follows:

```
[TurboIntegratorErrors]
fields=host
startswith="TM1.Process"
```

Once you've created and saved the file, you'll need to restart Splunk. Then, we can simply call the transaction type by name in our search, as follows:

```
sourcetype=TM* | Transaction name=TurboIntegratorErrors
```

This produces the same report, as shown in the following screenshot:

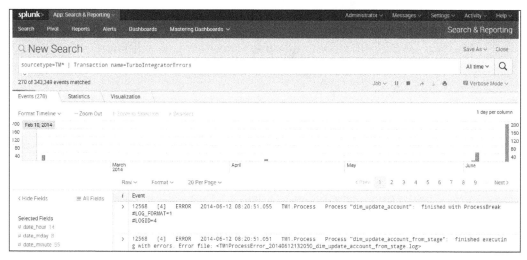

The search result

Of course, now, we can just add any overrides as we wish.

Grouping – event grouping and correlation

Throughout this book, we've mentioned that all data in Splunk is indexed as events. Part of the investigation of these events is the concept of event correlation.

> *"Event correlation is finding relationships between seemingly unrelated events in data from multiple sources to answer questions."*
>
> *Splunk.com, 2014*

Splunk supports event correlations not only with transactions and transaction types (the topics covered in this chapter), but also through various other means, most of which were covered within this book:

- You can identify relationships within events based on the time proximity or geographic location of the events. You can run a series of time-based searches to investigate and identify abnormal activity and then use the timeline to drill into specific time periods.

- You can trail a sequence of related events, even if they are sourced from separate data sources, as a single transaction.

- You can utilize a Splunk subsearch to take the (perhaps conditional) results of a search and use them in another search.

- You can correlate data to external sources using lookups.

- You can use SQL-like inner and outer joins to link two different sets of data based on one (or more) fields.

It is extremely important for you as a Splunk master to thoroughly understand each option that Splunk provides and which option will not only meet your requirements, but also be the most effective and efficient choice. In an enterprise environment, you'll need to understand the resource, concurrency, and performance implications of the choices you make (more on this topic in the next chapter).

In addition, it should be pointed out that transaction types (for example) are valuable as enterprise knowledge objects, and time should be spent developing transaction types that can be reused across the organization (as opposed to *singular, one time*, and *just for me* transaction type configurations).

Concurrent events

Concurrent events, in Splunk, refer to events that occur simultaneously or at the start time of the event (not the number of events that occurred during some overlying period of time). To be clearer, consider two events (we'll name them *E1* and *E2*); we can say that *E1* is concurrent with *E2* if *(E1.start, E1.start + E1.duration)* overlaps, in any way, with *(E2.start, E2.start + E2.duration)*.

Splunk 6.1 provides the `concurrency` command, which you should be familiar with. The `concurrency` command will use a `duration` field to locate the number of concurrent events (for each event).

The following is the command syntax:

```
concurrency duration=<field> [start=<field>] [output=<field>]
```

Let's take a closer look at each of the code terms in the preceding syntax:

- `duration`: This is a required field that indicates a span of time and depends on the field specified as the duration (for example, seconds)

- `start`: This is an optional field representing the start time (defaults to `_time`)

- `output`: This is an optional field that writes the resulting number of concurrent events (defaults to `concurrency`)

Examples of concurrency command use

Looking at our earlier example of the Splunk transaction type (we called it `TurboIntegratorErrors`), we see that it uses the duration or time span of the groups of events returned to count the number of other transactions that occurred at the same time. Consider the following example:

```
sourcetype=TM* | transaction name=TurboIntegratorErrors | concurrency
duration=duration | eval duration=tostring(duration,"duration")
```

The preceding example uses a transaction type (`TurboIntegratorErrors`), and then pipes all results (the grouped events) into the Splunk `concurrency` command. This then counts the number of events that occurred at the same time based on the timestamp and duration of the transaction. The results are shown in the following screenshot:

The search result

This search similarly uses the `eval` command as well as the `tostring()` function (reformatting the values of the `duration` field to a more readable format: `HH:MM:SS`).

Here is an example showing an unformatted `duration` field:

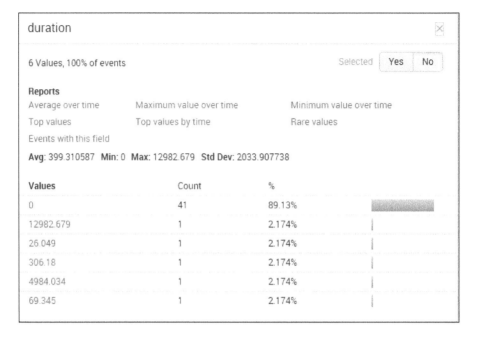

Here is an example showing a formatted `duration` field:

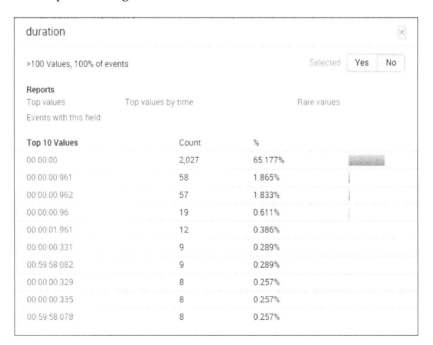

In this example, you can use the time between each event to count the number of different events that occurred at the same time, as follows:

```
sourcetype=TM* | transaction name=TurboIntegratorErrors | delta _
time AS timeDelta p=1 | eval timeDelta=abs(timeDelta) | concurrency
duration=timeDelta
```

Here, we see the Splunk `delta` command as well as the `_time` field. Running this command string will calculate the time between one TM1 event (returned from the configured transaction type) and the event immediately preceding it. The search also renames this change in time as `timeDelta`.

You might encounter some negative values using `timeDelta`, and as concurrency does not work with negative values, the `eval` command can then be added to convert `timeDelta` to an absolute value (using `abs(timeDelta)`). This `timeDelta` value can then be used as the duration to calculate concurrent events.

Note that the results from the preceding two examples are similar, but the fields' output will be very different.

Here is an example where we can calculate the number of concurrent events for each transaction and save the result as a field we define named `splunkmaster`:

```
sourcetype=TM* Error | transaction name=TurboIntegratorErrors |
concurrency duration=duration output=splunkmaster
```

This is also shown in the following screenshot:

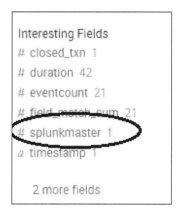

If you click on the **# splunkmaster** option, the following dialog box opens:

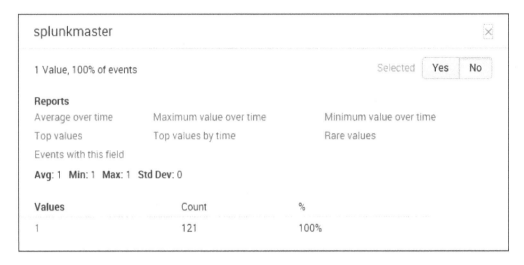

The following is an example that calculates the number of concurrent events that uses the et field as the start time and length as the duration:

```
sourcetype=TM* Error | transaction name=TurboIntegratorErrors |
concurrency duration=length start=et
```

The results are shown in the following screenshot:

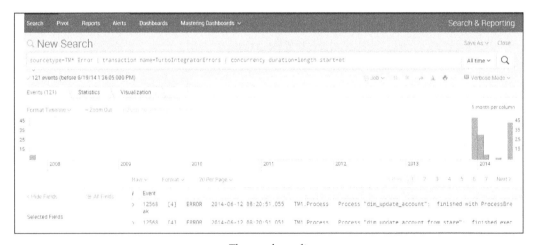

The search result

What to avoid – stats instead of transaction

We've discussed Splunk transactions and transaction types in detail in this chapter. Transactions are a powerful feature provided by Splunk. However, depending on your objectives, transactions might not be the most efficient approach to take. For example, if your intention is to compute aggregated statistics on transactional data that are defined using a single field, then the `stats` command is the most efficient option. So, let's take a look at an example.

To get the statistics of the duration of a defined transaction, which is defined by the `host` field, we can use the following query:

```
sourcetype=TM* Error | transaction name=TurboIntegratorErrors |
stats min(_time) AS earliest max(_time) AS latest by host | eval
duration=latest-earliest | stats min(duration) max(duration)
avg(duration) median(duration) perc95(duration)
```

Here are the results:

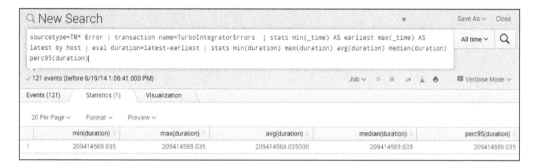

Similarly, if you want to compute the number of hits per host in your TM1 indexed logs, you can use the following query:

```
sourcetype=TM* Error | transaction name=TurboIntegratorErrors | stats
count by host| sort -count
```

Here are the results:

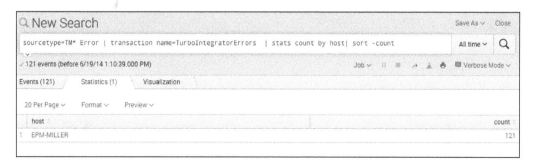

Hopefully, after reviewing the preceding examples, when you are generating statistics over transactional data, you will always consider using the `stats` command first.

Summary

In this chapter, we defined Splunk transactions and transaction types along with concurrent events. In addition, we covered different methods for grouping and configuring events into transactions.

In the next chapter, we will introduce the idea of best practices for Splunk development and provide some guidelines and working examples.

10
Splunk – Meet the Enterprise

This chapter will introduce you to the idea of Splunk from an enterprise perspective. Important best practices for development, such as naming, testing, and developing a vision are covered in detail.

The topics that will be covered in this chapter are as follows:

- General concepts
- Naming for documentation
- Testing
- Retrofitting
- The vision

General concepts

In this book, we started out by defining what Splunk is and what we believe it is becoming. In addition, we took a walkthrough of how to obtain and install Splunk and once installed, we covered searching, tables, charts, and fields as well as covered how to implement lookups, dashboards, indexing, apps, monitoring, and transactions.

At this point, you should be comfortable with all of this—which is referred to as "tactical Splunk". Now, it is time to discuss Splunk from a *strategic* (or enterprise) perspective. When we say strategic, we mean *doing things in a proven way and specifically looking for opportunities to gain an edge through the development and management of Splunk knowledge and knowledge objects*. This viewpoint is well defined in the much written about Capability Maturity Model (which is discussed later in this chapter, in the *A Structured Approach* section) and generally explains the progression of an organization's perspective from tactical to strategic.

Best practices

There is no shortage of recommendations and guidelines (really just opinions) when developing software components or solutions, regardless of the technology used. Anyone involved in the process of software design has their own ideas on what the best approach might be, and these ideas might change over time. Recently, a distinction has even been made between the concepts of best practices and proven practices, as what is considered to be the best might vary depending on organizational needs and priorities.

The practice guideline topics include the following:

- Requirements
- Architecture
- Design
- Coding
- Reviews
- Testing
- Performance profiling
- Configuration management
- Quality assurance
- Deployment
- Operations and support
- Data and migration
- Project management
- Measurement of success

Each of these topics are important to develop software components and solutions, and are based on knowledge (what works, what works best, and what doesn't work so well). Best practices really are a way of managing acquired knowledge. For Splunk masters, these practices focus on the concept of managing Splunk knowledge (knowledge management).

Definition of Splunk knowledge

Splunk, from a strategic perspective, starts with the understanding that as you use and develop Splunk technology within your organization, the knowledge a nd experience you and your co-workers acquire and/or advance are represented as knowledge or knowledge objects.

Splunk is a commanding search and analysis tool that helps organizations see both the details and the big picture (in the way of patterns) in the available data. Using Splunk, you are not just scanning log entries, but you also have the ability to leverage the insights that the data holds to find out more about the past, present, and future.

Throughout this book, we explained how Splunk automatically extracts knowledge from (most) any kind of data—events, fields, timestamps, and more—to help you harness the information in a better, smarter, and more concentrated way (some data is extracted at index time, as Splunk indexes data, while the majority comes at search time).

Different from mainstream or structured database tools that use predeterminations or preconfigurations (schemas) to decide what information to pull out or analyze from the data, Splunk enables you to dynamically extract knowledge from the data as you need it. In the beginning, Splunk enables you to perform simple searches, and as your organization continues to use Splunk, it creates additional organizational (Splunk) knowledge, such as event types, tags, lookups, field extractions, workflow actions, and saved searches.

Developed Splunk knowledge can be thought of a tool to be used to simplify the process of discovering and analyzing various aspects of the data. Think of an example such as Splunk transactions, which allow you to link events together as a single event on which you can perform precise analytical searches.

These tools or toolsets can be organized and maintained as the Splunk knowledge objects of your organization and are maintained and accessed through the Splunk Web interface (and/or through the Splunk configuration files). They can be used for the continual analysis of an organization's data. In other words, Splunk makes it easy to share this knowledge (or knowledge objects) throughout an organization. Have a look at the following diagram:

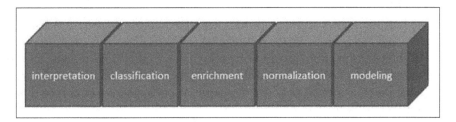

Splunk knowledge can typically be organized into one of the five different categories, which are explained in the following sections.

Data interpretation

The process of understanding data begins with the identification and extraction of certain data points or fields from the raw data. As discussed in *Chapter 3, Mastering Tables, Charts, and Fields*, Splunk automatically extracts specific (or default) fields from your data that will help bring meaning to the data, which otherwise might not always be evident. Additional fields might also be (manually) extracted from your data to expand upon and improve the organization's level of understanding.

Classification of data

As we saw in *Chapter 9, Transactional Splunk*, you can use Splunk event types and transactions to classify or group data together into interesting sets of corresponding data events. Splunk event types can be used to group together sets of events that your organization has discovered through its Splunk searches, while Splunk transactions can be configured as the data collections of conceptually related events within certain periods of time.

Data enrichment

Your data can be enriched through the use of Splunk lookups and workflow actions (see *Chapter 4, Lookups*). Lookups and workflows are categories of Splunk knowledge that can easily extend the helpfulness of data in numerous ways. You can add explicit information to your data in the form of additional fields from external data sources (such as a static CSV file) or Python-based executable commands. Workflow actions enable communication between the fields in your data and other applications or web resources, such as a WHOIS lookup on a field containing an IP address.

Normalization

You can use Splunk aliases and tags (which we discussed in *Chapter 3, Mastering Tables, Charts, and Fields* and *Chapter 4, Lookups*) to normalize your organization's collection of field information, group your sets of associated field values, and give tags to extracted fields which reflect different aspects of their identity. You can tag different fields (such as hosts) as being the same or perhaps give different field aliases to make Splunk treat them the same.

Modeling

A Splunk data model can be used to create a representation of one or more datasets. Based on the format and semantics of the specific indexed data, data models can include numerous Splunk objects (such as lookups, transactions, and calculated fields) and can enable users to (with Splunk pivot) quickly generate useful tables, complex visualizations, and robust reports.

In addition, Splunk knowledge management can also include what is referred to as jobbing and accelerating.

When you execute Splunk searches or perform pivots, the outputs are automatically erased within 10 minutes by Splunk, unless they are saved as jobs. Splunk knowledge managers have the ability to review and manage these recently run and saved jobs through the Splunk **Jobs** page.

If a Splunk search or pivot is determined to be too slow, Splunk knowledge managers can leverage summary-based acceleration strategies (for example, report accelerations for searches, data model accelerations for pivots, and summary indexing for special cases) offered by Splunk to improve performance.

Strategic knowledge management

Splunk knowledge management helps you to transition from *tactical individual use* to the *strategic empowerment* of the enterprise. Typically, knowledge management focuses on runtime (or search-time) event manipulation rather than the preindexed setup and processes, which are more Splunk administrative in nature.

Note that it is a good idea for someone involved in knowledge management to have an experience of working with Splunk's administrative matters or at least a fundamental understanding of the basic matters, listed as follows, and a strong understanding of the data and use cases.

Let's see what the prerequisites for knowledge management are:

- **Apps**: If your enterprise uses more than one Splunk app and it will (for example, network administration and website log review might be two completely different user groups with completely different goals), you need to understand how Splunk apps are organized and how app object management works within multi-app deployments.

- **Configuration files**: Although most configurations can be set using Splunk Web, you do need to understand where the configuration files are located, how they are organized, precedence, and so on. Working with the `.conf` files directly allows a more fine-tune control. Splunk administrators should be comfortable with this. Power users can rely on Splunk Web.

- **Indexing**: As more users come online and search pipelines become more intricate, it will be increasingly important to know what an index is and how it works. Perhaps, most significant is knowing the difference between index time and search time and why this distinction is so significant.

- **Getting data in**: Everything in Splunk begins with data, so it's critical to know all about Splunk's data inputs.

- **Forwarding and receiving**: The power of Splunk's forwarders and receivers makes it very important for you to understand what forwarders and receivers are and how and why they can be implemented.

- **Event processing**: Understanding how Splunk parses and indexes data can help to resolve processing issues or improve performance.

- **Default fields**: Splunk will extract, by default, fields such as host, source, and source type at index time (rather than at search time). Your Splunk knowledge should include an understanding of how default field extraction can be managed and leveraged for peak optimization and efficiency.

- **Roles and users**: Even if you do not have the responsibility of creating roles and users, it is recommended that you understand how they're set up within your environment, as this directly affects your ability to share and promote Splunk knowledge objects between user groups.

Splunk object management with knowledge management

If you are your organization's sole Splunker or are a part of a larger team or perhaps a Splunk administrator, sooner or later you will be faced with an ever-growing number of Splunk knowledge objects. In the most vivid example, organizations that have multiple teams of Splunkers will even have a number of objects that solve the same problem.

Splunkers, including you, might find themselves doing the following:

- Sorting through a large number of Splunk objects
- Interpreting misleading or conflicting names
- Struggling to just find the existing objects

- Adapting objects that have unevenly applied app assignments and permissions
- Recreating objects already existing elsewhere in the system

Hence, even a minimalist effort to organize and manage your organization's (or your own) Splunk knowledge can provide positive benefits. Organizational efforts include the following:

- **Simple inventory and organization**: Time should be taken to make an inventory of and monitor Splunk object creation (across teams, departments, and even deployments) in order to minimize the reinvention of objects that solve the same thing and promote the creation and sharing of useful general-purpose objects on a global basis across deployments.

- **Normalization of data**: The basic principles of normalization apply to Splunk. Adopt uniform naming conventions and the Splunk Common Information Model (a set of field names and tags that your organization can use to define its common interest data).

- **Splunk configuration files**: You have, at this point, found that most of the Splunk functionalities can be configured through Splunk Web, and you also know that there are certain features and functionalities of Splunk that are more effectively handled through the configuration files. Splunk configuration files need to be considered as knowledge objects and need to be monitored and managed as such.

- **Data modeling**: Splunk data models are developed by Splunk users who possess a thorough understanding of the data indexed by Splunk and are very familiar with the Splunk search language. These data models are used to drive the Splunk pivot tool (without a data model, Pivot has nothing to report) and should be organized and leveraged as Splunk knowledge.

- **Performance management**: A variety of circumstances (such as large amounts of indexed data) can result in sluggish Splunk performance. To speed up things, you can make use of report acceleration, data model acceleration, and summary indexing (all based on Splunk knowledge) to support the teams in your organization in order to get the results they need swiftly and efficiently. The monitoring of these strategies is required to ensure that Splunk objects are being used as effectively as possible.

Naming conventions for documentation

As with any technology, it is highly recommended that you develop naming conventions (sometimes referred to as a naming style) for your knowledge objects before you begin developing them. That's the trick.

Developing naming conventions for knowledge objects

It is difficult to create workable conventions or standards unless you have experience and are familiar with which objects can be created within Splunk and their purposes. Generally speaking, more mature organizations will adopt styles used with other technologies, which you'll need to learn and adhere to. In new or less mature shops, it'll be up to you to define naming styles.

You can cultivate naming conventions for almost every kind of knowledge object in Splunk, but what will this standard naming really do for us Splunkers?

Organized naming conventions

Using consistent naming, such as a prefix for all the objects intended for a specific purpose, will naturally show object associations. If I prefix all of the objects created for demonstration purposes in this book with `book_demo_`, then they will easily stand out from all the other objects in my Splunk environment. Additionally, I can be more specific, such as naming all the searches as `book_demo_searches_`, which will create groups within my *book demo* list of objects.

Object naming conventions

Object naming can also be used to describe the purpose of an object. For example, an object named `db_search_` indicates that the object is a database search. Other information that you might want to include in the object naming can be:

- Which groups of users use the object
- The locations that use the object
- Which technology it involves
- The purpose or application(s) involved

Hints

Start early. So, the sooner you start adopting a convention or style the better, as once there are potentially many, many objects already created and in use, it will be confusing to sift through them and rename them later.

Be consistent. Make sure that you choose a style that can be easily followed by all the users in your organization. If everyone consistently follows the convention, it will become easier to use as time goes by.

Be reasonable. Use a style/convention that makes sense and is easy to understand and use. If you don't, the convention will most likely be abandoned or at least avoided. In addition, use conventions only when it makes sense to do so, not just because it is the standard.

Think forward. At this time, I do not believe that there is any globally adopted Splunk standard naming convention or style, but it makes sense to adopt one of your own and offer it to the Splunker online community — this way, you might receive constructive feedback and perhaps play a role in standardizing the technology!

An example of naming conventions

As naming is so important, let's take a look at a little example (keep in mind that if your organization already has a style or convention, you should use it as much as it can be applied to your Splunk knowledge objects).

You should consider (as a knowledge manager for your Splunk team) a naming style that is simple to apply and logical. For example, most technologies will adopt a delimiter — meaning an agreed-upon method to separate the sections or parts of an object name. The most common are the dash and underline characters. Using the delimiter, the next step is to determine which sections should make up your object name and the order in which the sections should be.

Here are examples of reasonable section options:

- **User group**: This section will group together all the objects owned by a particular group of Splunkers. For example, you might have a corporate group, a finance group, a Cognos TM1 group, and so on. User groups can be CRP, FIN, or TM1.
- **Type**: This section will indicate the type of object — search, alert, report, field, tag, lookup, and so on.
- **Platform**: This section will correspond to the platform subjected to the object (MS Windows or Linux).

- **Category**: This section will indicate what Splunk refers to as "the concern areas" for the prevailing platforms (disk exchange, SQL, event log, CPU, jobs, subsystems, services, security, and so on).

- **Interval**: This section will indicate the interval over or on for the object (15 minutes, 24 hours, or on demand).

- **Explanation**: This section will provide a meaningful description of the context and the intent of the object, limited to one or two words.

These conventions can be listed in a table as follows:

User group	Type	Platform	Category	Interval	Explanation
CRP	Alert	Windows	Disk exchange	<arbitrary>	<arbitrary>
FIN	Report	Linux	SQL		
TM1	Field		Event log		
	Tag		CPU		
	Lookup		Jobs		
			Subsystems		
			Services		
			Security		

So, using the preceding convention, the format of an object might be `UserGroup_Type_Platform_Category_Interval_Explanation`.

Splunk's Common Information Model

The **Common Information Model** (**CIM**) add-on offers a standardized approach to parse, categorize, and normalize the information input into Splunk.

Splunk's CIM is really a set of categorized tables that are used to normalize data by ensuring the use of same field names and tags for comparable events. The CIM add-on implements these tables as Splunk data models, which are used for the following:

- Testing the accuracy of how your fields and tags have been normalized

- Generating reports and dashboard panels via Splunk pivot

There is plenty of information available online that describes Splunk's version of the IT industry's Common Information Model (this is an exercise for you). The main point is that this is actually an approach or strategy that you as a Splunk master should be comfortable with.

The process of normalizing your Splunk-extracted field names, event type tagging, and host tagging includes a discrete list of standard custom fields, an event type tagging system, and a list of standard host tags.

You can download the CIM add-on from Splunk Apps.

Testing

Software testing is defined as an investigation. This investigative effort is performed with the objective of providing information about the quality of the product or service being tested.

Carrying out testing activities can also offer an objective and an independent view of a technology (or a specific software tool), allowing the stakeholders to appreciate and comprehend the potential risks of implementation (this might be what you and your organization might be doing with Splunk). Evaluation testing is conducted in a different way and with different objectives than testing for quality. In this book, we focus on testing Splunk knowledge objects to determine the level of quality (looking for bugs).

Quality testing (or quality assurance) comprises exercising the software (or knowledge objects for Splunk). Generally, each component, feature, or property of an object is assessed independently and as part of the overall object to see the degree to which it:

- Meets the requirements that originally guided its design and development
- Responds acceptably to all types of inputs
- Achieves its functions within an acceptable time
- Is appropriately usable
- Can be installed and used in its envisioned environments
- Achieves the desired general outcomes

There are an endless number of approaches to test for quality; to ensure the best use of the available time and resources, it is recommended that you use a reasonable testing strategy. Typically, testing is defined by levels, with each level having its own objectives and timing. Overall, it is a good practice to test early and test often, meaning that your testing can begin as soon as there is anything that can be tested (even if what you have is only partially developed). Sometimes, how you develop your app will dictate when and how testing can be conducted. A mainstream approach is to begin testing after system requirements have been documented and implemented in testable programs. In an agile approach, requirements, programming, and testing can be done simultaneously.

Testing before sharing

If you intend to share your Splunk app or add-on outside your organization by uploading it to Splunk Apps, you'll need to test (actually, verify) whether it meets the specific approval criteria, as follows:

- Does the object follow sensible packaging and naming standards?
- Are all Splunk configuration files consistent and standardized?
- Have you followed Splunk's XML file standards?
- Does the entire source code meet acceptable standards?
- Did you follow the general version and installation standards?
- Did you follow the recommended operating system standards?
- How have you managed malware/viruses, malicious content, and user security?
- Are all external data sources consistent and standardized?
- What about support standards?
- Is this considered intellectual property? Does it involve any existing IP?

This kind of testing is required for submission, but you should also consider adopting this verification testing as part of your internally developed testing strategy to ensure that the knowledge objects you develop are of the highest quality.

Levels of testing

Tests are usually grouped by where they land in the software development cycle or by how precise the test is. Testing levels are classified by the objectives of the test. The most common levels of testing are unit, integration, system, acceptance, performance, and regression.

It is important to point out that with Splunk, all the basics of testing still apply and test objectives might include certifying that your Splunk app is not only suitable for use within your Splunk environments but also meets the criteria required to share it on Splunk Apps.

Unit testing

When we say unit (or module) testing, we mean testing that validates a specific segment of code, usually at a very rudimentary level. The developer (who created the code) should write the testing steps to be taken as they develop the code. This helps guarantee that a specific function will work as designed. Keep in mind that a unit test might have many test steps and might include code, data flow and metrics analysis, peer code reviews, code coverage analysis, and other software verification practices.

All of these apply to Splunk knowledge object testing. Even an individual search command line might be broken up into smaller subsearches and reviewed and analyzed before the complete search object is made available to other Splunkers.

Integration testing

Integration testing focuses on verifying the linkage between components within a solution. Components can be incrementally integrated or all at once. Integration testing verifies the correctness of the interactions between components, rather than the components themselves. With Splunk, an example of integration testing might be to test the interaction between the saved searches that make up a dashboard.

Component interface testing

Component interface testing focuses on the information that is passed between the components in a solution (not to be confused with integration testing that is focused on the actual component linkage). **Component interface testing (CIT)** uses the term *packets* to describe the information bits that are passed around between solution components.

These packets can be *ranged* (testing upper and lower limits), *typed* (certifying that the data being passed is the type expected by the component—numeric, string, and so on), or *validated* (based on certain defined business rules). Of course, all your Splunk knowledge objects can be tested in this way. What does a dashboard display when no events meet the search criteria? What happens when the number of events exceed expected levels during a specific time frame? What if unrecognized characters appear in a message log (Splunk data input)? What if events don't follow expected patterns? You should be confident that your Splunk component will react in an appropriate manner if (and when) any of these conditions occur.

System testing

System testing (often referred to as end-to-end testing) refers to a completely integrated solution test, verifying that the solution will meet your requirements. A part of the system test is to not only verify a solution, but also verify that the solution does not negatively (or unexceptionally) impact the environment it runs in, and of course, to determine that working within a solution does not impact other users within the solution itself.

A simple example might include logging into an application, constructing and perhaps modifying an input, then sending or printing results, followed by summary processing or deletion (or archiving) of entries, and then logging off.

You must verify that all of your Splunk objects completely work and do not impact your environment (or other users of the object or Splunk itself).

Acceptance testing

Acceptance testing is perhaps the final step, phase, or level in your testing effort. This is when your solution is actually delivered to the users for (hopefully) their blessings. Splunk knowledge objects are not excluded from this important process. As per my experience, this level or phase of testing is the most difficult and the most important. It is critical that before any testing begins, your users are identified.

Having the key stakeholders of your solution or Splunk knowledge object identified (not to mention, defining a timeline for the users to evaluate and rule on the tests) is absolutely critical. This level of testing is where you'll receive an acknowledgement that your developed solution or knowledge object really works and hopefully adds value (you should define everything about this level of testing early in your development process). It is important in any effort to know when you are done.

Performance testing

The objective of performance testing is to focus on determining at what level a particular component or the entire solution will perform when given expected workloads. Responsiveness and stability are keenly measured for each workload and then compared with predetermined acceptable baselines. Performance testing is also used to determine a component's (or solution's) ability to scale and maintain reliability and sustainability. Splunk performance testing will involve measuring its indexing and searching performance based on Splunk's configuration settings, operating systems, hard disk devices, and even specific server (physical or virtual) machines.

Splunk's performance test kit

True to its form, Splunk is now offering a downloadable test kit, whose purpose is to help with Splunk performance testing and tuning. *Splunkit*, as it is named, is an extendable app that streamlines your organization's process of Splunk performance testing by doing the following:

- Mechanically creating data for testing
- Generating patterned searches (simulating Splunk user running command-line searches)
- Producing collections of benchmark measurements and informational statistics

Splunkit is also configurable. You can do the following:

- Set the rate at which data is generated or just use your own data
- Set the number of simulated Splunk users
- Set specific usage patterns for each simulated user

Regression testing

Regression testing is the type of testing that is used to identify mistakes or errors (or regressions) in existing functional and nonfunctional areas of a component or the entire solution after modifications such as enhancements, patches, or configuration changes have been introduced. The objective is to ensure that these changes have not introduced errors (or otherwise invalidated any earlier remediation). Regression testing also helps to evaluate how changes in one area of a component or solution might affect other areas.

It is imperative to plan for reasonable regression tests and perform them when making changes to your Splunk environment or knowledge objects (just as you would when working with any other technology) in order to ensure stability and quality. Regression testing can be accomplished efficiently by systematically choosing the suitable minimum set of tests needed to adequately cover your changes.

Retrofitting

The act of retrofitting refers to the addition of new features or functionalities to existing components or solutions. Software developers will be familiar with the practice of (sometimes) continually adding more to an already developed component or group of components, based on changes to requirements or added requirements.

When working with overly complex designs, adding on can be difficult. In some cases, retrofitting might also mean the reuse of a developed component to meet a requirement that it was not designed specifically for (this is usually done to save development time and costs). Retrofitting is typical and, especially when using a RAD or rapid application development approach, might actually be expected.

From a Splunk perspective, the effective administration and management of your organization's knowledge objects minimizes the effort and impact of retrofitting. Retrofitting enables you to do the following

- Easily identify existing knowledge objects that might already meet (or are about to meet) the new requirements
- Easily identify existing knowledge objects that might be assembled into a new solution to meet the new requirements

To be clear, it is always more efficient to leverage an existing component than it is to design and develop a new one (that's where you'll see retrofitting come in), but the effort to retrofit might expand to a point where it would have been cheaper to create a new component. To control the effort/cost of retrofitting, you need to be sure you have a strategy for managing your knowledge objects.

The enterprise vision

The enterprise or strategic vision for Splunk (as with most tools and technologies) is based on an evolutionary roadmap that evolves from the initial evaluation and implementation to building and using and finally (hopefully) the management and optimization of the tool or technology:

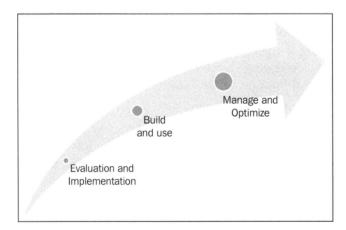

Evaluation and implementation

The evaluation and implementation phase will generally cover the discovery and evaluation that takes place with any new (to the organization) tool or technology. Testing should cover everything that is required to determine whether the tool/technology will meet or exceed the organization's needs now and in the foreseeable future. Once a decision is made to move forward, this phase also includes the installation, configuration, and everything that might be involved in deploying the new tool or technology for use by the intended users of the organization.

From a Splunk perspective, this phase might involve downloading and configuring an evaluation copy of Splunk and potentially multiple Splunk apps. It is best to determine the core requirements of your organization before you begin any downloading. In addition, Splunk should be tested in an environment comparable to the environment that it will eventually be installed in and using actual data samplings. It is also a very good idea to have a thorough understanding of which topology might best meet your specific needs.

Build, use, and repeat

Once a technology or tool is deployed, users will begin building and using the components. The effectiveness with which these components are created and the level of quality of the developed components will be contingent on the (hopefully escalating) level of exposure to the technology that the users possess. Characteristically, building and using is recurrent with success.

Splunk is a commanding instrument and in most cases, does not necessitate extensive training to begin using in order to execute searches. With human nature being what it is, once a search command line is validated as correct and valuable, it will be set aside for later reuse and hopefully, pooled as a valuable knowledge object across the group or entire organization. Although most organizations reach this phase, it is not unusual to see the following:

- Objects with similar or duplicate functionality
- Poor naming of objects (no one but the creator knows what it does)
- Objects that are not shared (objects visible only to specific groups or individuals)
- Objects that are obsolete or do not work properly or optimally

Management and optimization

At some point, usually while (or after a certain amount of) components are developed, the process will mature, most likely to the point that users will begin devoting time and perhaps dedicating resources to organize, manage, and optimize the developed components (or in other words, perform organizational knowledge management).

As a Splunk master, you should be committed to forming a Splunk governing committee to support the identification and management of Splunk knowledge within your organization to do the following:

- Record and appraise objects
- Establish suitable naming standards and styles
- Establish suitable development standards
- Create, implement, and impose a strict testing strategy
- Continually develop a vision for Splunk within your organization and the worldwide Splunk community

More on the vision

As I've mentioned before, part of taking a strategic or enterprise approach to Splunk, you need to develop a vision. This will ensure that your organization is leveraging Splunk to achieve the highest rate of return today and over time. This is not simply about administrating the environment, but involves everything (and more) that we've discussed in this chapter—best practices and continued and evolved improvement.

A structured approach

CMM or Capability Maturity Model is a structured approach to how an organization or individual approaches the software (component or solution) development process. According to popular opinion, the CMM model is based on a framework, the **process maturity framework** (**PMF**), and was created to assess not the performance but the performance capabilities of contractors and is specifically used to expedite and perfect software development processes and system improvement. This is a critical concept that should be instrumental in creating your vision.

CMM is the yardstick that is used to equate processes, habitually applied in information technology, commerce, as well as government, and advanced business processes such as software engineering, risk and project management, and even system engineering.

The CMM model is based on the following notions:

- **Key process areas or KPAs**: These refer to a collection of activities used for the achievement of goals
- **Goals**: These refer to the effective implementation of acknowledged KPAs, which then indicate the maturity (capability) level of an organization's development processes
- **Common features**: These refer to KPA performance commitment and ability, performed activities, measurement, implementation verification, and analysis
- **Key practices**: These refer to the infrastructure components used to enable KPA implementation and institutionalization
- **Maturity levels**: These refer to a five-level process, where the highest level is a perfect state and processes are systematically managed through optimization and continuous improvement

CMM advances through the following visionary phases:

- **Just started**: This is an unstable process environment, uncontrolled and almost entirely reactive.
- **Repeatable**: Repeatable processes deliver reliable results; basic project management techniques are repeatedly used.
- **Defined**: This encloses documented and distinct standards that continue to work but will change over time and still promote established consistency.
- **Managed**: This uses metrics and successfully controls all of the organization's processes. Management will routinely acclimate and amend for projects without specification deviation.
- **Optimizing**: This focuses on continuous process performance improvement through innovative and incremental technological improvements. Awesome!

Splunk – all you need for a search engine

As a part of your vision, you need to consider exactly what Splunk *brings*.

Who can imagine life without the Internet? Can you imagine trying to navigate even a small portion of the Internet's wealth of information and raw data without some form of Internet search engine? Using this analogy, can you even begin to think about what is required to successfully navigate the growing volumes and complexity of your organization's data and any externally available data that your organization might be interested in? If you think about it, it is a similar problem.

The answer lies in Splunk! Splunk is the search tool (or engine) that indexes and lets you search, navigate, alert, and report most of your data from any application, server, or network device (similar to an Internet search engine). As your Splunk expertise grows (you become the next Splunk master), I'm guessing you'll see more and more applications that are ripe for addressing with all that Splunk has to offer.

Summary

In this chapter, we introduced a vision for enterprise Splunk, defined Splunk knowledge, and stated its value to an organization and individual Splunk users. In addition, we touched on several key areas such as naming, the Common Information Model, and testing. Finally, we wrapped up by talking about establishing a strategy or roadmap to evolve Splunk within your organization.

Quick Start

In this appendix, we will give examples of the various resources you can use to become a Splunk master, from certification tracks, to the company's website and support portal, as well as everything in between. We will also walk you through the process of obtaining a copy of the latest version of Splunk and its default installation. Finally, we will discuss some ideas to set up an environment that is conducive to personal research and practice.

Topics

The topics that will be covered in this appendix are:

- Learning about Splunk (where and how)
- Obtaining the software
- Installation and configuration
- An environment to learn in

Where and how to learn Splunk

"Never become so much of an expert that you stop gaining expertise."

– Denis Waitley

Continued learning (gaining expertise) is a characteristic of success — even survival — in every field but especially for those with technology-related careers. There are numerous options that you can use to increase your Splunk knowledge and proficiency. We'll discuss just a few of these options, starting with the more obvious choices:

- Obtaining product certifications
- Attending formal training
- Reviewing the product documentation
- Visiting the company's website frequently

Certifications

To date, the Splunk community categorizes certifications by a generalized area discussed in the following sections.

Knowledge manager

A **knowledge manager** manages (and develops) *knowledge* objects. Knowledge managers might work at the project level, organization level, or practice level to manage:

- Saved searches
- Event types
- Transactions
- Tags
- Field extractions and transformations
- Lookups
- Workflows
- Commands
- Views

A Splunk knowledge manager will have a deep understanding of Splunk, its user interfaces, the objective of each type of knowledge object, and so on. Knowledge managers must also look beyond personal use or a particular project, extending the Splunk environment, through the management of a Splunk knowledge object library.

Administrator

As a Splunk administrator, you need to provide hands-on daily support of (perhaps) several Splunk installations, requiring hands-on knowledge of the best or proven practices and configuration techniques, and in addition, be able to construct and manage an organization's knowledge objects.

Architect

Splunk architects can design and create apps in Splunk. In addition, an architect needs to have both knowledge management experience and administration know-how. Additionally, architects need to be comfortable with large-scale deployments and an application's best practices for tasks such as forecasting, raw data collection, sizing, and documenting.

Supplemental certifications

Only available to Splunk partners, Splunk offers what is referred to as **supplemental certification**.

Splunk partners

Splunk offers partnerships that, if you wish, you can pursue based on your interests, such as:

- Powered associate
- Consulting partner
- Development partner
- Reseller partner
- Service provider partner
- Technology partner

Individuals or organizations who are Splunk partners can be sources of advice and useful information to you and your organization on your journey of mastering Splunk. In fact, you might want to target becoming a Splunk partner.

It is highly recommended that you establish an account at `http://www.splunk.com/` and log in regularly as a *returning Splunker*. On the website, you can find details on the partnering program or find an existing partner.

Proper training

As with other technologies, Splunk offers instructor-led classes. You can attend the "virtual classroom" or have the class presented at your location.

The complete Splunk curriculum is offered monthly, and all the classes consist of relevant, student-done exercises in:

- Advanced users
- Splunk (app) development
- Administration
- Architectural techniques
- Security

The Splunk documentation

Maybe the best training choice is to read though the Splunk documentation. The documentation of Splunk is excellent for providing explicit details and step-by-step examples that you'll find invaluable.

Take the time to browse `http://docs.splunk.com/Documentation/Splunk` (bookmark it!). Notice that you have the option to select the version of Splunk that you are interested in, and from there, you can continue your training at your own speed and on your own schedule by following these topics:

- Summaries of each release
- Searching data models and pivot (and other) tutorials
- Administration and alerting manuals
- Installation procedures
- Dashboards and visualizations
- Distributed deployments
- Forwarders
- Knowledge management
- Module system references
- Pivoting
- APIs
- Searching and distributed searching
- Debugging

- Developing views and apps for Splunk Web

- Getting your data into Splunk

- Indexing and clustering

- The modules system user manual

- Reporting

- Security

- Updating instances

www.splunk.com

This website is available 24/7 (the Internet never shuts down!) and is an easily searchable portal for all types of Splunk-related information, which is nicely ordered as follows:

- Basic products

- Various Splunk solutions

- Industries

- Partners

- All about Splunk

- How to get the right kind of support

- Available services

- More resources

The Splunk website includes the topics discussed in the following sections.

Splunk answers

Splunk answers give you the ability to interact with everyone within the Splunk communities for quick answers to all of your Splunk questions.

Splunkbase

Splunkbase is a **searchable knowledge base of apps** consisting of FAQs, answers, and good advice. An exceptional feature of Splunkbase is that you can earn points and badges of honor to improve your Splunkbase ranking, which creates a professional image on the site's leadership board.

The support portal

The Splunk support portal is available at http://www.splunk.com/ (look for it under **Support**). The portal is where you can become a spot-on "Splunker" by creating your own account to:

- Download versions of the Splunk software and updates
- Join online forums and discussions
- Submit support issues and/or questions
- Download copies of application guides and whitepapers
- Access the Splunk product roadmaps and add your own comments to the mix
- Access tech updates, the *SplunkVox* newsletter, and lots more Splunk-related useful information

You don't have to pay anything to create an account of your own. You need to just access the website and click on **Sign Up Now**, as shown in the following screenshot:

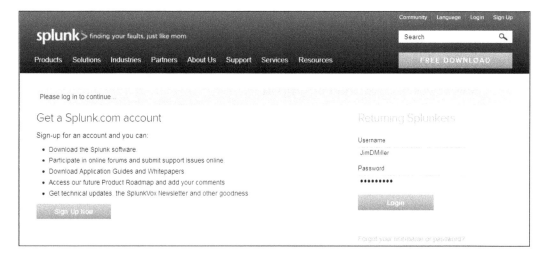

Here, you just need to create a (unique) username and password (and, of course, agree to the Splunk website's terms and conditions).

The Splexicon

The word "lexicon" is Greek and translates to "of or for words." The Splunk lexicon (or the "Sp-lexicon") explains all the technical terms that are used with the Splunk technology. All descriptions reference the Splunk product documentation (via links).

You can use Splexicon as an "intelligent user interface" to online Splunk reference manuals, tutorials, and related information, allowing you to easily look up Splunk terminology and then "jump right to" the documentation and informational details pertaining to that term.

Have a look at the following screenshot as an example of the documentation and informational details pertaining to the term **Alert Manager**:

Alert Manager

noun

A feature that enables you to see and manage records of triggered alerts. You access the Alert Manager by clicking the **Alerts** link at the upper right hand corner of the **Splunk Web** interface.

The Alert Manager only displays records for alerts that have **Tracking** selected in their alert definition. It includes a **Severity** column that enables you to quickly spot alerts that are high priority (this setting is also defined in the alert definition).

You can also click **View results** for a particular alert record to see the results for the **search job** artifact associated with it. This can be helpful if you want more information about the specific events that triggered the alert.

Alert records expire after a given amount of time; this is controlled by the **Alert expiration** setting in the alert definition. For example, you can have all records of a particular alert expire one day after they have been triggered.

For more information

In the Alerting Manual:

  * About alerts
  * Review triggered alerts

The "How-to" tutorials

Presently, the Splunk Education team offers more than 10 video instructional teachings by industry experts with topics that include:

* How to install MS Windows and Linux

* Getting your data into Splunk and getting it indexed

* Searching fundamentals

* How to use fields

* Saving and sharing your searches

* Tagging

* Dashboards and reports

Note that Splunk Education offers self-paced e-learning (free) to end users in order to teach various features through content, simulations, and quizzes. You only require your own Splunk account and profile. I greatly recommend that you invest your time to work through as many of these as your personal schedule allows.

User conferences, blogs, and news groups

You will find infinite amounts and limitless assortments of Splunk conferences. All these conferences are open to anyone who desires to attend in an effort to increase one's experience of Splunk and its growing communities. The most popular conference is **SplunkLive!**

SplunkLive! is your chance to hear the most recent announcements, the many ways to extend the platform, and what's hot, such as:

- Cloud
- Mobile
- Hadoop
- The app store

SplunkLive! always includes general sessions, speakers, and workshops. Perhaps, most importantly, it is also an opportune method of meeting other Splunkers!

Professional services

Don't forget to consider the Splunk professional services team. They can provide services based on your needs. These might include the development of custom Splunk applications, the implementation of use cases specific to your environment or needs, workshops and design sessions, or almost anything that demands Splunk talent.

Obtaining the Splunk software

To obtain the Splunk software, you need to carry out the steps explained in the following sections.

Disclaimer

The first step is to read the *Splunk Software License Agreement* (which can be found at `http://www.splunk.com/view/SP-CAAAAFA`; once you install the software, you'll find it in the installation folder).

 Note that although you have the ability to download a full-featured copy of Splunk Enterprise for free, the software license agreement rules the installation and uses, and it is incumbent on you to understand.

Disk space requirements

The next step is typical for any software installation, that is, evaluating your hardware to ensure that you can successfully run Splunk to meet your requirements. Though Splunk is extremely optimized, a best practice is if you are evaluating Splunk, you should use hardware typical of the environment you intend to employ to. The hardware you use for evaluation should meet or exceed the recommended hardware capacity specifications for your intentions (check the Splunk website or talk to a Splunk professional to be sure).

Beyond the minimal physical footprint of Splunk itself, you will need some "operational space." When you add data to Splunk, it creates a compressed/indexed form of your "raw data," and this is approximately 10 percent of the needs of the original data. Also, Splunk will create index files that point to the compressed file. These associated index files can range in size from approximately 10 percent to 110 percent of the raw data file, based on the number of unique terms in the data that affect this value. Again, rather than getting into sizing specifics here, if your goal is to explore Splunk, go ahead and install Splunk on your local machine or laptop—it'll be sufficient.

To go physical or logical?

Today, most organizations will run a combination of physical and virtual machines. Generally speaking, Splunk runs just fine on both. It is imperative to understand the needs of any software and to ensure that your environment is configured suitably.

From the Splunk documentation:

> *"If you run Splunk in a virtual machine (VM) on any platform, performance does degrade. This is because virtualization works by abstracting the hardware on a system into resource pools from which VMs defined on the system draw as needed. Splunk needs sustained access to a number of resources, particularly disk I/O, for indexing operations. Running Splunk in a VM or alongside other VMs can cause reduced indexing performance."*
>
> *– Splunk.com*

Splunk Version 6.0.2 runs on both MS Windows and Linux operating systems, but for this discussion, I'm going to focus only on the MS Windows version.

The Splunk architecture

You can run Splunk as either 32- or 64-bit; be sure to choose the version you need.

Let's get the software! You can download the installation package (.msi for MS Windows) from the website.

I recommend that you read the release notes for the version that you intend to install—release notes list the known issues along with possible workarounds, and this information can save plenty of time later.

 Note that you'll need to visit the Splunk website for detailed instructions if you upgrade Splunk.

Creating your Splunk account

You need to have a Splunk account to download any version of Splunk. I've already suggested that you create your own user account for support and for your own education. If you have, then you are all set. If not, set one up now by following these steps:

1. Visit http://www.splunk.com/.
2. Click on **Sign Up**—yes, it's really that easy!

Once you have set up a Splunk account, click on **Free Download**. From here, you will be directed to the **Download Splunk Enterprise** page, where you can review the list of available downloads. Click on the link of the Splunk version you want to install.

Next, you will be redirected to the **Thank You for downloading** page and will be asked to save the installation file to your location:

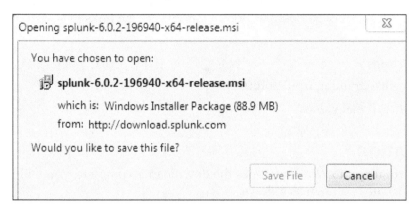

Installation and configuration

After downloading Splunk, you'll see a screen as follows. Let's get started now.

After navigating to the (http://www.splunk.com/) website, download and save the Splunk installation file (the one that is appropriate for your system); you can then begin the installation process.

You should have already received the *Thank You for Downloading* e-mail.

This e-mail provides valuable information about the limitations of your free Splunk license (don't worry, you can upgrade it later) as well as provides links to get you up and running just as fast as possible. Some examples of the links provided include the following options:

- Lectures
- Free live training from Splunkers
- Instructional videos

Installation

If you are running MS Windows, once the download is complete, you will be prompted to run it, shown as follows:

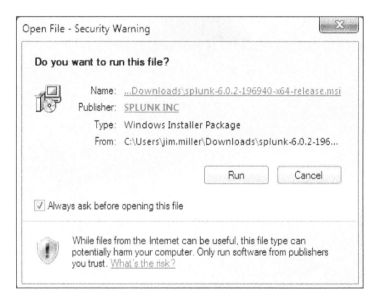

After you click on the **Run** button, you will see the **Welcome to the InstallShield...** screen, as shown in the following screenshot:

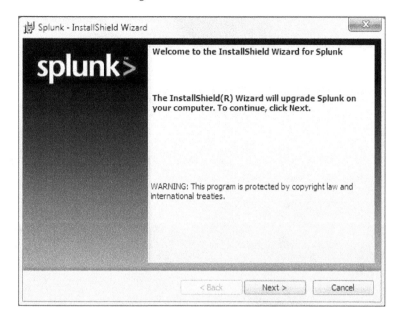

Next, click on **I accept the terms in the license agreement** (you have read the agreement and accept the terms, right?) and then on the button labeled **Next>**, as shown in the following screenshot:

[Alert! If you do not accept the terms, you will not be able to proceed (the **Next>** button remains disabled until you accept the terms).]

Once you've accepted the terms and clicked on the next button, the process informs you that it intends to install at the default location, C:\Program Files\Splunk.

Note that the destination folder you choose is important as it is required for multiple reasons. For this installation—education and evaluation—I recommend that you stay with the default destination.

Keep in mind that wherever you choose to install Splunk, that location will be referred to as $SPLUNK_HOME or %SPLUNK_HOME%.

After you click on **Next>**, the installation process will ask if you'd like to create a shortcut on your MS Windows **Start** menu.

I always check the checkbox and then click on the button labeled **Install**.

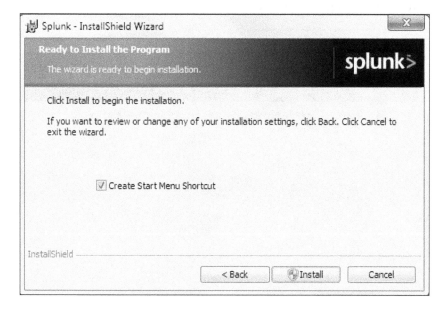

The process should then begin by performing a validation. The validation attempts to verify that you are installing the version of Splunk that is correct for your operating system and that the appropriate support files that Splunk expects are present. You'll see a screen similar to the following screenshot:

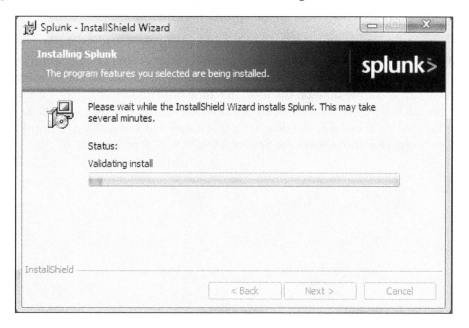

Depending on your hardware, the entire process might take several minutes, as shown in the following screenshot:

During the installation, Splunk will install (and configure) two MS Windows services:

- **Splunkd**: This is the Splunk server that accesses, processes, and indexes the streaming data and handles all search requests
- **Splunk Web**: This provides the Splunk user interface

Both the services will install and run (by default) using the machine's local system user (but can be set up to run using another user account). The Splunk user is significant and determines what it can monitor, whereas the local system user has access to all the data on the local machine only and nothing else. A user other than the local system user has access to whatever data the user wants to access, but you must provide the user with this access before installing Splunk. The following screenshot shows the Splunk installation in progress:

In the last step, the process will start the two (new) MS Windows services it has added to your machine (explained earlier). On successfully starting them up, it will give you the successful installation dialog, as shown in the following screenshot, and prompt you for permission to launch Splunk within your default web browser:

Once you open Splunk in your web browser, you are ready to sign in for the first time. Splunk makes this very easy by including the question **First time signing in?**, which is located beneath the username and password, as shown in the following screenshot:

When you click on the **First time signing in?** link, Splunk will give you a one-time password (After you use it to sign in, Splunk will *force* you to change the password: write it down) for the username admin, as shown in the following screenshot:

If this is your first visit, you will see a **What's new in 6.0** banner, as shown in the following screenshot:

Are you a new Splunker? If yes, then I recommend that you take the time to explore these topics by clicking on the **Learn More** button before proceeding to Splunk's **Home** page.

Splunk home

Once you've closed the **What's new** banner (either after selecting the **Learn More** button and taking the tour, or by clicking on the **x** button in the upper-right corner to close the window), you will find yourself on Splunk's home page, ready to begin with Splunking, as shown in the following screenshot:

Splunk home is the entry point to all the apps and data accessible from the installation (referred to as a **Splunk instance**).

Home has been redesigned in Version 6.0, and includes a handy search bar, **Add Data**, and the **Help** panel.

> Note that after signing in to Splunk for the first time, you can configure your instance to "go directly to" a particular view that might be the most efficient for you and your needs—such as search or pivot (keep in mind that you can always jump back to Splunk's Home page by clicking on the Splunk logo).
> Happy Splunking!

An environment to learn in

Generally speaking, most of us obtain a copy of the software we are interested in learning and quickly install it, anxious to get started right away and discover all that it might have to offer. This usually provides some amount of instantaneous gratification, but it also provides some eventual reworking, reinstalling, reconfiguring, or even revisiting the source (of the software) to secure a new copy once the initial discovery phase has passed.

In addition, it is always advisable to thoroughly understand the environmental cost, configuration options, and perhaps how to troubleshoot or diagnose certain behaviors of any software you install and use.

Lastly, to make the most productive use of your time, it is a good idea to understand the bigger picture or the long-term vision for where the technology is now, how it is being used, and what might be the future opportunities for it and for someone who is proficient in it.

To this end, the following are some general tips on establishing a formal ongoing learning process and sustainable environment:

- Understand any software prerequisites
- Understand any hardware requirements (for the installation and for ongoing use)
- Know how to determine the specific version and build numbers of the version you install and potentially upgrade to
- Understand specifically what occurs during the installation process
- Understand what you are agreeing to when you acknowledge the software licensing agreement, including what to do if/when evaluations expire

- Know what to do to uninstall and how to restore your system to an appropriate state

- Know what the (at least most popular) configuration options might be

- Be aware of performance baselines—know how to tell whether the response times that you are experiencing are reasonable or not

- Know how to diagnose errors or exceptions during use

- Know where to go for help and support

- Learn the product roadmap, where the experts see it going, so that you can best position yourself to take advantage

- Be aware of general industry-proven or best practices and become familiar with them, making them a habit from your first exposure to the software, rather than retraining yourself later

The preceding points are just a few suggestions for optimizing your Splunk learning experience. These suggestions apply to any computer software but warrant mentioning as part of your experience in mastering Splunk.

Summary

In this appendix, we provided:

- A list of resources to increase your knowledge and level of expertise with Splunk

- Where and how you can obtain a copy of the latest version of Splunk Enterprise

- A walkthrough of a default Splunk Enterprise (for MS Windows) installation

- Some general recommendations for setting up an environment for focused learning

Index

custom apps
  building 191
  URL, for uploading 191
Customer Relationship
      Management (CRM) 22
custom indexes
  using 165
customization, user interface (UI)
  advanced views 192
  dashboards 192
  form search 192

D

Dashboard Editor
  about 124
  used, for creating dashboards 123
dashboard panel
  inline search 139
  time range picker 128, 129
  used, for searching 139
  visualizations, specifying 127, 128
dashboards
  access, controlling 130, 131
  cloning 131
  constructing 125
  context, selecting 131
  creating 115, 116
  creating, Dashboard Editor used 123
  customization 132
  Dashboard Editor 124
  deleting 131
  framework, constructing 125
  modules 117
  panel content, adding 126
  Panel Editor 123
  panels 117
  panels, adding 126, 129
  panels, editing 133
  panels, using 132
  real-time solutions 149, 150
  real-world solutions 149, 150
  search form 118
  versus forms 122
  views 116
  visualization 134
  Visualization Editor 123

data
  classifying, with Splunk knowledge 272
  enriching, with Splunk knowledge 272
  interpreting, with Splunk knowledge 272
  modeling, with Splunk knowledge 273
  normalizing, with Splunk knowledge 272
data inputs, for monitoring
  apps 216
  Splunk CLI 215
  Splunk configuration files 215
  Splunk Web 215
data location 217, 218
data sources, Splunk
  files and/or directories 8
  network events 8
  other sources 8
  Windows sources 8
Decision Support System. *See* DSS
dedup command
  used, for handling duplicates 99, 100
default fields 248
default indexes
  about 155, 156
  Audit (_audit) 156
  Internal (_internal) 155
  Main (main) 155
delete operator
  about 169
  using 173
dense searches
  versus sparse searches 31
directories
  monitoring 15
disaster recovery (DR) 23
documentation, naming conventions
  Common Information
      Model (CIM) 278, 279
  developing 276
  developing, for knowledge objects 276
  example 277, 278
  hints 277
  object naming conventions 276
  organizing 276
documentation, Splunk 292
drilldowns
  about 64, 65
  cell drilldown 69, 70

chart drilldowns 70, 71
functionality 67
legends 71
options 66, 67
row drilldown 67, 68

DSS
about 19, 20
ETL analytics 20
ODBC 22
preconceptions 20

dynamic drilldowns
about 144
disabling 149
example 146-149
implementing 145

dynamic lookups 100

E

enterprise data warehouses (EDW) 21
enterprise vision
about 284
building 285
developing 286
evaluation 285
implementation 285
management 286
optimization 286
repeating 285
search engine 287
structured approach 286, 287
using 285

escapes
using 33, 34

eval statement
example 44
using 43

eval statement, parameters
eval-expression 43
eval-field 43

event correlation 261, 262

event data 248

event processing
about 154
indexing 155

parsing 154

events
deleting 169-171
sending, to be indexed 165-167

event timeline
used, for investigational searching 14

examples, naming conventions
category 278
explanation 278
interval 278
platform 277
type 277
user group 277

expiration, Splunk 245

extended functionalities, Splunk
about 244, 245
expiration 245
Splunk acceleration 245
summary indexing 246

Extensible Markup Language. *See* **XML**

external lookup
example 104

F

features, indexes
frozen archive path 163
index names 162
max sizes 163
path locations 162

field lookup
automatic lookups 90
configuration files 94, 95
configuration files, using instead of Splunk
    Web 103, 104
configuring 85
defining, in Splunk Web 85-90
duplicates, handling with dedup
    command 99, 100
duplicate table names, preventing 110
dynamic lookups 100
implementing, configuration
    files used 96, 97
Splunk Web, using 101-103
tables, populating 97
time-based lookup 105

S

Thank you for buying
Mastering Splunk

About Packt Publishing

Packt, pronounced 'packed', published its first book, *Mastering phpMyAdmin for Effective MySQL Management*, in April 2004, and subsequently continued to specialize in publishing highly focused books on specific technologies and solutions.

Our books and publications share the experiences of your fellow IT professionals in adapting and customizing today's systems, applications, and frameworks. Our solution-based books give you the knowledge and power to customize the software and technologies you're using to get the job done. Packt books are more specific and less general than the IT books you have seen in the past. Our unique business model allows us to bring you more focused information, giving you more of what you need to know, and less of what you don't.

Packt is a modern yet unique publishing company that focuses on producing quality, cutting-edge books for communities of developers, administrators, and newbies alike. For more information, please visit our website at www.packtpub.com.

About Packt Enterprise

In 2010, Packt launched two new brands, Packt Enterprise and Packt Open Source, in order to continue its focus on specialization. This book is part of the Packt Enterprise brand, home to books published on enterprise software – software created by major vendors, including (but not limited to) IBM, Microsoft, and Oracle, often for use in other corporations. Its titles will offer information relevant to a range of users of this software, including administrators, developers, architects, and end users.

Writing for Packt

We welcome all inquiries from people who are interested in authoring. Book proposals should be sent to author@packtpub.com. If your book idea is still at an early stage and you would like to discuss it first before writing a formal book proposal, then please contact us; one of our commissioning editors will get in touch with you.

We're not just looking for published authors; if you have strong technical skills but no writing experience, our experienced editors can help you develop a writing career, or simply get some additional reward for your expertise.

Implementing Splunk: Big Data Reporting and Development for Operational Intelligence

ISBN: 978-1-84969-328-8   Paperback: 448 pages

Learn to transform your machine data into valuable IT and business insights with this comprehensive and practical tutorial

1. Learn to search, dashboard, configure, and deploy Splunk on one machine or thousands.

2. Start working with Splunk fast, with a tested set of practical examples and useful advice.

3. Step-by-step instructions and examples with a comprehensive coverage for Splunk veterans and newbies alike.

Splunk Operational Intelligence Cookbook

ISBN: 978-1-84969-784-2   Paperback: 414 pages

Over 70 practical recipes to gain operational data intelligence with Splunk Enterprise

1. Learn how to use Splunk to effectively gather, analyze, and report on the operational data across your environment.

2. Expedite your operational intelligence reporting, be empowered to present data in a meaningful way, and shorten the Splunk learning curve.

3. Easy-to-use recipes to help you create robust searches, reports, and charts using Splunk.

Please check **www.PacktPub.com** for information on our titles

Big Data Analytics with R and Hadoop

ISBN: 978-1-78216-328-2   Paperback: 238 pages

Set up an integrated infrastructure of R and Hadoop to turn your data analytics into Big Data analytics

1. Write Hadoop MapReduce within R.

2. Learn data analytics with R and the Hadoop platform.

3. Handle HDFS data within R.

4. Understand Hadoop streaming with R.

5. Encode and enrich datasets into R.

Hadoop Real-World Solutions Cookbook

ISBN: 978-1-84951-912-0   Paperback: 316 pages

Realistic, simple code examples to solve problems at scale with Hadoop and related technologies

1. Solutions to common problems when working in the Hadoop environment.

2. Recipes for (un)loading data, analytics, and troubleshooting.

3. In depth code examples demonstrating various analytic models, analytic solutions, and common best practices.

Please check **www.PacktPub.com** for information on our titles